Bare-Bones Tarot

An In-Depth Study to Key Elements of the Tarot

Pitisci

CreateSpace Independent Publishing Platform

Dedication

To those who have led the way

Contents

Quick Reference card meanings on last two pages of book.

Contents

Quick Reference card meanings on last two pages of book.

Preface

– I was a Teenage Tarot Reader! –

A lot of things happened that year. The Woodstock rock concert was in the news. Charles Manson went nuts. Chicago police and the FBI raided and shot dead Black Panther leader Fred Hampton. We even went to the moon! Nixon was President and Vietnam was going strong. Next year I might get drafted!

"Join the Army!....See the World!....Meet new and interesting people! And kill them!" I wasn't concerned about having to go to Vietnam and kill people as much as I cared about getting my hair cut and probably losing my girlfriend if I got drafted.

As a 16 year old teenager I had an insatiable urge to know more about the paranormal, metaphysics, ghost and all the other typical things a teenager would be interested in. One day after about 15 minutes of some careful study and research I decided it was time to learn how to read Tarot cards.

I called Kroch's & Brentano's book store located downtown Chicago and asked "Do you have Tarot cards?" The man on the other line told me "Yes we do." I said "Will you hold a deck for me? I will be there in an hour to pick them up." He replied "Certainly."

I checked my wallet. I was loaded. Must have at least $10 here! I put on my Levis, dago tee, slipped into my Cuban heeled *points*, ran some Brylcreem through my long hair, threw on my black leather Cabretta and hopped on a train to the loop.

Walked down to Wabash Ave. and Madison St. to the ultimate bookstore known to man. Kroch's & Brentano's! Went through the doors to the front counter and told the man sitting there "I'm the guy who called about a deck of Tarot cards." He swung his swivel chair around to a counter right behind him, picked up the deck, swung back around to me and said "Here you are."

I thought to myself ... WOW.... I got Tarot cards! I left the store....after I paid the man $4.50 of course. Got a Coke at the train station and got on board back home. I must have looked like *Gollum* from *Lord of the Rings* with his *preciousssss* sitting there fondling the box of cards in my hands all the way home. *My precioussss*!

That's how it all started. The deck was the Tarot of Marseilles by B.P. Grimaud.

Imagine plunging out into the vast unknown without so much as a credit card in my pocket. Not even a cell phone! With that kind of determination and courage I must have been destined to be a card reader!

The year was 1969.

Introduction

A tilted look at the Tarot

To the best of my knowledge, the Tarot of Marseilles is the oldest Tarot deck on record used for divination. That goes back to the 1770's with names like Jean-Baptiste Alliette and Antoine de Gebelin. I think it's ironic that this book will be sharing some major breakthroughs found on my journey with the Tarot and I will be doing that using this classic deck. The Tarot of Marseilles. Sorta going full circle back to it's roots.

Since the late 1960's, I have seen first hand the Tarot being pulled into all sorts of different directions. This has caused a lot of confusion today to the point where people find it difficult knowing where to start! My guess is that most of you have already purchased and tried a number of different Tarot decks and still don't feel like you have a real grip on this whole "Tarot thing."

Just the selection of decks available today is amazing and the art work is beautifully done by many inspired and talented artists. I was fortunate enough not to have all that confusion when I started with the cards.

There were no decisions to be made on which decks work best. The Tarot cards that were readily available was only the Tarot of Marseilles and we didn't judge them in any way at all. They were just Tarot cards and that was how Tarot cards looked. Like I said – a whole different time.

At no time in it's history has the Tarot seen such a surge of various styled Tarot decks like the last 50 years. Today you have to decide between hundreds of different Tarot decks. How do you know? That can become overwhelming in itself. So if you are considering the Tarot of Marseilles deck to be your main choice it feels like a big weight has been lifted off your shoulders.

You were able to make a choice! You're going back to the original Tarot. It makes things so simple. So basic. Do they work? Of course they do. They have been around for centuries.

You might wonder if the newer decks have something more. After all, improvements do happen in many things over time. Why not Tarot cards. Maybe today's decks have more capability than this old Marseilles version has. I can honestly say that I feel that is not the case. You just can't get more "Tarot" than the Tarot of Marseilles.

Here's a secret. All Tarot decks work. It just comes down to what is your personal preference. Over time I have jumped from Tarot deck to Tarot deck and I felt very comfortable using these newer decks. They work just fine. But I always go back to what I trust the most as being the true "Tarot." So if I had to make a choice the Tarot of Marseilles always feels right. It's like home to me.

It is time tested and it has remained with us for centuries. Will any of these newer decks do that? Who knows. But the Marseilles deck already has. It's just plain classic Tarot. It screams Tarot right at you loud and clear.

I have been fortunate enough to see many changes in the way we view Tarot cards over the decades. And I've watched those transitions grow right from the beginning.

The Rider/Waite Tarot deck was reintroduced into circulation right after I got involved with Tarot in 1970. That amazing deck opened up the floodgates to newer decks. That was when we really started studying the images on Tarot cards. I feel all of our attention went in that direction. The images of the cards.

I feel looking so closely at the symbolism of those images has limited our focus to just the cards. The other aspects of reading Tarot cards are not given too much thought. Studying the rich symbolic images of Tarot cards under a microscope and interpreting them in various ways by all sorts of different sources became the new thing. New Tarot authors came about having their own little twist here and there about the meanings of the cards since my beginning with the cards.

There was never any confusion with the Marseilles deck. There wasn't much written about them at all. Nothing had to be written about them. They were just Tarot cards. No flood of opinions on card meanings. It just sat quietly and remained a simple and classic Tarot deck.

I love looking at the new Tarot decks that come out every year just as much as the next person. It's so easy to look deep into them.
But have we spent too much focus on the cards and not enough on their application?

The amazing Rider Waite deck has inspired many other new decks and it has become a standard. It is the Tarot deck widely accepted and all Tarot enthusiast are familiar with it. Not so much with the older Tarot of Marseilles. Because of this, I have taught mostly using the Rider Waite deck in my classes. My books up to this release all use the Rider deck to show the cards as well.

It is a wonderful deck and I have used it myself many times professionally over time. Most newer decks will use the Rider as a guide to their renditions today as well. The Tarot can fit into any scenario. Today we have Native American Tarot, Egyptian Tarot, Tarot of Baseball, (really we do!) Gay Tarot, Lord of the Rings Tarot, Housewives Tarot, James Bond Tarot, Gummie Bear Tarot and the list keeps growing every year.

For the most part these newer decks come and go but seem to follow the Rider theme. The Tarot of Marseilles doesn't follow any previous theme. It is not swayed in any way. It was out there before all this started. It's just Tarot cards plain and simple.

The Marseilles deck has no known author. It was not trying to compete with anyone. It just was. The titles of the cards today have changed as well. In the Marseilles, The High Priestess was called The Lady Pope and is depicted as a woman dressed in Pope garments including the Mitre on her head.

The Hierophant was called The Pope himself and was dressed accordingly. The Lovers card today was called The Lover. Singular. A lover can be seen as a threat coming into the picture or maybe a positive thing. It meant a choice will be made.

The Magician was known as The Trickster. He is seen as a street performer who is a master of tricks right before your eyes. Which cup is the bean hidden under now? 3 card monty and other traps of the time. Watch your purse!

Strength was titled Force. The Wheel was known as The Wheel of Fortune. The Tower was The House of God or The Tower of Destruction.

The Fool was depicted as a struggling fool being attacked and humiliated by some small wild creature ripping his pants off his backside. Not the care free traveler with his little doggie friend at his side.

The Chariot was sometimes known as The Cart and Death didn't dare have a title. Just the number 13. Knowing these differences over time helps us understand the Tarot in a better light. Why? Because the newer meanings work just as well as the original meanings did. They all work.

They are just labeled card meanings and they can change over time and still be useful to us as we read them. So the ideas and insight we receive as we do a reading are coming from our own mind not a deck of cards. The cards spark insightful, intuitive ideas to us no matter what meanings are assigned to them.

The Lover....or The Lovers. The High Priestess ...or The Lady Pope. It makes no difference. They are just random ideas. Suggestions for possible answers to the position they are placed into.

So after all this time do I know the Tarot well? Sometimes I still wonder. After all they still surprise me all the time. Like they know what I'm looking for!
There is something about the Tarot of Marseilles that keeps me thinking it has more to tell me. And it cannot tell it all in one sitting. It will take a life time. So many more ideas and concepts. It offers so many more answers that I want to find. I just have to spend time with it.

After 50 years of reading the Tarot I even created my own version of this classic Tarot of Marseilles. I scratched in every line in every card and it is used in this book you're holding right now. But if I am ever known in some small way as contributing to the Tarot community I hope it is not because of a deck of cards. The deck of cards is a very small addition to the Tarot compared with something else I found.

I came across a remarkable discovery on my Tarot journey. And I want to share it with you in these pages. Yes, this book is about how to read Tarot cards and it will cover all of that. But it also has something else added.

Since it's beginning there has always been one big mystery to the Tarot cards. Why does it work? What would you give to know the answer to that one Tarot question?

That secret has been the main Tarot mystery for centuries. No one could ever explain it. If you could answer that one question you unlock the biggest mystery of the Tarot. Your readings could be refined. Improved with a better understanding of what you're doing with these curious cards if you could understand the mechanics behind it.

Knowing that secret would answer and explain much about the Tarot. Actually that is probably what causes such interest in the Tarot! That unexplainable knack to see into the future. How does a deck of cards do that? What would you give to be one of the first to peek behind that curtain?

That one big mystery that none of the Tarot masters, occultists, mystics, even prophets over time could never explain. "WHY" does this deck of cards do what it does? How can 78 cards actually tell me things that will happen in the future? Well now that centuries old mystery has been unlocked and I share it with you in these pages.

My work on this subject is a first of its kind. But it would be hard to deny once it is explained to you.

This is an amazing revelation that will alter our understanding of the Tarot. The conclusive facts are there. This new revelation allows us to advance with the Tarot in ways never before thought possible.

It will open up new innovative ideas about these cards and allow more effective applications. This creates a whole new understanding of the Tarot. A new understanding that we are just scratching the surface of. I do hope that my work will stimulate others to delve into this new insight on the Tarot cards more deeply.

Although this book uses the Tarot of Marseilles, it is my goal to show you the Tarot clearly regardless of the Tarot deck you choose to use. But I would like to finish this introduction by saying if you decide to read with the Tarot of Marseilles – You're not playin around. You're a Tarot reader!

1. The Winds of Change 1969

I have a 50 year history with the Tarot and through all that time the perception of the Tarot has shifted in many ways. So I thought I would share my experience and opinions on the subject with you here.

Our understanding of the mind has moved in great leaps since 1969. Approximately 90% of what we know about the mind has been found in the last 50 years.

1969 is when I started reading the Tarot. It was a different world at that time in many ways including the Tarot. The Tarot of Marseilles was the standard Tarot deck and was widely accepted that way just like playing card styles have a standard look today. No one questioned the look of the deck. It was just Tarot cards and that is what Tarot cards looked like.

Sure, there were some novelty type decks just like you might find some novelty playing card decks today but the Marseilles was the standard and most authentic Tarot deck in circulation at the time. We didn't question the way Tarot cards looked. We didn't judge them. They just were. There was no selection to choose from.

Then something happened in 1970. U.S. Games Systems, Inc. re-released the Rider Waite Tarot deck, originally published in 1910 by Arthur Waite and beautifully illustrated by Pamela Coleman Smith. These images were more curious to look at than the standard Marseilles deck.

Almost simultaneously, that same year, Eden Gray released her book on the Tarot "*A Complete Guide to the Tarot*" using this new Rider Waite deck. The book was a first as far as clear instruction on how to use Tarot cards and I feel that book also legitimized the Rider Waite deck as an acceptable alternative to the Marseilles deck.

For the first time, we had a book where things were easy to understand on the subject. It also had about 25 pages dedicated to just three specific card spreads applications. One of them was the Celtic Cross. Eden Gray called it "*The Ancient Keltic Method*" in her work.

By todays' standard 25 pages used to describe the application of just 3 card spreads is rare. Most work today will set aside just a few pages to describe applications of applying Tarot card spreads. Most of the focus will be on describing the beautiful images and their symbolic meanings on each card.

The reason not much is written on card spreads is because we could never explain why card spreads work. Even Eden Gay admits that in her book stating the following in chapter 5 titled "How to Read the Cards:"

"In some way that we do not understand, your subconscious mind seems to direct the shuffling but can do this correctly only after you have implanted the meaning of each card in your memory."

"In some way that we do not understand?" So right from the get-go we are trying to learn something that we don't completely understand. We start out with a confusing situation that can't be clearly explained. Seeing we have never been able to explain conclusively why the Tarot works we have put all our concentration on the card meanings and what the images on those cards depict. A focus on the symbolism in the cards. Not how they are used.

What followed was other talented and inspired artist creating more beautiful and curious looking examples of Tarot cards with their own spin on the symbolic meanings of the images the cards now seemed to depict. At no time in it's history has the Tarot seen such a surge of various styled Tarot decks like the last 50 years. What's interesting is that all of them seem to work just fine no matter who the artist was and how the cards are portrayed.

With all this wide selection of different styled Tarot cards out today we seem to be focused on the various styles of artwork illustrated in each deck. What symbolism, color palette, style, themes and other artistic factors do they show. The symbolism in the cards is where our focus has been drawn to. And we spend a lot of effort studying that.

But is the actual art work of a Tarot deck really that important? Or is the application and its unexplainable ability to find answers what we should be looking at. I feel it's essence of success can be found in the latter. In 1969 you had basically one common Tarot deck to choose from. The Tarot of Marseilles.

And although the artwork and symbolism in that classic deck is different than most Tarot decks today it works just as well as the newer decks do.

Is the images on Tarot cards really the key? Or is there some other reason this system works the way it does. Something we're not looking at. Most Tarot decks seem to work just fine even though the images are different and the symbolism varies from one to another. They all will do a successful card reading. So is the look really that important?

I feel what makes a Tarot reading successful is something we haven't really studied deeply over the years. The application. That thing that we just accept as not being able to explain. Back to Eden Gray's words. *"In some way that we do not understand."* And we just accept that without any thought to look deeper.

But today we can look deeper. We have the resources to understand this centuries old mystery and explain it. Although the cards are necessary, the secret has never been in the cards. Now it can be seen that it's secret has been in the application.

All Tarot readers use the same basic procedures we call card spreads. The card spread is an application that is very effective in showing us answers we didn't see before we sat down with those cards.

Why this works so well has always been the mystery of the Tarot. It could never be explained. With today's easy access to information through the internet that mystery is now unraveled. I stumbled across this treasure in 2012 and I've enjoyed sharing this new insight with you ever since.

Knowing why the Tarot works makes it easier to understand what you're doing while you're learning. It makes concepts a lot clearer.

We've been looking in the wrong place trying to understand the Tarot. Study the Tarot cards all you want – it will never show you why they work. But it's application has been something we just skim over briefly since my involvement with the Tarot.

Explaining that subject we've been told is *something we do not yet understand*. I felt it was fitting to explain this mystery with the most authentic Tarot deck in circulation today. The Tarot of Marseilles.

Today this application of thinking that in 1970 we didn't understand is an established psychological study used in artificial intelligence, science, medicine, technology. It is used by inventors, authors, artists and many other creative sources looking for answers to something they seek.

It has also been unknowingly used for centuries by the Tarot reader.
I said unknowingly....until now. Because that's all about to change.

A Tarot reading is all about finding answers. Answers we didn't have information on before hand. Finding fresh insight. New ideas to be accomplished in the future. To predict.

So how do we find ways of predicting new ways of looking at a question? New answers to a goal? How do we find new answers to something we are stuck on?

Today we've researched this question with many advancements on the study.
So now I'll invite you to step through the looking glass to a dimension of the Tarot that has remained a secret throughout it's history.

~ Why it works ~

2. Revealing the Mystery

I would like to start by saying that the application and purpose of a Tarot card reading would be accurately defined and explained today in psychology as a widely used and very powerful creative thinking technique commonly known as Conceptual Blending. Not a mystery at all. The procedures and purpose of Conceptual Blending are identical to the procedures and purpose of a Tarot card reading. Which means with today's understanding of how the mind works we can explain why a Tarot card reading is so effective.

Not only is this intentional application of thinking taught in our colleges as a creative thinking technique, Conceptual Blending is used to explore new ideas into artificial intelligence, medicine, science, technology, the arts, advertising, and many other disciplines.

It is used in branches of our government like NASA, the CIA, The Pentagon, the FBI. It's purpose is to find innovative and useful answers to specific questions we previously did not have an answer for. It is also used by most of your Fortune 500 companies to find new and better ways to enhance their product or services.

Others that use this application of thinking are inventors, comedy writers, novelists, artists, and the list goes on. Today we know that genius minds throughout history have used this same procedure of thinking to find new ideas. Answers to what they sought. Names like Darwin, DaVinci, Einstein, Galileo, Edison all have used this application of thought to find new answers and solutions to what they sought to know.

And this intentional application of thought is identical to the applications and procedures used in a Tarot card reading. Today we know enough about the mind to explain why these mysterious cards can do what they do. The Tarot reading is not a unique way of finding answers that are hidden from us. This identical application is used all over the world by many people that never picked up a deck of Tarot cards.

So what's the difference between this established creative thinking technique known as Conceptual Blending and reading the Tarot cards? There isn't any. The two procedures are identical. And both are used to predict the future.

How is Conceptual Blending done?

Conceptual Blending is done by adding what is known as a *"random stimulus"* to elements of a question. Then making associations between this "randomness" and the element of the question it was placed with. Any random subject is acceptable (including a Tarot card.) *How can this random subject help me find new answers? How can this randomness be associated to my question in some useful way?* Ideas are usually found by associating the random subject metaphorically to our question in some way that makes a useful connection.

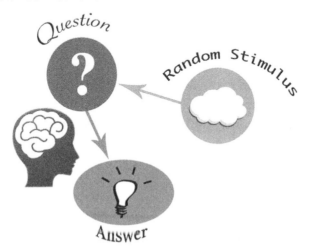

Making associations between some random subject to an element of our questions forces us to use our imagination. *A new idea is nothing more than two known subjects blended together.* We have to mentally reach to connect the dots some how between these two elements. This forces us to look at our question in ways we wouldn't normally think about it. We blend the two subjects metaphorically until some connection is made that fits with the question it is placed with.

Random Stimulus:

"A random stimulus is any class of creativity techniques that explores randomization. Most of their names start with the word "random," such as random word, random heuristic, random picture and random sound. In each random creativity technique, the user is presented with a random stimulus and explores associations that could trigger novel ideas. The power of random stimulus is that it can lead you to explore useful associations that would not emerge intentionally."
~Wikipedia

Conceptually Blending is done by adding a Random Stimulus to elements of a question to spark new and innovative ideas not seen before.

Conceptual Blending is a structured and deliberate procedure of creative thinking to stir up new and original answers to a question someone is looking into. When we are stuck for an answer, stuck for a solution, this procedure finds answers not previously seen.

Conceptual Blending is done by randomly connecting anything in our world to our question and blending them together metaphorically for new ideas to come to us. Anything used is acceptable including Tarot cards. A random stimulus that has nothing to do with your question works best. That random subject forces us to use our imagination until we make a connection in some way that is helpful.

This application is capable of finding dynamic answers.
Answers that we would normally never begin to consider. It opens up our mind in very effective ways. Imagination and intuition are both highly used in this application. It taps into that part of the mind very well. Actually it forces us to intentionally use that part of the mind.

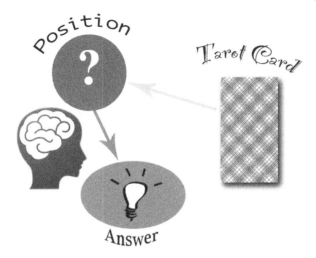

When using the Tarot, we blend ideas from random Tarot cards placed into elements of our questions known as card spread positions. From this blending process we find answers we didn't see before. The Tarot cards are a random stimulus blended into aspects of our question to spark insight not seen before.

This creates a very strong illusion as if the cards are actually telling us something. In reality we are finding answers within our own mind we didn't know were there. Conceptual Blending simply brings them out.

After centuries of mystery we can now explain clearly...with conclusive facts...why the Tarot reading is so effective in finding answers to the future. Not being able to explain why Tarot worked has limited our advancement with Tarot card readings immensely. We have been forced to mimic what has been done in the past without question. Step-by-step instructions to insure nothing will go wrong.

With no understanding into why it works all we can do is repeat what's been done before and hope for the best. With no room for advancement.

You cannot improve something if you don't understand why it works to begin with. With this new understanding of the Tarot card reading we can now open up doors to better applications with more accurate results. Each of us can make these changes ourselves, to our liking. Why? Because we will know...for the first time... what we're doing when we read Tarot cards.

This new understanding of why the Tarot reading works creates a quantum leap in our advancement into the Tarot. It is a major breakthrough in our understanding of what has always been considered a mysterious power held within Tarot cards.

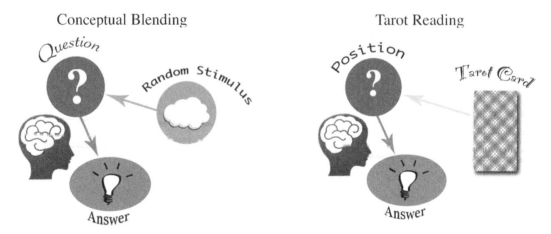

I hope that my work in this study will stimulate others to delve deeper into this advanced understanding of the Tarot cards and the amazing insight we receive from reading them. Google the term *"Conceptual Blending"* and you will start to easily connect the dots that link reading Tarot cards to this well studied creative thinking technique.

Tarot cards have been a perfect Random Stimulus for this application for centuries.

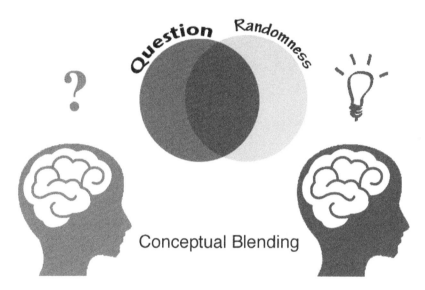

The card position is a question. The card placed into it is used for an answer.
A card spread is never seen on the table until cards are placed into it. I feel that is why this important part of the process is not given much thought.

Positions of a card spread are not just a place to lay Tarot cards into. Positions of a card spread are meant to be important aspects of the question being looked into. Each position has meaning and purpose.

The Tarot cards that are laid into those positions are meant to represent suggestions and ideas for possible answers to the position they are placed into. They are two separate things.

That process would be defined today as Conceptual Blending. A very effective way of finding answers to future objectives and goals. To predict. To see into the future!

The earliest record we have of Tarot cards being used to perform readings is in the late 1700's. The term Conceptual Blending did not become officially recognized in the field of psychology until 1993. So this study is fairly new when compared to reading Tarot cards. This could explain why none of the master Tarot names from the past ever noticed the strong comparison between these two applications. The study of Conceptual Blending was not yet known.

3. Card Meanings & Maps

I think Peter Demianovich Ouspensky (1878 – 1947) said it best...”The Tarot is not a dictionary.” He was considered a forerunner of the new breed of scientist-mystic philosopher of his time. You don't just look up what a specific Tarot card means. We have to look within ourselves to find what the card can tell us. The key to finding meaning in the Tarot lies in your imagination. It touches our creative, intuitive and artistic part of the mind that we are all capable of tapping into.

So putting into words what each Tarot card can mean becomes a challenge. Actually each and every Tarot card can encompass meaning to everything in our world! So finding a specific meaning for each card can limit its range of insight. We each find our own meanings to the cards. As you get to know other readers you will see that we all see the cards a little different from each other. We are all unique in our thinking.

The key to the Tarot lies in your imagination. Not in my words but in your unique and wonderful way of seeing the cards. The meanings are within you and only you. My words are OK to consider. To get you started. To get you on your path. But you will expand my words into your own eventually.
"We do not seek to imitate the masters......we seek what they sought."

I have decided to use the same approach to card meanings as I did in my second book *"The Essential Tarot – Unlocking the Mystery."* I feel that method works so well I would be reaching if I tried to perfect it any more than it is. The only difference is I used the Rider Waite deck in that book. Here I will be using the Tarot of Marseilles.

NOTE:

How card meanings are used in this chapter.

Each card is shown in two page spreads. A left and right hand page. The page on the left will show a "Keyword" meaning under the title of the card. You will also see a traditional type card interpretation agreeable with most other sources today. You will also see listed how the card was interpreted in the 1980's and the 1960's. Additionally, you will see a group of keywords meanings for the card listed as *"At A Glance."* This is a quick look at what the card represents for your convenience at a glance.

The right hand page will show a second "Keyword" meaning under the title of the card and twenty other keywords surrounding the card in a mapped out fashion.

This allows you to see how a meaning can drift into a vast array of meaning a card can have. Keywords can drift into associations to ultimately encompass everything in our world. This method allows your mind to drift to other words that come directly from you.

The keyword meanings surrounding each card shows how your mind can drift into many useful variables the card can mean.

This learning approach allows you to see the cards through your own eyes instead of trying to memorize what I'm seeing as a card definition.
Although you are welcome to use my keywords on these pages I'm sure you will start to "drift" into your own "keywords" in time.

The Major Arcana

The 22 Major Arcana are seen as the most mysterious suite of the deck. The meanings of these cards are thought to represent deep metaphysical aspects and universal principles as opposed to every day affairs. Although the cards can be metaphorically watered down to fit into our worldly questions. It is common to see these cards as more significant in the reading as well.

Many people think that the definitions of Tarot cards hasn't changed over the years. Not true. I personally have seen the card meanings change over the last 50 years. I decided to list separately what the cards meanings were in the 1960's and the 1980's as well as their meanings today.

The older meanings are taken from the instruction pamphlets that came with the cards back at that time. I do this to show that we have come far in our interpretations since I started reading 50 years ago. Some of these older meanings will actually seem odd, confusing and even comical today. Some might even seem like typo errors by the author. They aren't. It's just what they were. I wonder what card meanings will look like 50 years from now. Maybe we're all still learning to see the Tarot better.

Additionally 6 of the Majors were also considered more important than the other 16. They were #5, The Hierophant, #10, The Wheel of Fortune, #15, The Devil, #20, Judgement, #21, The World, and #22, The Fool (commonly numbered today as #0) I have listed The Fool last in this chapter. It can be seen as either 0 or 22, or both. But that is just one variable that has been lost over time and no longer used today.

I felt it would be interesting for you to see that things do change with the Tarot and nothing is etched in stone. Including the meanings and procedures in reading over the last 50 years.

I feel my meanings work with any deck you decide to use and will be agreeable with most other sources you come across on your Tarot journey.

Major Arcana
The Magician I
~ *Awareness* ~

At a Glance
~ Mastership
~ Strong Focus
~ Planned Execution
~ Misdirection
~ Harmonious Activity
~ Strong Capability

~ Meaning ~

Direct and deliberate intention. A persuasive influence.

Precise execution prevails and persuades others.

Unconventional but convincing approach to a challenge is taken.

Meaning from the past – 1980's

Practical and intelligent action, Quick reflexes, Selfishness in sentimental matters, Resistance to illness.

If placed near #5 **The Hierophant** it could mean "Unwisely inspired"

If placed near #10 **The Wheel** it could mean "A good Journey"

If placed near #15 **The Devil** it could mean "Irresponsible decisions"

If placed near #20 **Judgement** it could mean "A Happy Ending"

If placed near #21 **The World** it could mean "Getting rich with ease"

If placed near #22 **The Fool** it could mean "Mistakes, Uncontrollable desires.

Meaning from the past – 1960's

Uncertainty, Hesitation, Change caused by chance.

If placed near #13 **Death** the **Magician** card becomes inactive and not used at all.

Major Arcana
The Magician I
~ *Focus* ~

—— Keyword Associations ——

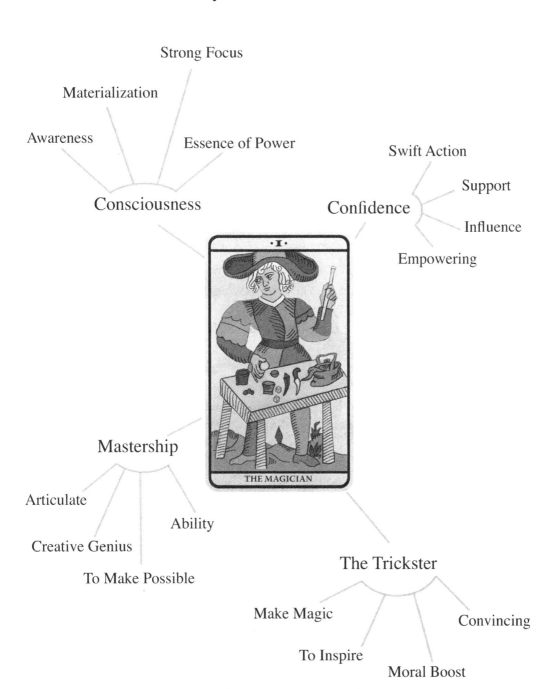

Strong Focus

Materialization

Awareness

Essence of Power

Consciousness

Swift Action

Support

Influence

Confidence

Empowering

Mastership

Articulate

Ability

Creative Genius

To Make Possible

The Trickster

Make Magic

Convincing

To Inspire

Moral Boost

Major Arcana
The High Priestess II
~ *Mystery* ~

At a Glance
~ Mystery
~ Unknown
~ Intuitive foresight
~ Intuitive Guardianship
~ Premonition
~ Dreams

~ Meaning ~
Hidden and mysterious knowledge. Value of the unexplainable. A path of least re-sistance. A feminine authority. Mystery of the subconscious. A time to listen to your dreams carefully. Subtle hints of insight are close at hand.

Meaning from the past – 1980's
Sense of duty. Family devotion. Selfishness in sentimental matters.
If placed near #5 ***The Hierophant*** it could mean "Desires fulfilled"
If placed near #10 ***The Wheel*** it could mean "Success in all matters"
If placed near #15 ***The Devil*** it could mean "Impossible to change"
If placed near #20 ***Judgement*** it could mean "Change of decision"
If placed near #21 ***The World*** it could mean "Triumph over obstacles"
If placed near #22 ***The Fool*** it could mean "A lost opportunity"

Meaning from the past – 1960's
The occult, intuition, the forces of nature. Safety, power over events. Something hid-den is revealed. If placed next to the ***Wheel of Fortune***
it can mean a secure future.

Major Arcana
The High Priestess II
~ *Wisdom* ~

—— Keyword Associations ——

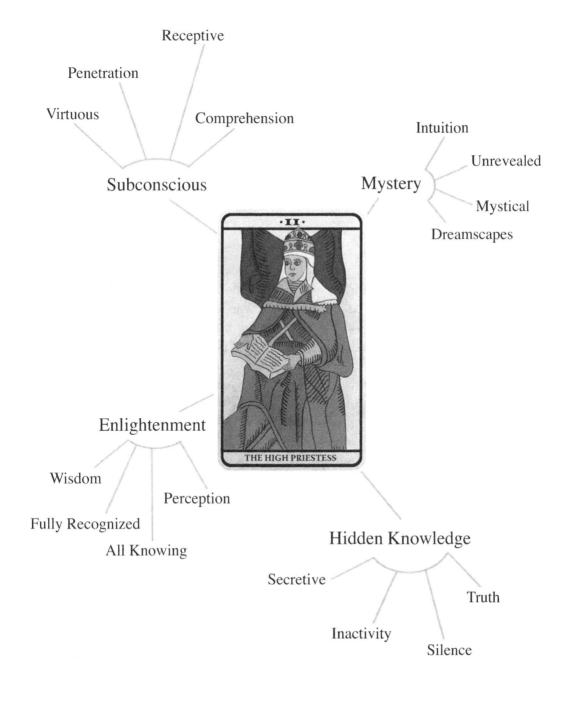

Receptive

Penetration

Virtuous

Comprehension

Subconscious

Intuition

Unrevealed

Mystery

Mystical

Dreamscapes

Enlightenment

Wisdom

Perception

Fully Recognized

All Knowing

Hidden Knowledge

Secretive

Truth

Inactivity

Silence

THE HIGH PRIESTESS

Major Arcana
The Empress III
~ *Creativity* ~

At a Glance
~ Abundance
~ Bountiful
~ The Mother
~ Nurturing Energy
~ The Cycle of Life
~ Fertility

~ Meaning ~
Flowing creativity, New life. Start of a new inspiration. Growing in abundance. Plentiful concepts and ideas to be had. Ideas become realities. Incubation creates new concepts. The mother of invention. Creative energy flows freely.

Meaning from the past – 1980's
Ambition with finesse. Successful business journeys.
If placed near #5 **The Hierophant** it could mean "Physical resistance"
If placed near #10 **The Wheel** it could mean "Growth in wealth"
If placed near #15 **The Devil** it could mean "Sensuality, Jealousy"
If placed near #20 **Judgement** it could mean "Unexpected reward"
If placed near #21 **The World** it could mean "Birth of a boy, Sly one"
If placed near #22 **The Fool** it could mean "Carelessness and waste"

Meaning from the past – 1960's
A force against which one cannot react. A state of affairs that nothing can alter. This is a strong card which influences the cards around it, but is not influenced by them. If it precedes **The Chariot** it means Victory.

Major Arcana
The Empress III
~ Nurturing ~

—— Keyword Associations ——

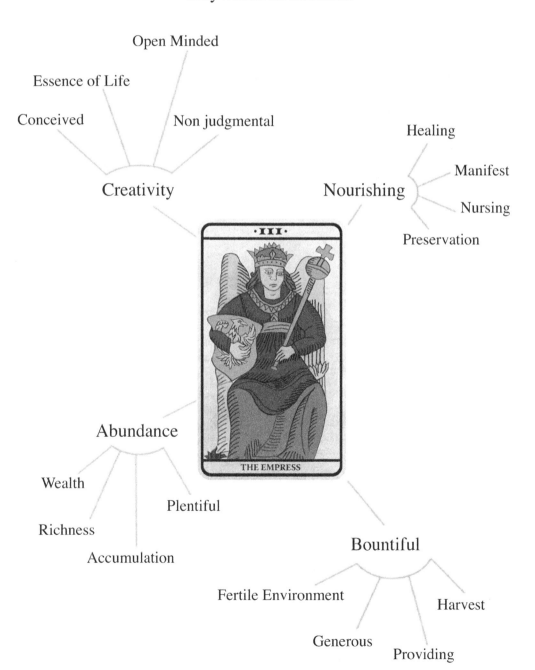

Open Minded

Essence of Life

Conceived

Non judgmental

Creativity

Nourishing

Healing

Manifest

Nursing

Preservation

Abundance

Wealth

Plentiful

Richness

Accumulation

Bountiful

Fertile Environment

Harvest

Generous

Providing

THE EMPRESS

Major Arcana
The Emperor IV
~ Leadership ~

At a Glance
~ Visionary
~ Manifestation
~ Strong Authority
~ Structured Reality
~ Established Environment
~ Strong Principles

~ Meaning ~
Responsibility is taken. Turning concepts into realities. Overseeing all that is needed.
Building new alliances. Taking charge of needed environments. Manifesting ideas
into realities. A person in position of authority. The building of a new concept.

Meaning from the past – 1980's
Perseverance, Kindness. A tendency towards excesses.
If placed near #5 ***The Hierophant*** it could mean "Triumph"
If placed near #10 ***The Wheel*** it could mean "Efforts rewarded"
If placed near #15 ***The Devil*** it could mean "Accepting adversity"
If placed near #20 ***Judgement*** it could mean "Disciplined instinct"
If placed near #21 ***The World*** it could mean "Comfort. Security."
If placed near #22 ***The Fool*** it could mean "Fear of the future."

Meaning from the past – 1960's
Wealth and power. Divisions are reunited.
If near ***The World***: Peace, but only temporary.

Major Arcana
The Emperor IV
~ *Authority* ~

—— Keyword Associations ——

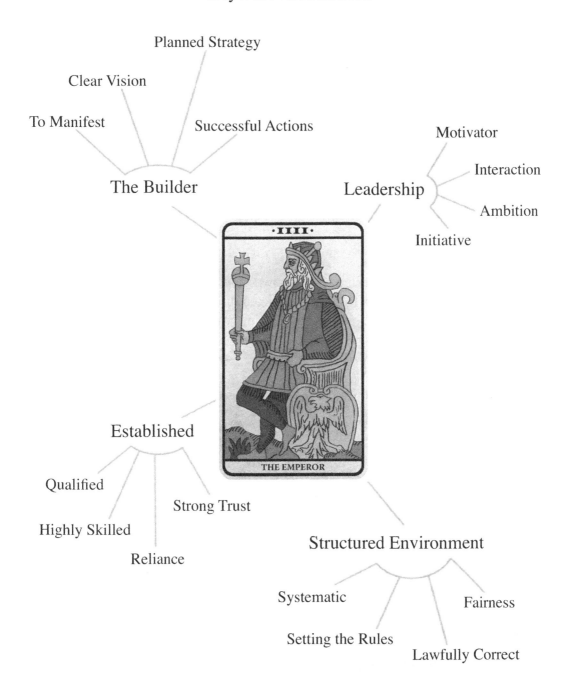

Planned Strategy

Clear Vision

To Manifest

Successful Actions

The Builder

Motivator

Interaction

Leadership

Ambition

Initiative

Established

Qualified

Strong Trust

Highly Skilled

Reliance

Structured Environment

Systematic

Fairness

Setting the Rules

Lawfully Correct

Major Arcana
The Hierophant V
~ *Spiritual Guidance* ~

At a Glance
~ Tradition
~ Universal Connection
~ Established Counsel
~ Spiritual Peace
~ Teacher of Knowledge
~ Conformity

~ Meaning ~
The common known link between a higher power and mankind. An all knowing source. A guidance of authority. Definite instructed direction. Laws and instruction abided. Ritualistic spirituality. Spiritual leadership. Traditional ceremony.

Meaning from the past – 1980's
Loyalty, Organized ability. Enthusiasm. A successful professional trip leads to promotion. Health troubles.
*If placed near **X The Wheel*** it could mean "Great joy. Profit"
*If placed near **XV The Devil*** it could mean "Rheumatism. Regret"
If placed near #20 ***Judgement*** it could mean "Material reward"
If placed near #21 ***The World*** it could mean "Triumph over evil."
If placed near #22 ***The Fool*** it could mean "Unexpected help."

Meaning from the past – 1960's
A secret revealed. The occult power of man. Religious or scientific vocation. If ***The Emperor*** is placed before ***The Hierophant*** in a spread, ***The Emperor*** turns his back on a good situation.
If ***The Hierophant*** is placed before ***The Emperor*** in a spread, knowledge will separate him from wealth and earthly power.

Major Arcana
The Hierophant V
~ *Tradition* ~

—— Keyword Associations ——

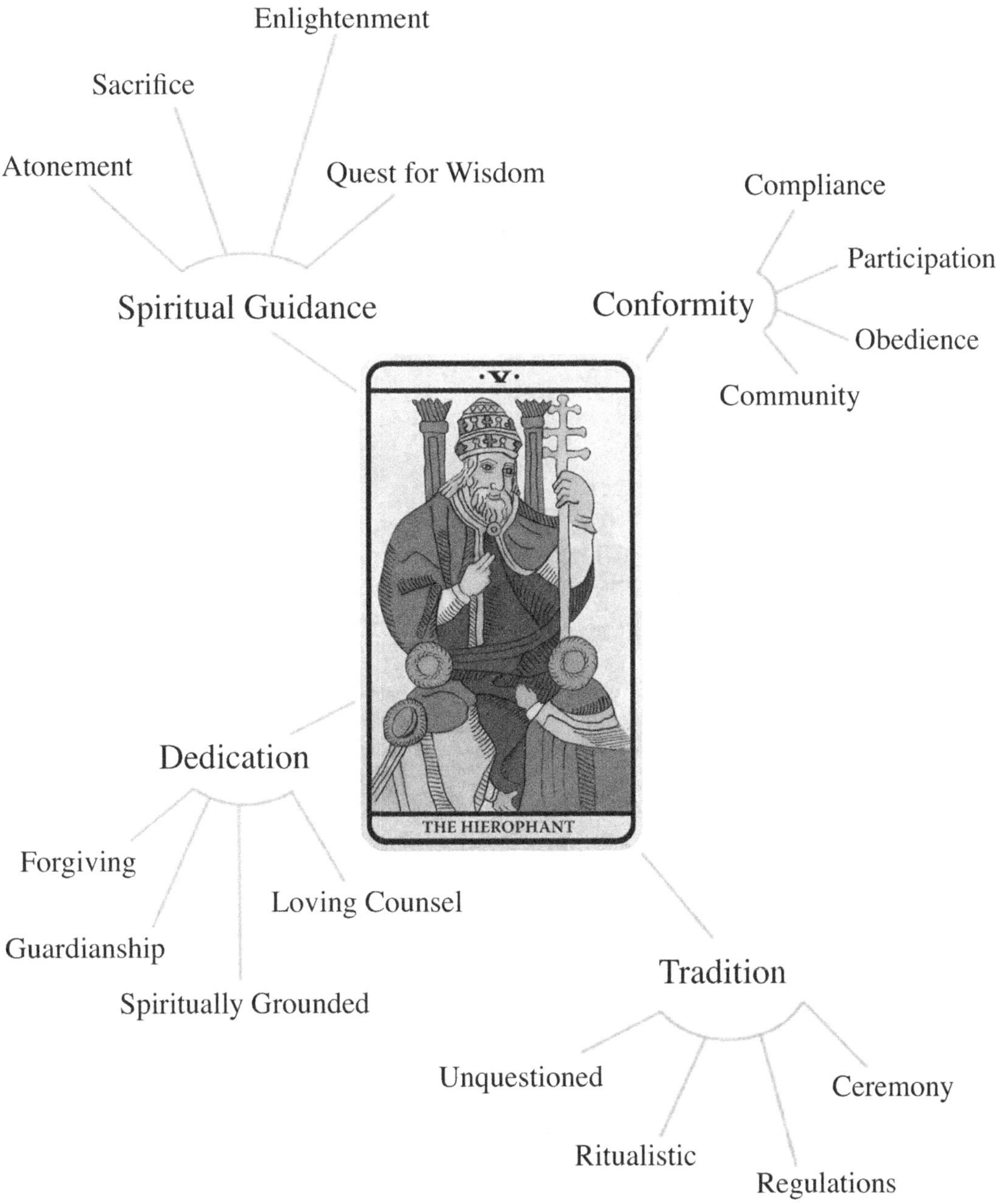

Enlightenment

Sacrifice

Atonement

Quest for Wisdom

Spiritual Guidance

Compliance

Participation

Conformity

Obedience

Community

THE HIEROPHANT

Dedication

Forgiving

Loving Counsel

Guardianship

Spiritually Grounded

Tradition

Unquestioned

Ceremony

Ritualistic

Regulations

Major Arcana
The Lover VI
~ Duality ~

At a Glance
~ Choice
~ Polarity
~ Attraction
~ Soulful Connection
~ Harmonious Interaction
~ Strong Bond

~ Meaning ~
A deep bond of commitment. A touching of the soul brings a fulfilling experience. Universal attraction. Love between two souls.
Choices bring happiness. Trust allows a shared life experience. A choice of trust. A meaningful unity. A mix of dualities.

Meaning from the past – 1980's
Hesitation, Anxious, indecisive pessimistic nature. Poor health.
If placed near #5 **The Hierophant** it could mean "Protection"
If placed near #10 **The Wheel** it could mean "Unhappiness in love"
If placed near #15 **The Devil** it could mean "Material worries"
If placed near #20 **Judgement** it could mean "Ambition fulfilled"
If placed near #21 **The World** it could mean "Cheers you up."
If placed near #22 **The Fool** it could mean "Mistakes. Unhappiness."

Meaning from the past – 1960's
Marriage. A choice to be made. A strong positive card.
If **The Lover** precedes **The Magician**: Indecision.
If **The Lover** precedes **The Chariot**: Betrayal, infidelity

Major Arcana
The Lover VI
~ *Magnetism* ~

—— Keyword Associations ——

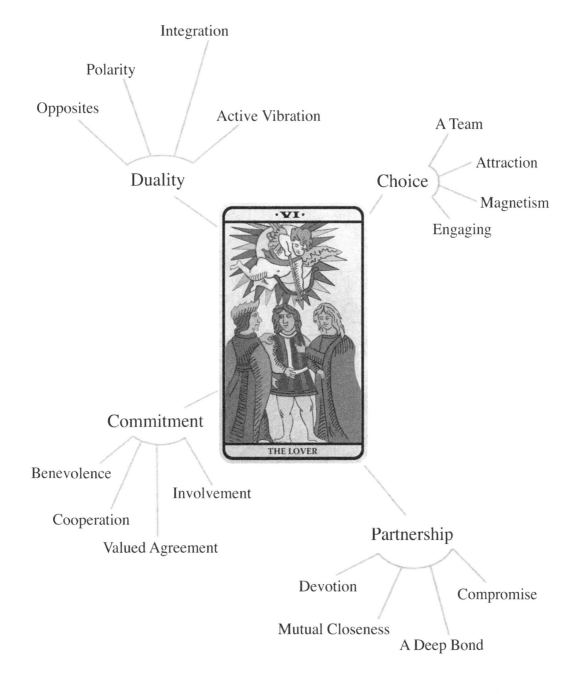

Integration

Polarity

Opposites

Active Vibration

Duality

A Team

Attraction

Choice

Magnetism

Engaging

Commitment

Benevolence

Involvement

Cooperation

Valued Agreement

Partnership

Devotion

Compromise

Mutual Closeness

A Deep Bond

THE LOVER

Major Arcana
The Chariot VII
~ Ability ~

At a Glance
~ Advancement
~ Progress
~ Successful Venture
~ Strong Influence
~ Set in motion
~ Knowledge

~ Meaning ~
The Chariot moves quickly without hesitation. Power to advance beyond others. An unbeatable force. Able to create the situation needed. Creating your own opportunities. Confidence is with you.

Meaning from the past – 1980's
Moral strength. Talent. Intuition. Long life
If placed near #10 **The Wheel** it could mean "Definite success"
If placed near #15 **The Devil** it could mean "Aimless journey"
If placed near #20 **Judgement** it could mean "Violence. Passion."
If placed near #21 **The World** it could mean "Marriage. Attachment."
If placed near #22 **The Fool** it could mean "Possibility of an accident. Avoid flying"

Meaning from the past – 1960's
Conquest. Unexpected good news. The truth will spread quickly.
According to its position it can be interpreted – a timely good word or slander.

Major Arcana
The Chariot VII
~ Execution ~

—— Keyword Associations ——

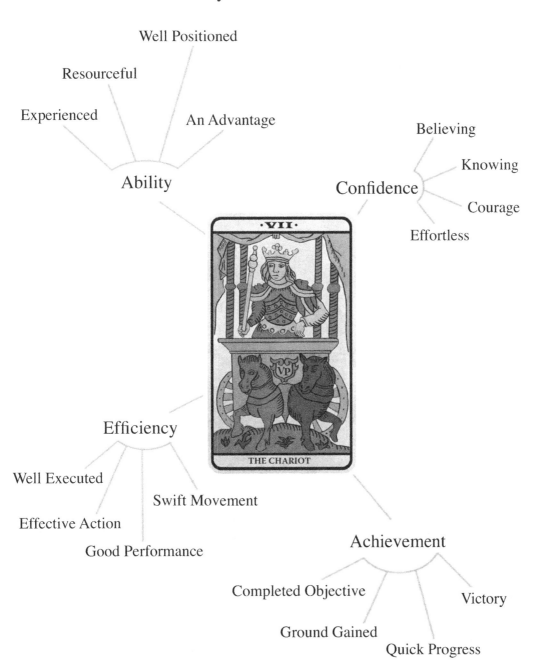

Well Positioned

Resourceful

Experienced

An Advantage

Ability

Believing

Knowing

Confidence

Courage

Effortless

Efficiency

Well Executed

Effective Action

Swift Movement

Good Performance

Achievement

Completed Objective

Victory

Ground Gained

Quick Progress

THE CHARIOT

Major Arcana
Justice VIII
~ *Truth* ~

At a Glance
~ Universal Laws
~ Fairness
~ Harmonious Principles
~ Retribution
~ Spiritual Justice
~ Quest for Truth

~ Meaning ~
Established regulations. Meanings based on principles. For the good of all involved. Many aspects and many truths. Enforced and structured judgment. Equal and impartial action. The authority of truth prevails. Ultimate realities are faced.

Meaning from the past – 1980's
Force and cunning for eventual good. Violence. Brutality.
If placed near #5 ***The Hierophant*** it could mean "Influence gained"
If placed near #10 ***The Wheel*** it could mean "Hardship"
If placed near #15 ***The Devil*** it could mean "A quarrel resolved"
If placed near #20 ***Judgement*** it could mean "A stark revelation"
If placed near #21 ***The World*** it could mean "Determination wins out."
If placed near #22 ***The Fool*** it could mean "A balance is broken."

Meaning from the past – 1960's
Equilibrium. Justice performed. Honesty prevails.
If ***Justice*** is placed before ***The Empress*** in a spread they cancel each other out.
If ***Justice*** is placed before ***The High Priestess*** in a spread a new revelation will be seen in a trial.

Major Arcana
Justice VIII
~ Universal Law ~

—— Keyword Associations ——

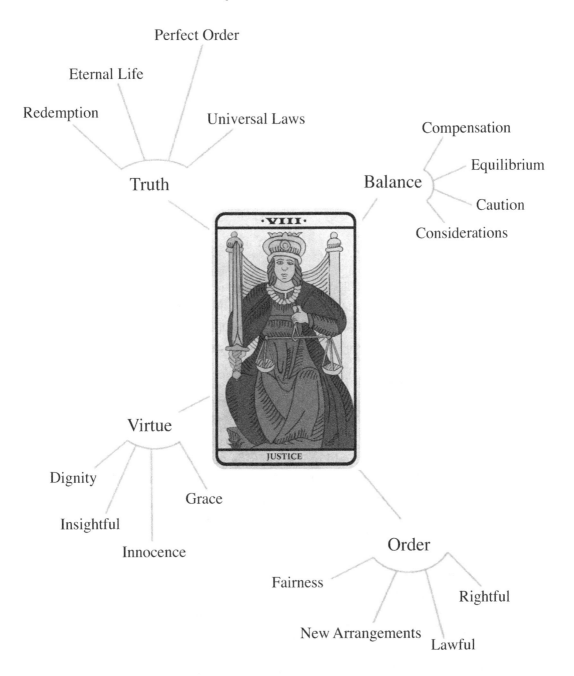

Perfect Order

Eternal Life

Redemption

Universal Laws

Truth

Compensation

Equilibrium

Balance

Caution

Considerations

Virtue

Dignity

Grace

Insightful

Innocence

Order

Fairness

New Arrangements

Rightful

Lawful

Major Arcana
The Hermit IX
~ *Inner Searching* ~

At a Glance
~ Guiding Light
~ Focus on Self
~ Search for Truth
~ Life's Journey
~ Experienced Wisdom
~ The Sage

~ Meaning ~

The Hermit seeks universal knowledge. Answers are found in solitude. A seeker of wisdom. A journey of enlightenment. The Hermit's path shows the way. A need for isolation to bring about clear thinking. Solitude will open doors of insight.

Meaning from the past – 1980's

Long life but troubled by chronic disease. Wisdom, respectability.
If placed near #5 ***The Hierophant*** it could mean "Physical resistance."
If placed near #10 ***The Wheel*** it could mean "Inclined to depression."
If placed near #15 ***The Devil*** it could mean "Sentimental frustration."
If placed near #20 ***Judgement*** it could mean "Difficulties surmounted"
If placed near #21 ***The World*** it could mean "Someone returns."
If placed near #22 ***The Fool*** it could mean "Medical advise required."

Meaning from the past – 1960's

Secluded life. A secret which will be revealed.
If ***The Hermit*** is placed before ***The World*** they cancel each other out. If ***The Hermit*** is placed before ***The High Priestess*** in a spread it means a secret that will never be revealed.

Major Arcana
The Hermit IX
~ *Enlightenment* ~

—— Keyword Associations ——

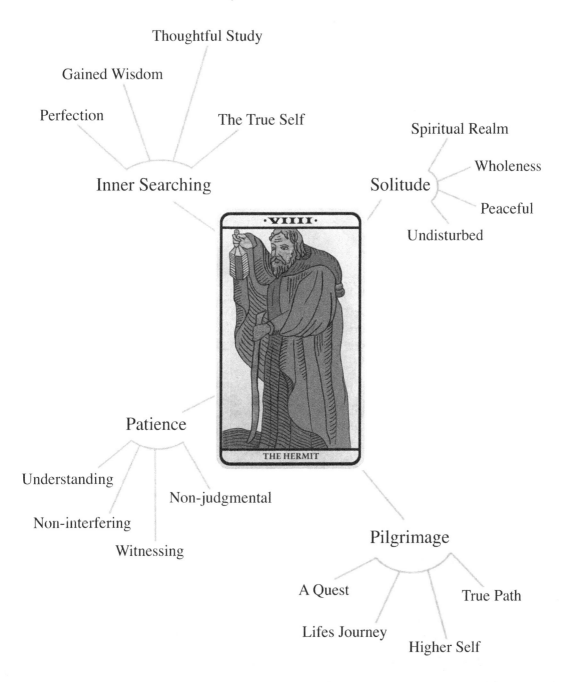

Thoughtful Study

Gained Wisdom

Perfection

The True Self

Inner Searching

Spiritual Realm

Wholeness

Solitude

Peaceful

Undisturbed

Patience

Understanding

Non-judgmental

Non-interfering

Witnessing

Pilgrimage

A Quest

True Path

Lifes Journey

Higher Self

Major Arcana
The Wheel X
~ *Evolvement* ~

At a Glance
~ Cycles of consciousness
~ Eternal Motion
~ Pre-Destined
~ Winds of Change
~ Turn of Events
~ Ever Changing

~ Meaning ~

Opportunities will reveal themselves in time. Ever changing circumstances turn the tables in your favor. Positions shift with actions taken. Motion finds slots of chance to take hold of. Evolutionary changes for the better take place. Lady Luck is nearby.

Meaning from the past – 1980's

Instability, love of traveling and love of discovery. Exuberant nature.
If placed near #5 **The Hierophant** it could mean "Stay at home."
If placed near #15 **The Devil** it could mean "Caution with finances."
If placed near #20 **Judgement** it could mean "Financial luck"
If placed near #21 **The World** it could mean "Inheritance. Promotion."
If placed near #22 **The Fool** it could mean "Definite danger."

Meaning from the past – 1960's

Evolution. Moving towards change. Happy outcome.
If **The Wheel** is placed before **The Magician** in a spread, A happy but unsettled situation. Much is happening.
If **The Magician** is placed before **The Wheel** in a spread, Many mishaps but all ending successfully in the end.

Major Arcana
The Wheel X
~ *Motion* ~

—— Keyword Associations ——

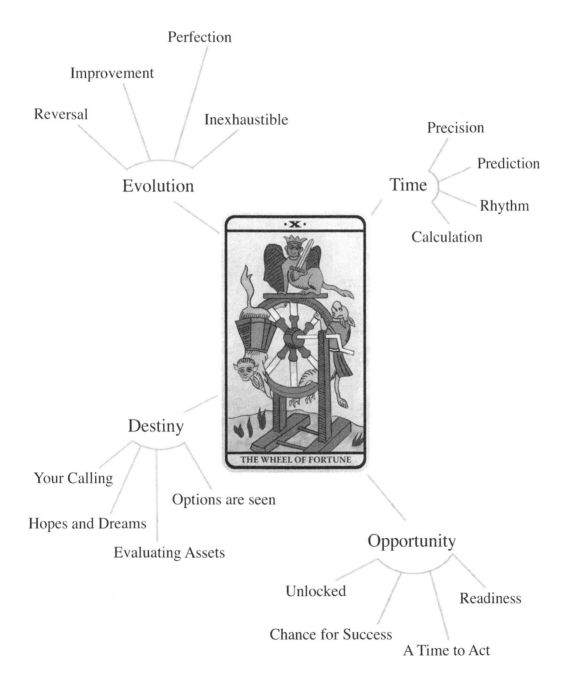

Perfection

Improvement

Reversal

Inexhaustible

Evolution

Precision

Prediction

Time

Rhythm

Calculation

THE WHEEL OF FORTUNE

Destiny

Your Calling

Options are seen

Hopes and Dreams

Evaluating Assets

Opportunity

Unlocked

Readiness

Chance for Success

A Time to Act

Major Arcana
Strength XI
~ Mind & Body ~

At a Glance
~ Inner Strength
~ Overcoming the physical
~ Mind development
~ Higher self awareness
~ Mastering the self
~ Inner conflict

~ Meaning ~

Mind and body working together in harmony. The conflict between spirit and the physical worlds. An understanding of what is reality. The soul prevails. The physical body's connection to the higher self. Harmony between the physical and spiritual worlds. Perfect balance.

Meaning from the past – 1980's

Boldness, anger, violence. Risk of injury.
If placed near #5 *The Hierophant* it could mean "Enthusiasm."
If placed near #10 *The Wheel* it could mean "Complicated journey"
If placed near #15 *The Devil* it could mean "Preoccupation of assets"
If placed near #20 *Judgement* it could mean "Creative work"
If placed near #21 *The World* it could mean "Many improvements"
If placed near #22 *The Fool* it could mean "Danger from carelessness"

Meaning from the past – 1960's

Matters are thought through. A time of will power. Deep focus. Destiny is near.
The Strength card voids out *The Devil* card and *The Death* card in all spreads, The *Strength* card is a strong card and can amplify all positive and negative cards placed near it.

Major Arcana
Strength XI
~ *Control* ~

—— Keyword Associations ——

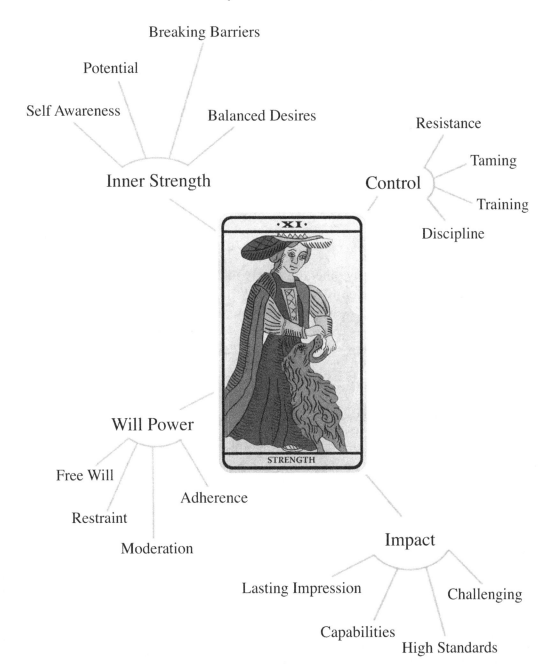

Breaking Barriers

Potential

Self Awareness

Balanced Desires

Inner Strength

Resistance

Taming

Training

Control

Discipline

Will Power

Free Will

Adherence

Restraint

Moderation

Impact

Lasting Impression

Challenging

Capabilities

High Standards

Major Arcana
The Hanged Man XII
~ Sacrifice ~

At a Glance
~ Reversed Thinking
~ Unorthodox Perception
~ Enlightened Understanding
~ Strong Beliefs
~ A Twist in Values
~ Major Transition of Thought

~ Meaning ~
A sacrificial act not understood by others. A lonely understanding. A harsh but enlightened reality. Thinking differently than others brings challenges. A swift reversal of views may take place. A new awareness brings sudden changes. Truths may not be accepted by others.
A state of limbo.

Meaning from the past – 1980's
Misjudgment, Infidelity, Hard work, Fear
If placed near #5 **The Hierophant** it could mean "Improvement."
If placed near #10 **The Wheel** it could mean "Bad luck"
If placed near #15 **The Devil** it could mean "Empty hopes"
If placed near #20 **Judgement** it could mean "Unexpected solution"
If placed near #21 **The World** it could mean "Kindness & protection."
If placed near #22 **The Fool** it could mean "Mounting unhappiness."

Meaning from the past – 1960's
Confusing situation. A bad card always indicating abandonment. Bound by fate with no way out.
If **Temperance** is placed before **The Hanged Man** in a spread, it means indecision.
If **Death** is placed before **The Hanged Man** in a spread, it means bad consequences.

Major Arcana
The Hanged Man XII
~ *Reversal* ~

—— Keyword Associations ——

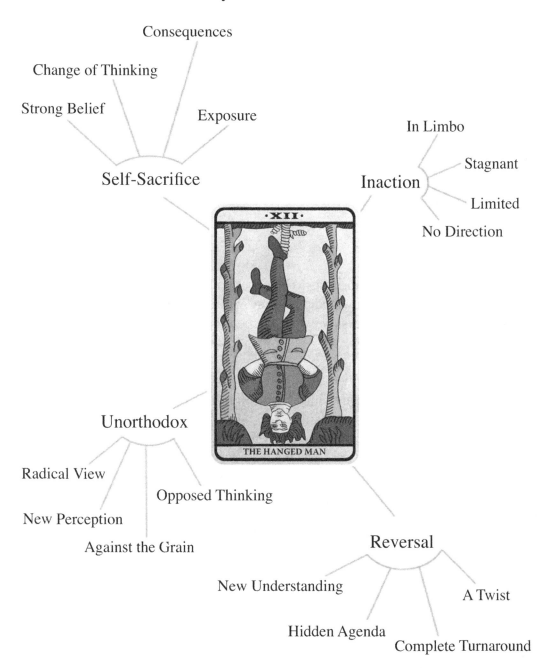

Consequences

Change of Thinking

Strong Belief

Exposure

In Limbo

Stagnant

Self-Sacrifice

Inaction

Limited

No Direction

Unorthodox

Radical View

Opposed Thinking

New Perception

Against the Grain

Reversal

New Understanding

A Twist

Hidden Agenda

Complete Turnaround

THE HANGED MAN

Major Arcana
Death XIII
~ *Transformation* ~

At a Glance
~ Cleansing
~ New Birth
~ Limitations are lifted
~ Voluntary Surrender
~ Changed Perception
~ Transformation

~ Meaning ~
A major shift in identity. New horizons to be experienced. The rising sun brings new life. Changes in spirit release new understanding. Spiritual transition. Bringing in the new and releasing the old. Necessary cycles are coming to an ultimate closure.

Meaning from the past – 1980's
This card is not frightening. It only indicates death if the draw of other cards confirms it. Otherwise it means the end or a change. Fears. Loss of vitality.
If placed near #5 ***The Hierophant*** it could mean "Protection."
If placed near #10 ***The Wheel*** it could mean "Fatal ending"
If placed near #15 ***The Devil*** it could mean "Completely drained"
If placed near #20 ***Judgement*** it could mean "Quick improvement"
If placed near #21 ***The World*** it could mean "Cancels Death card."
If placed near #22 ***The Fool*** it could mean "Failure."

Meaning from the past – 1960's
Death taken in its current meaning. The end of something.
If ***The Tower*** is placed before ***Death*** in a spread it means a great disaster followed by the death of others.

Major Arcana
Death XIII
~ Cleansing ~

—— Keyword Associations ——

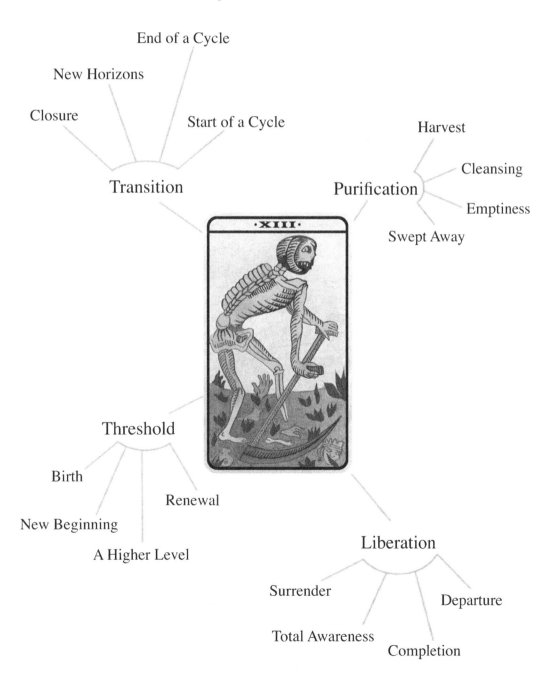

End of a Cycle

New Horizons

Closure

Start of a Cycle

Harvest

Cleansing

Transition

Purification

Emptiness

Swept Away

Threshold

Birth

Renewal

New Beginning

A Higher Level

Liberation

Surrender

Departure

Total Awareness

Completion

Major Arcana
Temperance XIIII
~ Inspiration ~

At a Glance
~ Awe inspiring
~ Flowing effortlessly
~ Grounded spiritually
~ Higher power understood
~ Experienced bliss
~ Finding your center

~ Meaning ~

A sense of free flowing inspiration is with you. The power of knowing the full potential of self. Awe inspiring awareness. A belief in capabilities. All looks well. True inspiration. Eternal happiness. Contentment. Eternal peace and rest. Life's flow is strengthened within you.

Meaning from the past – 1980's

Lack of energy. Shortness of breath. Strong reasoning.

If placed near #5 ***The Hierophant*** it could mean "Emotional love."

If placed near #10 ***The Wheel*** it could mean "Plans fulfilled"

If placed near #15 ***The Devil*** it could mean "Hurt pride"

If placed near #20 ***Judgement*** it could mean "Danger is avoided"

If placed near #21 ***The World*** it could mean "Misjudgment resolved"

If placed near #22 ***The Fool*** it could mean "Disillusionment"

Meaning from the past – 1960's

A decision is carefully made. Both sides are considered fairly.

If ***Justice*** follows ***Temperance*** in a spread decisions take time but resolved well. If ***The Lover*** follows ***Temperance*** in a spread it shows instability and debauchery.

Major Arcana
Temperance XIIII
~ *Angelic* ~

—— Keyword Associations ——

Having Purpose

Gratification

Remarkable

A Worthy Quest

Inspiration

Protector

Steadfast

Guardianship

Alliances

Care Giver

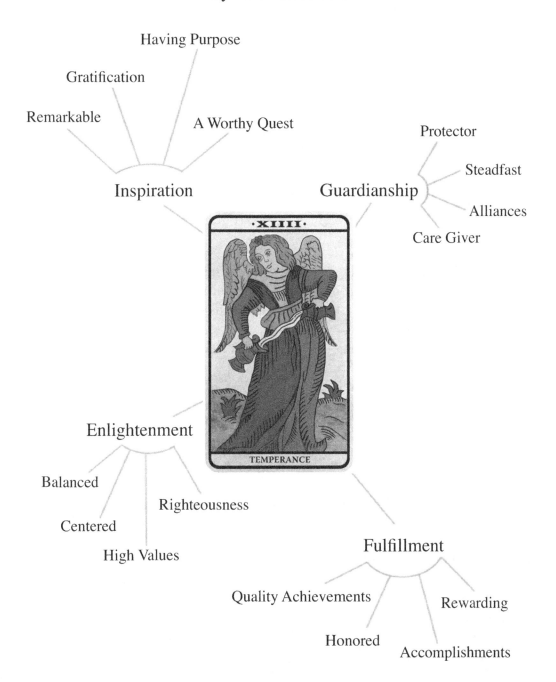

Enlightenment

Balanced

Centered

Righteousness

High Values

Fulfillment

Quality Achievements

Rewarding

Honored

Accomplishments

Major Arcana
The Devil XV
~ *False Truths* ~

At a Glance
~ Delusion
~ Procrastination
~ Self Limitation
~ False Values
~ Denial
~ Pessimism

~ Meaning ~

Self imposed limitations. Focusing on short comings instead of strengths. Seeking guidance in negative places. Dependency on others for self worth. Low self-esteem and negative outlook creates a dark reality. False truths may be close at hand. Things may not be as they appear to be.

Meaning from the past – 1980's

Lack of control. Bad impulses. Encourages excess towards pleasure.
If placed near #5 ***The Hierophant*** it could mean "Level headedness."
If placed near #10 ***The Wheel*** it could mean "Alternating feelings"
If placed near #20 ***Judgement*** it could mean "A time of healing"
If placed near #21 ***The World*** it could mean "Others of influence help"
If placed near #22 ***The Fool*** it could mean "Dishonest business deals"

Meaning from the past – 1960's

Triumph obtained by wicked means. Fortune acquired by fraud. Unscrupulous actions brings destruction of others. This card promises punishment as the powers it holds are only temporary and will be exposed. ***The Devil*** proceeded by the ***Emperor*** in a spread shows forces of evil are unleashed. ***The Devil*** preceding ***Justice*** in a spread shows a wrongful arrest, betrayal.

Major Arcana
The Devil XV
~ Shadows ~

—— Keyword Associations ——

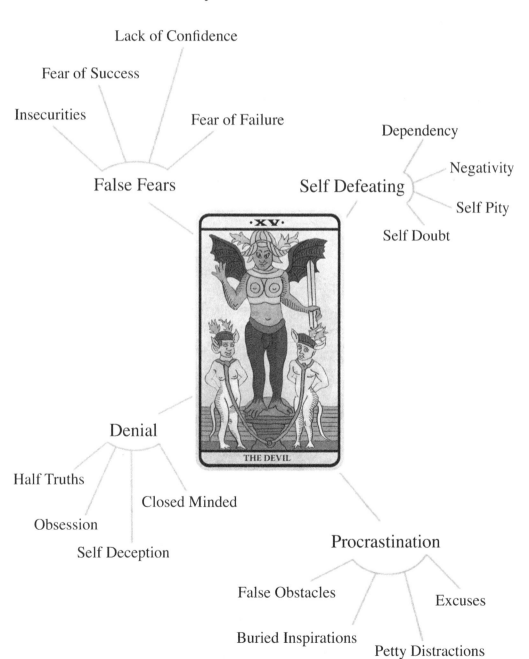

Lack of Confidence

Fear of Success

Insecurities

Fear of Failure

False Fears

Dependency

Negativity

Self Pity

Self Defeating

Self Doubt

Denial

Half Truths

Closed Minded

Obsession

Self Deception

Procrastination

False Obstacles

Excuses

Buried Inspirations

Petty Distractions

Major Arcana
The Tower XVI
~ Disruption ~

At a Glance
~Abrupt Changes
~ Sudden Shift
~ Vulnerability
~ Jeopardized Situation
~ Intimidating Circumstances
~ Challenging Surprise

~ Meaning ~
Riding out the storm. Preparing for what may come is wise. Resistance to a goal. Imposing influence against an idea. Sudden change of events. Tables are turned. A storm approaching on an issue. A time to prepare for a worse case scenario. A time of cautious action.

Meaning from the past – 1980's
Carelessness. Possible loss of consciousness. Psychic troubles.
If placed near #5 *The Hierophant* it could mean "Good self-control"
If placed near #10 *The Wheel* it could mean "Uninteresting contacts"
If placed near #15 *The Devil* it could mean "Inaction. No effort made"
If placed near #20 *Judgement* it could mean "A positive change"
If placed near #21 *The World* it could mean "A ray of hope"
If placed near #22 *The Fool* it could mean "Complications"

Meaning from the past – 1960's
This is a very powerful card. Imaginary creations created by desires and wishful thinking. Plans brought to abrupt halt. Unexpected shock.
When *The Tower* is preceded by *The World* card it means physical disaster. When *The World* card is preceded by *The Tower* it means disaster of a general order.

Major Arcana
The Tower XVI
~ Overwhelming ~

—— Keyword Associations ——

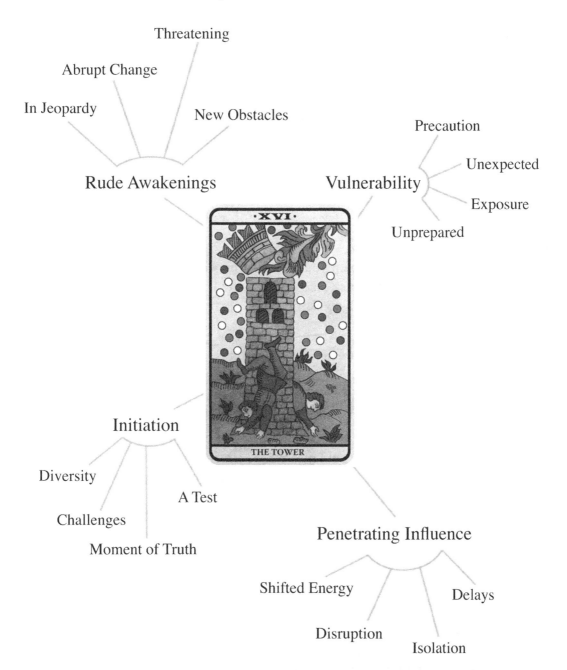

Threatening

Abrupt Change

In Jeopardy

New Obstacles

Rude Awakenings

Precaution

Unexpected

Vulnerability

Exposure

Unprepared

Initiation

Diversity

A Test

Challenges

Moment of Truth

Penetrating Influence

Shifted Energy

Delays

Disruption

Isolation

Major Arcana
The Star XVII
~ Direction ~

At a Glance
~ Good Sign
~ Relief
~ Rest before moving forward
~ Peace of Mind
~ Refreshed Environment
~ Positive Signs

~ Meaning ~
Your shining star. Following a path you know is true. Good direction is seen. Guiding light is shown. Brighter situations come after troubled times. A time of hope. Promise of success as things progress. Changes for the good are approaching. The way home is shown to you.

Meaning from the past – 1980's
Occult protection. Serenity. A dynamic nature. Quick recovery.
If placed near #5 **The Hierophant** it could mean "Strong willpower."
If placed near #10 **The Wheel** it could mean "Disorganization"
If placed near #15 **The Devil** it could mean "Ungranted request"
If placed near #20 **Judgement** it could mean "Timely opportunity"
If placed near #21 **The World** it could mean "Success is certain"
If placed near #22 **The Fool** it could mean "An error in judgement"

Meaning from the past – 1960's
Harmony based on a spiritual influence. Satisfaction. Love of life.
If **The Tower** precedes **The Star** in a spread it can mean the death of a feeling. If **The Star** precedes **The Magician** it can mean your hopes look promising. If **The Magician** precede **The Star** it can mean harmony will be restored by fate and destiny. If **The Star** precedes **The Empress** it can mean a happy destiny is assured.

Major Arcana
The Star XVII
~ *Hope* ~

—— Keyword Associations ——

On Course

Destination

Trust

Preparation

Faith

Knowing

Guidance

Hope

Drawn To

A Message

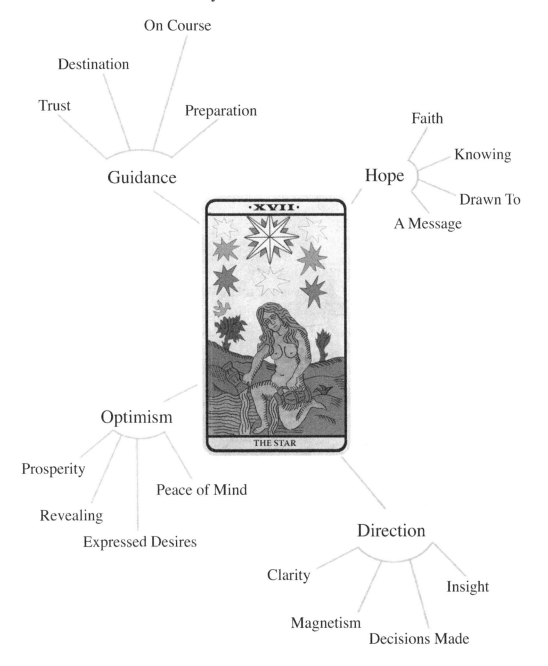

Optimism

Prosperity

Revealing

Peace of Mind

Expressed Desires

Direction

Clarity

Insight

Magnetism

Decisions Made

Major Arcana
The Moon XVIII
~ *Mysterious Paths* ~

At a Glance
- *Deep Reflection*
- *Curious Understanding*
- *Dreamscape*
- *Path is Shown*
- *Twilight of Understanding*
- *Sense of Direction*

~ Meaning ~

A feeling of knowing. A curious path comes from an intuitive insight. Following your instinct on a decision. Important decisions are made with little more than trusting your intuition. Knowing this is the right way without a rational explanation. Following a mystery.

Meaning from the past – 1980's

Disappointment. Anxiety. Obsession. Delicate state of health.
If placed near #5 **The Hierophant** it could mean "Illness is healed."
If placed near #10 **The Wheel** it could mean "Bad luck is overcome"
If placed near #15 **The Devil** it could mean "An operation on the genital organs. Impotence. Frigidity. "
If placed near #20 **Judgement** it could mean "A moral deliverance"
If placed near #21 **The World** it could mean "A hardship ends soon."
If placed near #22 **The Fool** it could mean "Pain. Upset."

Meaning from the past – 1960's

Illusion. A bad card because it corresponds to scandal, denouncement, or a secret revealed. If **Justice** precedes **The Moon** it can mean false witnesses bringing about a wrong condemnation.

Major Arcana
The Moon XVIII
~ *Hidden* ~

—— Keyword Associations ——

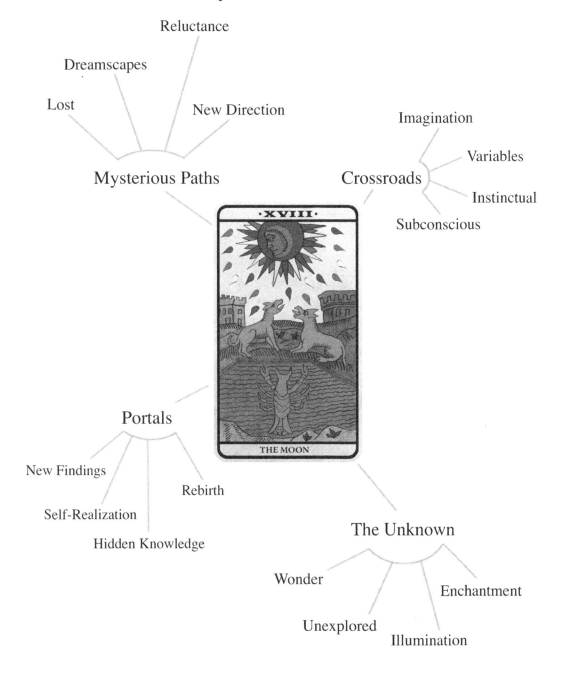

Reluctance

Dreamscapes

Lost

New Direction

Mysterious Paths

Imagination

Variables

Instinctual

Crossroads

Subconscious

Portals

New Findings

Rebirth

Self-Realization

Hidden Knowledge

The Unknown

Wonder

Enchantment

Unexplored

Illumination

Major Arcana
The Sun XVIIII
~ *Nurturing* ~

At a Glance
~ *New Life*
~ *Good Position*
~ *Bright Outlook*
~ *Strong Progress*
~ *Positive Environment*
~ *Seen Clearly*

~ Meaning ~

Healing energy. A vibrant position. A place of good surroundings and influence. Promise of future advancements. A turn in the right direction. Nurturing self aware-ness and happiness. Things start to blossom from your efforts.

Meaning from the past – 1980's

Happiness. Intellectual tendencies. Artistic gifts. Strength. Vitality.
If placed near #5 ***The Hierophant*** it could mean "Long life."
If placed near #10 ***The Wheel*** it could mean "Satisfying journey"
If placed near #15 ***The Devil*** it could mean "Increased vitality"
If placed near #20 ***Judgement*** it could mean "Mutual love"
If placed near #21 ***The World*** it could mean "New stimulation."
If placed near #22 ***The Fool*** it could mean "Disappointment."

Meaning from the past – 1960's

Universal radiance. Triumph and success. This is a very powerful card which is in no case influenced by the cards around it and which can be applied to all cards. ***The Tower*** card preceding ***The Sun*** card means a certain triumph prevails.

Major Arcana
The Sun XVIIII
~ *Light* ~

—— Keyword Associations ——

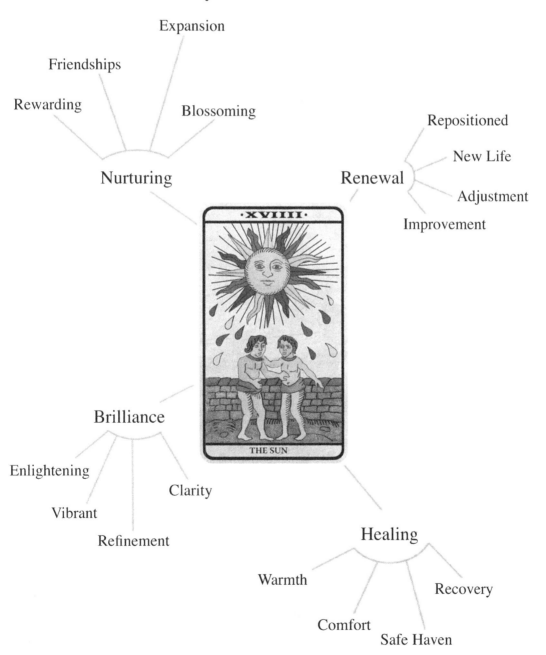

Expansion

Friendships

Rewarding

Blossoming

Repositioned

New Life

Adjustment

Nurturing

Renewal

Improvement

Brilliance

Enlightening

Clarity

Vibrant

Refinement

Healing

Warmth

Recovery

Comfort

Safe Haven

Major Arcana
Judgement XX
~ *New Awareness* ~

At a Glance
- *Enlightenment*
- *Higher Understanding*
- *Advancement*
- *Uplifting*
- *Experienced Truth*
- *Fully seen reality*

~ Meaning ~

A time of true judgment of affair's. A realization of significant importance. Moving to a higher level of awareness. A complete understanding makes life easier to navigate through. A sense of worth. An undeniable happiness. Positioned in a better environment.

Meaning from the past – 1980's

Straightforwardness. Love of beauty. Good health.
If placed near #5 **The Hierophant** it could mean "Aims are achieved."
If placed near #10 **The Wheel** it could mean "Travel will work"
If placed near #15 **The Devil** it could mean "Worry over the children"
If placed near #21 **The World** it could mean "Love and friendship."
If placed near #22 **The Fool** it could mean "False friends."

Meaning from the past – 1960's

Fame of an intellectual order and having good influence. Tendencies to be in a higher physical plane. If **Judgement** precedes **The Chariot** it means great news and public acclaim. **Judgement** preceding **The Hermit** it means Fame, glory, triumph, but hidden, almost inner glory. Scientific discoveries. Work performed in obscurity. This card is not affected by other cards near it other than **The Hermit** and **The Chariot**.

Major Arcana
Judgement XX
~ Inevitable ~

—— Keyword Associations ——

Accountability

Enlightenment

Realization

Truth

New Awareness

Opening Up

Summoned

Awakening

A Calling

Surfacing

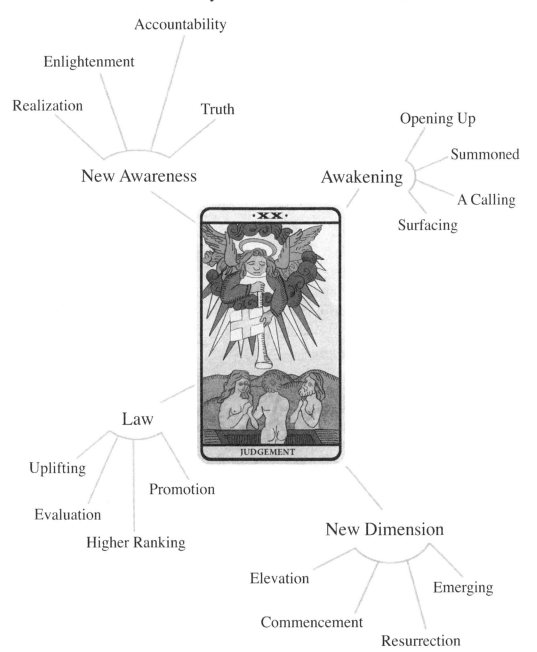

Law

Uplifting

Promotion

Evaluation

Higher Ranking

New Dimension

Elevation

Emerging

Commencement

Resurrection

Major Arcana
The World XXI
~ *Perfect Balance* ~

At a Glance
- *End of a Journey*
- *Final Destination*
- *Peace and Tranquility*
- *Celebrated Accomplishment*
- *Acceptance*
- *Understanding*

~ Meaning ~

All becomes understood. A joyful accomplishment. Perfect balance. Harmonious reunion. The finality of a wonderful journey. A state of perfection. A feeling of unity. An understanding of self. A happy ending to a wonderful experience.

Meaning from the past – 1980's

Capacity for making decisions. A practical mind. A long and quiet life.
If placed near #5 **The Hierophant** it could mean "A protector comes"
If placed near #10 **The Wheel** it could mean "Fortified actions"
If placed near #15 **The Devil** it could mean "Selfish decisions"
If placed near #22 **The Fool** it could mean "Temporary extravagance."

Meaning from the past – 1960's

The perfection of man. Perfect scenario. The individual representing their thoughts. Clear thinking and focus.
Combines well with most other cards.

Major Arcana
The World XXI
~ *Glory* ~

—— Keyword Associations ——

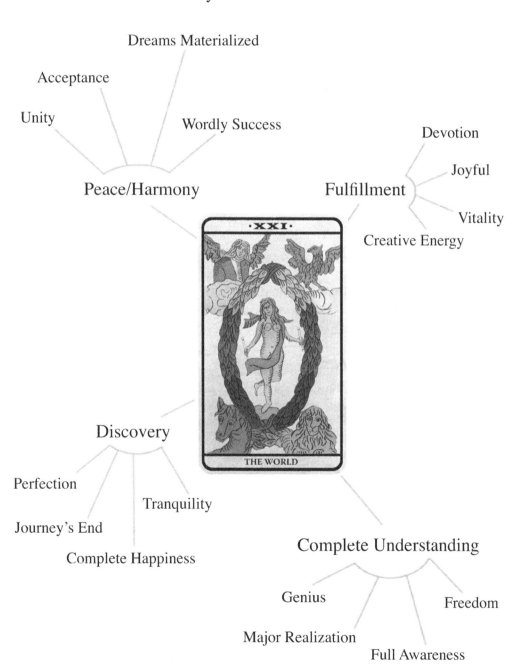

Dreams Materialized

Acceptance

Unity

Wordly Success

Devotion

Joyful

Peace/Harmony

Fulfillment

Vitality

Creative Energy

Discovery

Perfection

Tranquility

Journey's End

Complete Happiness

Complete Understanding

Genius

Freedom

Major Realization

Full Awareness

Major Arcana
The Fool XXII
~ *Believing* ~

At a Glance
~ *Acting on Impulse*
~ *Blind Trust*
~ *Unexpected Situation*
~ *Leap of Faith*
~ *Care Free*
~ *High Hopes*

~ Meaning ~
Moving forward without specific direction. Optimism and trust without planning. Unpredictable influences can bring positive or negative results. Un-conforming attitude. Following your bliss without worry or precaution.

Meaning from the past – 1980's
Inconsistency. Unawareness. Thoughtlessness. Listlessness. Neurasthenia.
If placed near #5 *The Hierophant* it could mean "Back on track"
If placed near #10 *The Wheel* it could mean "Better health"
If placed near #15 *The Devil* it could mean "Unhappy love-affair"
If placed near #20 *Judgement* it could mean "Unexpected help"
If placed near #21 *The World* it could mean "Improvement overall."

Meaning from the past – 1960's
Man progressing towards evolution. Thoughtlessness, lack of order, carelessness in promises, insecurity. *The Fool* preceding *The Hermit* means news of the past is buried. *The Fool* preceding *The Chariot* means important piece of news coming from afar. *The Fool* preceding *The Sun* means an event unexpected brings clarity.

Major Arcana
The Fool 0
~ *Trust* ~

—— Keyword Associations ——

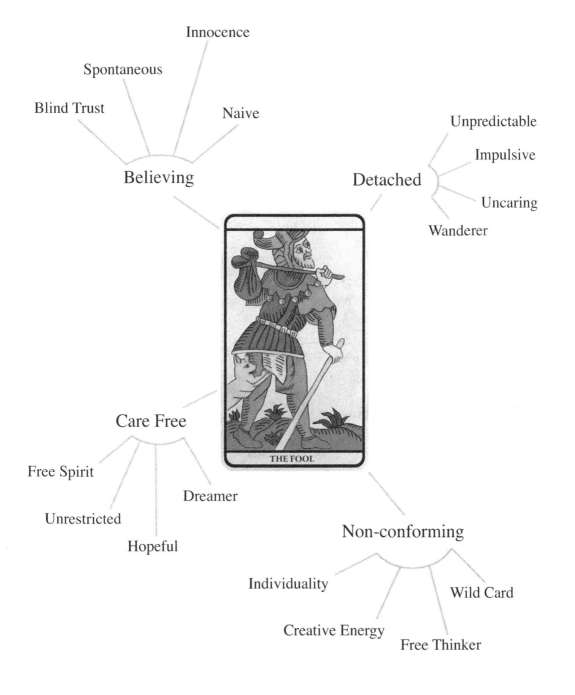

Innocence

Spontaneous

Blind Trust

Naive

Believing

Unpredictable

Impulsive

Detached

Uncaring

Wanderer

Care Free

Free Spirit

Unrestricted

Dreamer

Hopeful

Non-conforming

Individuality

Wild Card

Creative Energy

Free Thinker

THE FOOL

The 56 Minor Arcana

Each suit has Ace through ten and four court cards for a total of 56 cards. Think of a deck of playing cards only with an additional card court in each of the four suits. This additional court card is The Knight.

My work blends all four suits into the same root meaning in each of the 14 numeric values in the Minor Arcana, Ace through King.

So we have a King a Queen a Knight and a Page for court cards along with Ace through Ten in each of the four suits. The way I read and teach is the four suits represent the four basic functions of consciousness. Thought, Emotion, Spirit and our Material/Physical world.

Thought is represented by the suit of Swords. How you think. How you reason and your rational, logical choices you make in life. Emotion is represented by the suit of Cups. How you feel about your life. What moves you. What touches your heart. What and who you love.

Your spirit is represented in the suit of Wands. What you yearn for in life. What inspires you. What you thirst for. What enriches your spirit.

Lastly your physical world is represented in the suit of Pentacles. Your place in society. Your career. Your assets, finances, physical relationship, How you belong and interact in your community are represented in the suit of Pentacles.

These four functions of consciousness all interact with each other in our daily lives. As we move along in life. I can love my career and can pursue my happiness in my spirit. If I buy a house it effects my material world, how I think, my feelings and lift my spirit as well. If I get involved in a new relationship it will effect my emotional world but it also effects my material, physical world, my thinking, my spirit, pursuits of happiness. So they are all interconnected to some degree.

Because of this connection in our consciousness to the four suits I feel the numeric value of the Minor Arcana have a common meaning for each number regardless of the suit. All Aces have a basic common meaning. All of the Fives will have a basic common meaning. All the Tens, The Pages, The Queens and so on will have a basic commonality in regards to their numeric value.

Meanings are endless so even though the numeric value links a common meaning to the other three cards in the deck they will all have different meanings in these pages. You will see The Knight of Swords will have different key-word meanings than the Knight of Cups. But the basic meaning will be shown as a common meaning for all the knights. *"Action"* is the basic key word for the Knights in my work.

Therefore The Knight of Cups would be action from the heart. The Knight of Swords would be action based on careful thinking. The Knight of Wands would be action based on fulfilling what I yearn for. The Knight of Pentacles would be action on my material world. The physical aspects, money, career, my place in society.

I have never used reverse meanings in my work and the pips of The Tarot of Marseilles is not designed to be used that way. If a card is placed upside down in a reading I simply turn it right side up. All cards face me, the reader, right side up. Therefore only 14 basic keywords are needed to know the base meaning of the Minor Arcana's 56 cards. Ace through 10 and four court cards. One direction, right side up.

This way of seeing the Minor Arcana has worked very well for me in my teaching and in my readings as a professional. It is also capable of finding dynamic answers and insight in your readings.

I am adding the meanings from the 1980's and the 1960's like I did with the Majors to show how we have changed and improved our meanings over time. Now let's look at the Minors!

Where the Major Arcana represent metaphysical, universal principles, the Minor Arcana are more grounded to our life experiences in the physical plane. Our everyday concerns and goals.

The Minor Arcana can represent the four basic functions of consciousness nicely. Thought (Swords), Emotion (Cups), Spirit (Wands), and the Physical (Pentacles). *Carl Jung, Isabel Myers, Kathryn Briggs* and other great thinkers of psychology have claimed that we are all born with one of these four basic functions of consciousness being our primary personality type. However all four aspects do affect us all to some degree. Some aspects in our lives will bring out one aspect more strongly than the other three. This will depend on who we are and how we think. I see the four suits of the Tarot representing this way of thinking very well.

Which Suit are you?

Where you are strong in one suit makes you weakest in its opposite suit.
Cups and Swords are opposite personality types. So are Wands and Pentacles.
Note the five categories these personality types are viewed from:
• Being
• Trusting
• Yearning
• Seeking
• Prizing

The Suit of Cups

The Cups are the suit of Romance. The suit of Cups represents emotion, love, empathy, and compassion. They are the suit of creative energy. Family, friendships and relationships of love. They are the true romantic. Cups make up approximately 10% of the population.

Suit of Cups
~ The Heart ~

Cups value:
Being – *enthusiastic*
Trusting – *intuition*
Yearning for – *romance*
Seeking – *identity*
Prizing – *recognition*

Suit of Swords
Swords value:
Being – *calm*
Trusting – *reason*
Yearning for – *achievement*
Seeking – *knowledge*
Prizing – *deference*

Suit of Pentacles
Pentacles value:
Being – *concerned*
Trusting – *authority*
Yearning for – *belonging*
Seeking – *security*
Prizing – *gratitude*

Suit of Wands
Wands value:
Being – *excited*
Trusting – *impulse*
Yearning for – *impact*
Seeking – *stimulation*
Prizing – *generosity*

Minor Arcana
The Ace of Cups
~ *New Concept* ~

At a Glance
- *Fresh Start*
- *A New Look*
- *A First Step*
- *Good Direction*
- *Turn of Events*
- *New Possibilities*

~ Meaning ~

A heartfelt inspirations becomes clear.

New arrangement and change of plans. New influence with good energy. Time is good to shift direction to more promising opportunities. A new influence may become substantial. Keep aware of opportunities of the heart. A bright vibration is around you.

Meaning from the past – 1980's

Talent and communicability. Joy in intimacy. Useful conversations.

If placed near #5 ***The Hierophant*** it could mean "Vain hope"

If placed near #21 ***The World*** it could mean "The seeker asserts himself and attracts sympathy."

Meaning from the past – 1960's

Great psychic protection and knowledge which will be realized. Plans, latent thoughts, ready to be put into action, but whose meaning is still hidden.

Minor Arcana
The Ace of Cups
~ *Awareness* ~

—— Keyword Associations ——

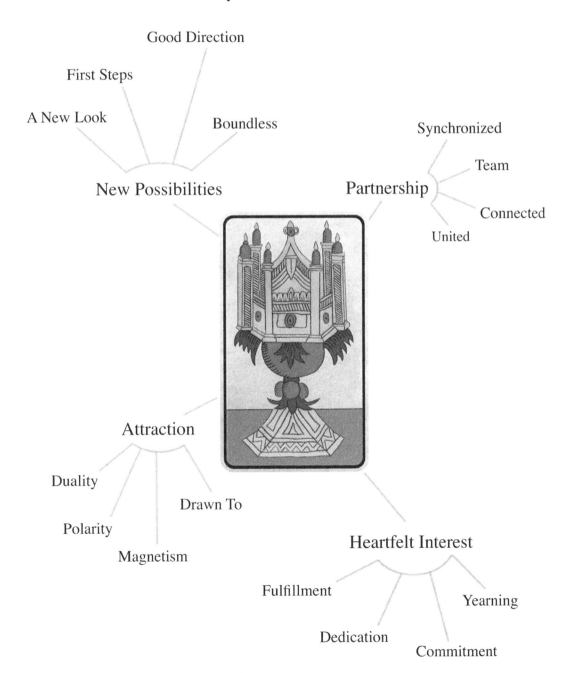

Good Direction

First Steps

A New Look

Boundless

New Possibilities

Synchronized

Team

Partnership

Connected

United

Attraction

Duality

Drawn To

Polarity

Magnetism

Heartfelt Interest

Fulfillment

Yearning

Dedication

Commitment

Minor Arcana
The Two of Cups
~ Choice ~

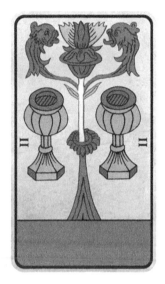

At a Glance
- *Partnership*
- *Commitment*
- *Polarity*
- *Wholeness*
- *A Trust*
- *Mutual Understanding*

~ Meaning ~

A commitment from the heart.
Good choices are clearly seen. A decision is made to move forward from the heart. A bond is established. New awareness and understanding of another. Mutual cooperation to a common goal. Sincere intentions are seen.

Meaning from the past – 1980's

Animosity. Incompatibility. Poor health. No communication.
If placed near #5 **The Hierophant** it could mean "Better prospects"
If placed near #21 **The World** it could mean "Harmony restored to a relationship."

Meaning from the past – 1960's

Man can elevate himself by thought. His success on a physical plane will be subordinated to his actions on a psychic plane, when these are in agreement with his conscience. Alliance in every sphere. Spiritual and physical riches.

Minor Arcana
The Two of Cups
~ *Opportunity* ~

—— Keyword Associations ——

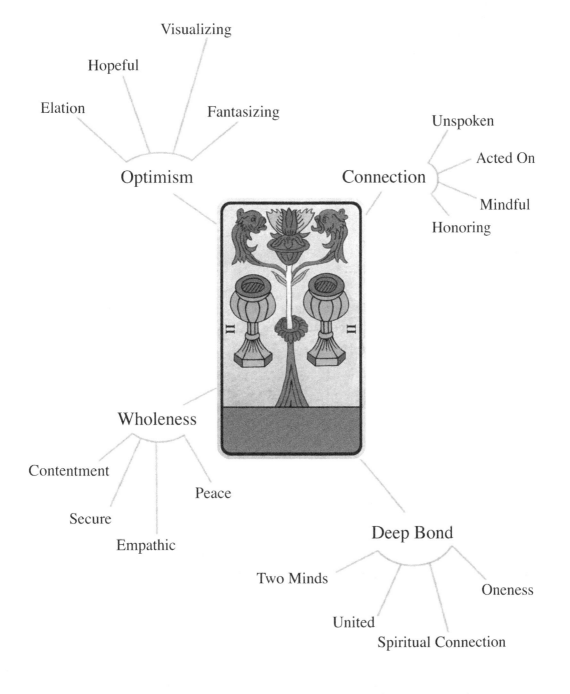

Visualizing

Hopeful

Elation

Fantasizing

Unspoken

Acted On

Optimism

Connection

Mindful

Honoring

Wholeness

Contentment

Peace

Secure

Empathic

Deep Bond

Two Minds

Oneness

United

Spiritual Connection

Minor Arcana
The Three of Cups
~ Creativity ~

At a Glance
~ New Growth
~ Nurturing
~ Creative Passion
~ Nourishing
~ Heartfelt Energy
~ Engagement

~ Meaning ~
Happy celebration.
A realization of potential is made clear. Plans continue forward with enthusiasm. Vision is made clear of future goals and ideas. The duality of the situation keeps things moving forward effortlessly.

Meaning from the past – 1980's
Body and mind at peace. Happy ending of an event.
If placed near #5 **The Hierophant** it could mean "Your studies will prove beneficial. Better health. "
If placed near #21 **The World** it could mean "Your plans will soon materialize."

Meaning from the past – 1960's
Spiritual riches brought about by a balance between the physical and the mental. Irregular, intermittent, plenty. Fruitful contribution by a union of two beings.

Minor Arcana
The Three of Cups
~ *Conception* ~

—— Keyword Associations ——

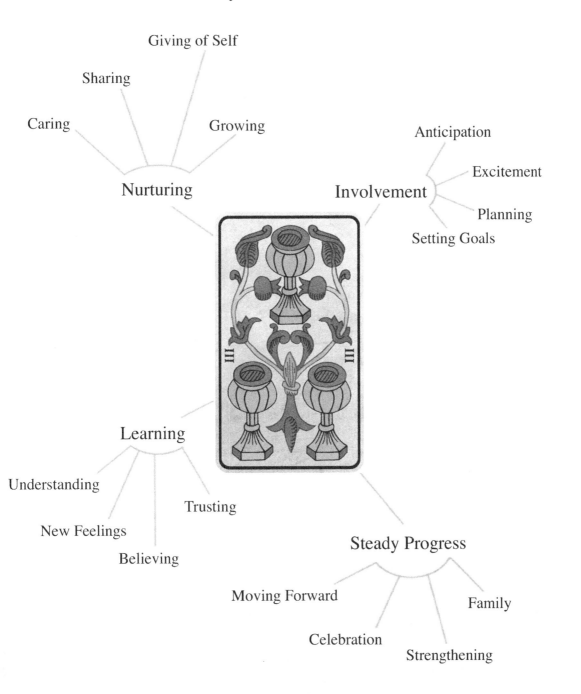

Giving of Self

Sharing

Caring

Growing

Nurturing

Anticipation

Excitement

Involvement

Planning

Setting Goals

Learning

Understanding

Trusting

New Feelings

Believing

Steady Progress

Moving Forward

Family

Celebration

Strengthening

Minor Arcana
The Four of Cups
~ *Stability* ~

At a Glance
• *Dedicated*
• *Sacrifice*
• *Known reality*
• *Unchanged*
• *Mutual Understanding*
• *Dependable*

~ Meaning ~

Predictable and steady situation. Routines and schedules become the norm. Lack of vision can bring unexpected challenges. A time to slow things down. Stability may bring a lack of vision and diminish motivation.

Meaning from the past – 1980's

Disappointment and neurasthenia. Beware of physical danger and sentimental disappointment.

If placed near #5 ***The Hierophant*** it could mean "Gives you courage."

If placed near #21 ***The World*** it could mean "The seeker frees themselves from obligations."

Meaning from the past – 1960's

Plenty as a result of agreement and equilibrium. Difficult agreement.

Minor Arcana
The Four of Cups
~ *Patterns* ~

—— Keyword Associations ——

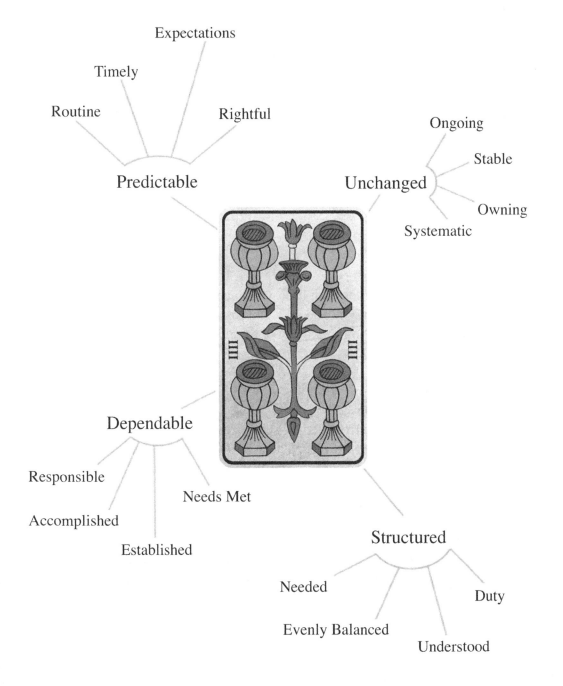

Expectations

Timely

Routine

Rightful

Predictable

Ongoing

Stable

Unchanged

Owning

Systematic

Dependable

Responsible

Needs Met

Accomplished

Established

Structured

Needed

Duty

Evenly Balanced

Understood

Minor Arcana
The Five of Cups
~ Change ~

At a Glance
- *A Shift*
- *Absence*
- *Change of Heart*
- *Situation in Jeopardy*
- *New Direction*
- *Heartfelt Loss*

~ Meaning ~
A time of challenge. A sense of loss can limit vision and inspiration. A time to believe in self. Inspiration is still within you and all is not lost. Something may still be saved. A time to count blessings. Moving forward will bring rewards not yet seen. A time of healing and acceptance.

Meaning from the past – 1980's
Separation and tears. You are surrounded by jealous people.
Gossip endangers your happiness. If placed near #5 **The Hierophant** it could mean "Slight improvement." If placed near #21 **The World** it could mean "The heart is at peace. Luck returns."

Meaning from the past – 1960's
Lack of harmony. Indefinite plan which comes to nothing. It also means prosperity in material things, but not a lasting one. A plan which does not achieve its aim.

Minor Arcana
The Five of Cups
~ *Reversal* ~

—— Keyword Associations ——

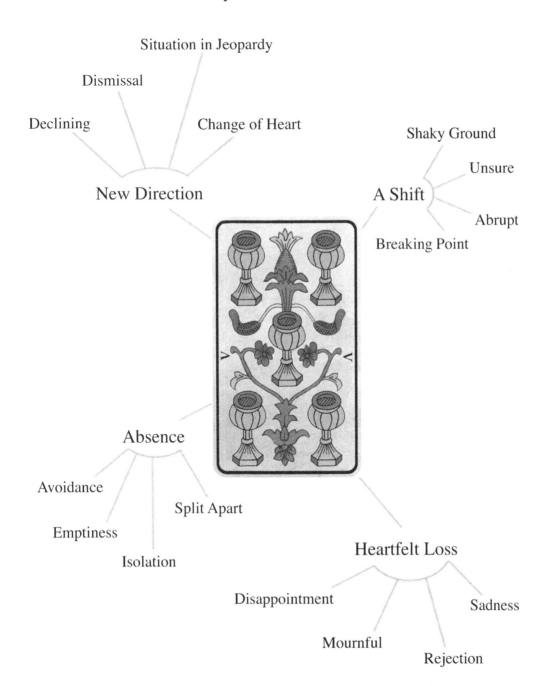

Situation in Jeopardy

Dismissal

Declining

Change of Heart

Shaky Ground

Unsure

New Direction

A Shift

Abrupt

Breaking Point

Absence

Avoidance

Split Apart

Emptiness

Isolation

Heartfelt Loss

Disappointment

Sadness

Mournful

Rejection

Minor Arcana
The Six of Cups
~ *Perseverance* ~

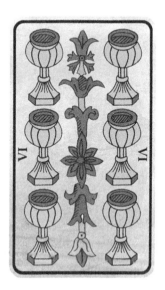

At a Glance
~ *Making Amends*
~ *Forgiveness*
~ *Empathy*
~ *New friendships*
~ *Rebuilding*
~ *Caring*

~ Meaning ~
A better understanding restores trust. The situation becomes peaceful. Acceptance brings back happiness into ones life. Important issues are addressed and dealt with. A coming to terms on the situation brings back peace and harmony.

Meaning from the past – 1980's
Hesitation and inferiority. More losses than profit.
If placed near #5 **The Hierophant** it could mean "Less unhappiness."
If placed near #21 **The World** it could mean "Influential people help the seeker."

Meaning from the past – 1960's
Equilibrium. Assured and durable success because it is perfectly balanced. Immobility. A state of affairs which cannot be deranged.

Minor Arcana
The Six of Cups
~ *Prevailing* ~

—— Keyword Associations ——

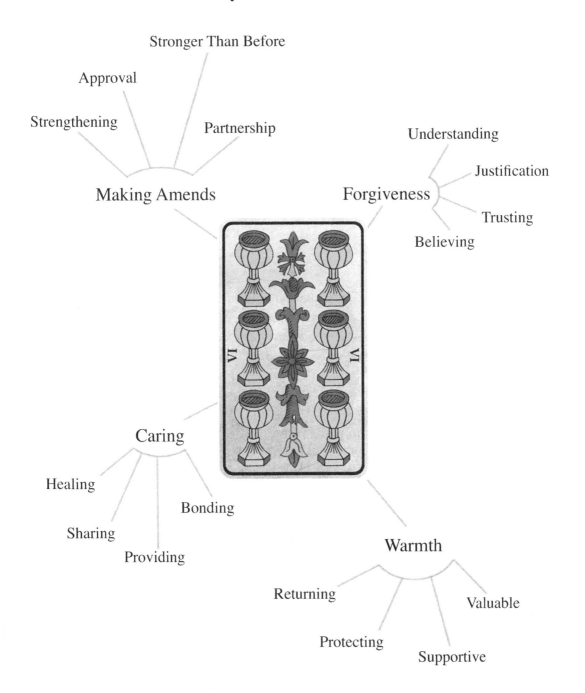

Stronger Than Before

Approval

Strengthening

Partnership

Making Amends

Understanding

Justification

Forgiveness

Trusting

Believing

Caring

Healing

Bonding

Sharing

Providing

Warmth

Returning

Valuable

Protecting

Supportive

Minor Arcana
The Seven of Cups
~ Confidence ~

At a Glance
~ Self-esteem
~ Satisfaction
~ Reaching for
~ Gratification
~ Self Worth
~ Recognition

~ Meaning ~

Evaluation of self brings clarity to the quest at hand. Re-evaluating progress brings insight for moving forward. Endless possibilities are realized. A time to focus on past successes not failures. Your experience becomes an asset. Your ability is known and looked for by others. Confidence will be gained as you move forward.

Meaning from the past – 1980's

Mutual love. Satisfaction concerning the heart and the senses.
If placed near #5 **The Hierophant** it could mean "Increase of energy."
If placed near #21 **The World** it could mean "Triumph over all obstacles."

Meaning from the past – 1960's

Difficulty in the realization of a happiness of the mind and the raising oneself above matter. Pleasure, transient joys. Realizations believed durable and which are not. Disappointments.

Minor Arcana
The Seven of Cups
~ *Vigilance* ~

—— Keyword Associations ——

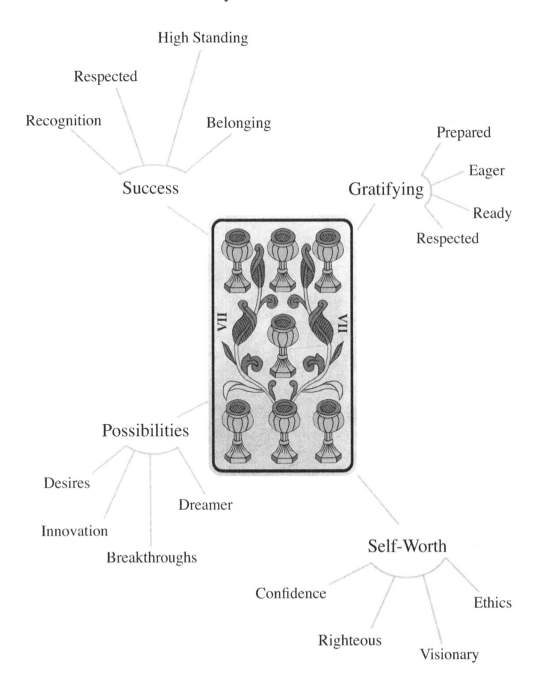

High Standing

Respected

Recognition

Belonging

Prepared

Eager

Success

Gratifying

Ready

Respected

VII   VII

Possibilities

Desires

Dreamer

Innovation

Breakthroughs

Self-Worth

Confidence

Ethics

Righteous

Visionary

Minor Arcana
The Eight of Cups
~ *Advancement* ~

At a Glance
~ *Moving Forward*
~ *Doing More*
~ *Quality*
~ *Flowing Progress*
~ *Refinements*
~ *New goals*

~ Meaning ~

A quest coming from the heart. Searching for refinement of a good situation. Holding on to assets as you move to acquire more. Stability mixed with positive changes. All will stay together as you strengthen what is already yours.

Meaning from the past – 1980's

Sentimental disappointment. Broken engagement.
If placed near #5 ***The Hierophant*** it could mean "Triumph of reason over hostility."
If placed near #21 ***The World*** it could mean "A marriage or an association would lead to social ascension."

Meaning from the past – 1960's

Abandon of the psychic return to matter, mental imbalance. Alone, in a game it means agreement and success unless influenced by the cards around it.

Minor Arcana
The Eight of Cups
~ *Strengthened* ~

—— Keyword Associations ——

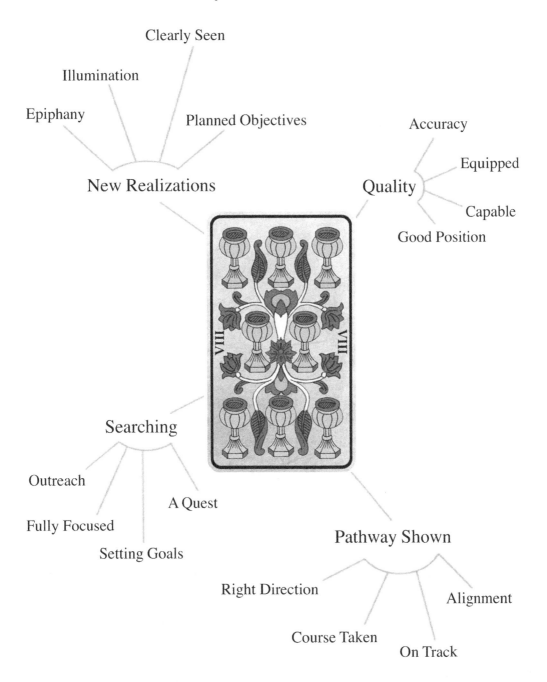

Clearly Seen

Illumination

Epiphany

Planned Objectives

New Realizations

Accuracy

Equipped

Quality

Capable

Good Position

Searching

Outreach

A Quest

Fully Focused

Setting Goals

Pathway Shown

Right Direction

Alignment

Course Taken

On Track

Minor Arcana
The Nine of Cups
~ *Attainment* ~

At a Glance
~ *Happiness*
~ *A Pinnacle*
~ *Peace of Mind*
~ *Contentment*
~ *Sound Decisions*
~ *Gratification*

~ Meaning ~

A heartfelt achievement is accomplished.

A time to enjoy what you've created. Stop and smell the roses. Your hard earned efforts are ready to be enjoyed. Happiness will be yours. A time to share good fortune with others.

Traditional Meaning from – 1980's

Joy for women, fecudity. Improves private life.

If placed near #5 ***The Hierophant*** it could mean "End of a period of doubt. Return of the beloved."

If placed near #21 ***The World*** it could mean "Happiness, Good health. (For women wished for pregnancy)."

Traditional Meaning from – 1960's

The joy of realization or aspirations of the mind. Success in the realm of intellect. Success in all projects, especially those based on, and concerning, matters of the heart.

Minor Arcana
The Nine of Cups
~ *Aspiration* ~

—— Keyword Associations ——

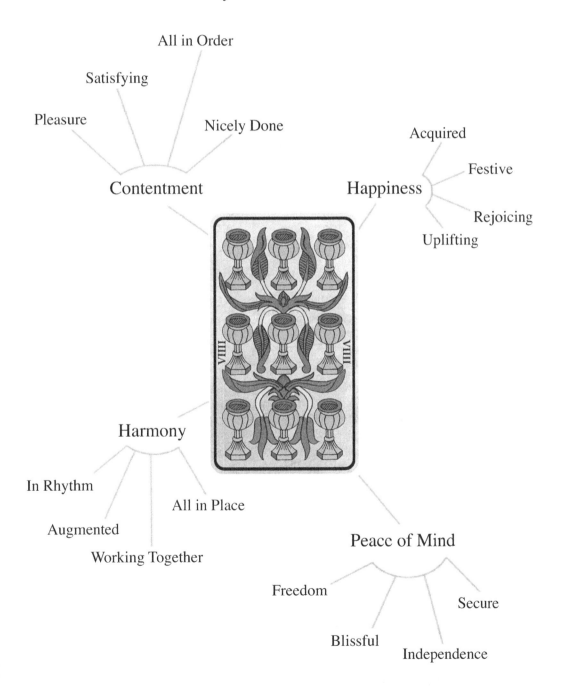

All in Order

Satisfying

Pleasure

Nicely Done

Contentment

Acquired

Festive

Happiness

Rejoicing

Uplifting

Harmony

In Rhythm

All in Place

Augmented

Working Together

Peacc of Mind

Freedom

Secure

Blissful

Independence

Minor Arcana
The Ten of Cups
~ Completion ~

At a Glance
~ Family
~ Togetherness
~ Uplifting
~ Peace
~ Reunion
~ The destination

~ Meaning ~

An established setting is created. A rewarding end. A completion to something beautiful. Fulfilling spirit. An experience well worth doing. A time to look back at what has been accomplished. Sense of pride is deservingly felt. A job well done.

Meaning from the past – 1980's

Friendship. Brief love affairs. The family is protected. Children (especially girls) are wanted..

If placed near #5 **The Hierophant** it could mean "Success in the Arts. Birth of a daughter who will be very pretty."

If placed near #21 **The World** it could mean "The person you love is unattainable."

Meaning from the past – 1960's

Separation of matter and mind. Burning need for evolution. Violent separation of all material links in view of a spiritual evolution. Transition, passage from life to death, halt.

Minor Arcana
The Ten of Cups
~ *Fulfillment* ~

—— Keyword Associations ——

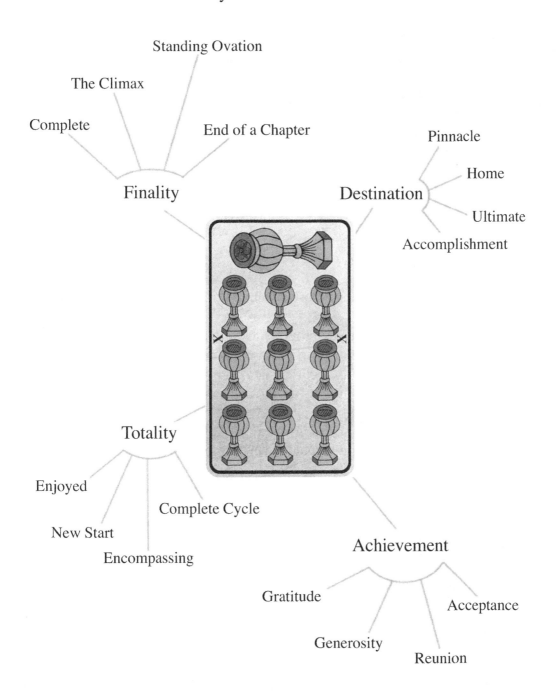

Standing Ovation

The Climax

Complete

End of a Chapter

Finality

Pinnacle

Home

Destination

Ultimate

Accomplishment

Totality

Enjoyed

Complete Cycle

New Start

Encompassing

Achievement

Gratitude

Generosity

Acceptance

Reunion

Minor Arcana
The Page of Cups
~ *New Path* ~

At a Glance
~ *Imagination*
~ *Spontaneity*
~ *Learning*
~ *Servitude*
~ *Diversity*
~ *Enthusiasm*

~ Meaning ~

Opportunities for what you seek are close at hand. A time to look for advancement. The cup is yours to take.

Your goals will be made clear as you progress. New experiences of the heart will open your eyes. New path from the heart is close by.

Meaning from the past – 1980's

Passionate and fickle young girl. Breaking away of the beloved, sentimental mistake. If placed near #5 **The Hierophant** it could mean "Curbs base instincts and checks hitherto uncontrollable impulses."
If placed near #21 **The World** it could mean "More security, more freedom."

Meaning from the past – 1960's

Spiritual and moral riches obtained as a reward and giving full satisfaction. Work is rewarded and gives wealth.

Minor Arcana
The Page of Cups
~ *Pilgrimage* ~

—— Keyword Associations ——

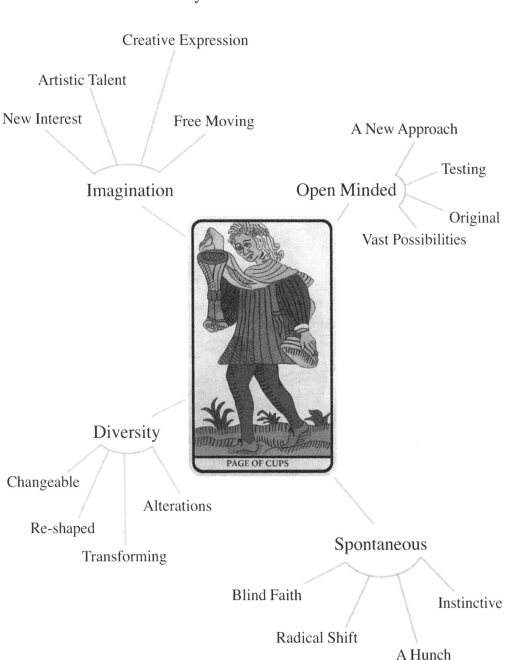

Creative Expression

Artistic Talent

New Interest

Free Moving

Imagination

A New Approach

Testing

Open Minded

Original

Vast Possibilities

Diversity

Changeable

Re-shaped

Alterations

Transforming

PAGE OF CUPS

Spontaneous

Blind Faith

Radical Shift

Instinctive

A Hunch

Minor Arcana
The Knight of Cups
~ *Action* ~

At a Glance
- *Passion*
- *Loyalty*
- *Excitement*
- *Humility*
- *Devotion*
- *Alliance*

~ Meaning ~

Action taken from the heart. Progress is made based on emotion. A clear sense of direction and purpose. A time to take action on goals. Moving forward with no hesitation. A belief in what seems to be effortless. Seeing the answers and moving on them quickly.

Meaning from the past – 1980's

Seductive and sentimental man. Love is enhanced, transformed and protected.
If placed near #5 **The Hierophant** it could mean "Pleasant evolution of feelings and wishes."
If placed near #21 **The World** it could mean "Total happiness. Joy of living."

Meaning from the past – 1960's

Frail destiny. Passing destiny which must be seized.

Minor Arcana
The Knight of Cups
~ *Activity* ~

—— Keyword Associations ——

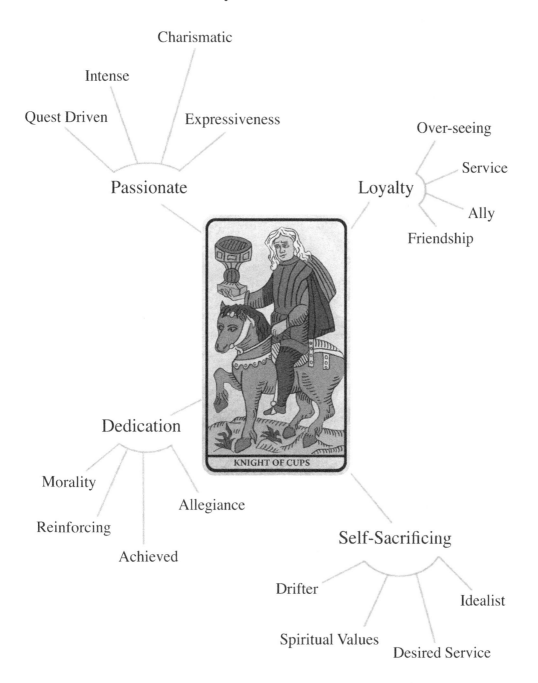

Charismatic

Intense

Quest Driven

Expressiveness

Passionate

Over-seeing

Service

Ally

Loyalty

Friendship

Dedication

Morality

Reinforcing

Achieved

Allegiance

Self-Sacrificing

Drifter

Idealist

Spiritual Values

Desired Service

KNIGHT OF CUPS

Minor Arcana
The Queen of Cups
~ *Patience* ~

At a Glance
- *Kindness*
- *Sensitivity*
- *Compassion*
- *Generosity*
- *Serenity*
- *Understanding*

~ Meaning ~

Seeing other aspects of a situation can be helpful in making progress.
Empathic awareness makes things clear. Motives are sincere. Care of the situation will be felt. Feelings need to be considered before acting. Consideration is remembered and appreciated

Meaning from the past – 1980's

Housewife. Affectionate and devoted wife and mother. Gives us courage and sometimes resignation.
If placed near #15 **The Devil** it could mean "She lowers herself through excesses due to the card representing the Devil."
If placed near #21 **The World** it could mean "Fulfills ambitions and brings comfort."

Meaning from the past – 1960's

Her wisdom prevails. Prudence, good advice.

Minor Arcana
The Queen of Cups
~ *Understanding* ~

—— Keyword Associations ——

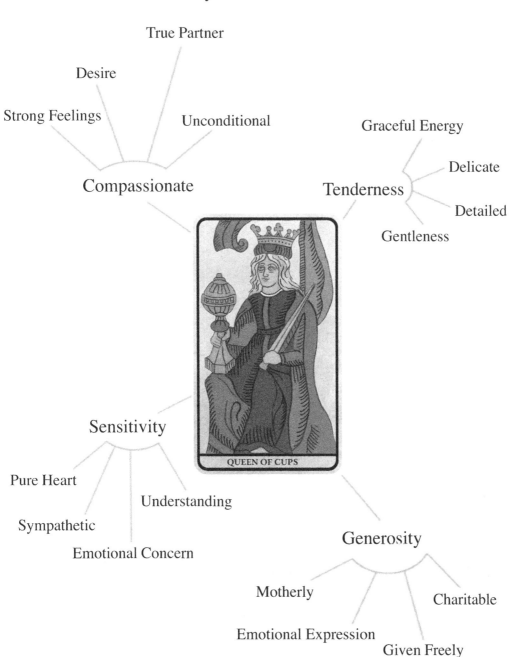

True Partner

Desire

Strong Feelings

Unconditional

Compassionate

Graceful Energy

Delicate

Tenderness

Detailed

Gentleness

Sensitivity

Pure Heart

Understanding

Sympathetic

Emotional Concern

Generosity

Motherly

Charitable

Emotional Expression

Given Freely

Minor Arcana
The King of Cups
~ *Knowledge* ~

At a Glance
- *Order*
- *Authenticity*
- *Diplomacy*
- *Wisdom*
- *Authority*
- *Structure*

~ Meaning ~

A positive influence on the situation. Clear alliances to a goal. Mutual friendship becomes an ally. You have the knowledge to make needed changes. Facts seem clear enough to move forward. In a good position to make clear decisions.

Meaning from the past – 1980's

Man who is fundamentally good but rather domineering in emotional matters. Easily carried away by his impulses.

If placed near #5 ***The Hierophant*** it could mean "With more wisdom your health improves."

If placed near #21 ***The World*** it could mean "Love, help and honours."

Meaning from the past – 1960's

Knowledge and abundance. Possessions safeguarded and protected, inalienable riches.

Minor Arcana
The King of Cups
~ *Insight* ~

—— Keyword Associations ——

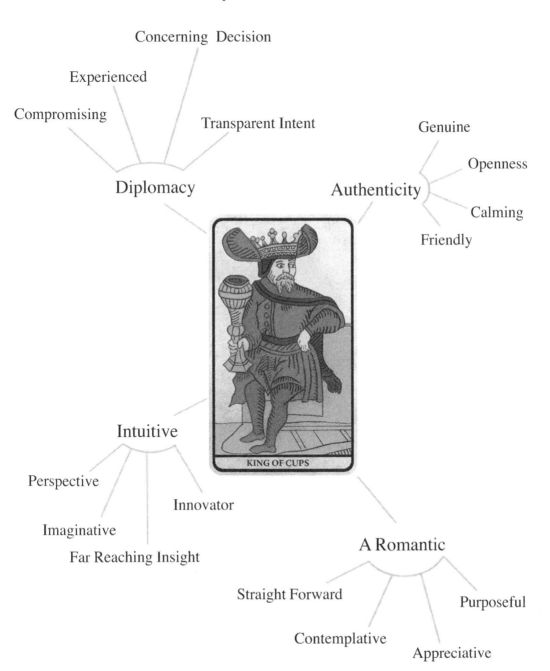

Concerning Decision

Experienced

Compromising

Transparent Intent

Diplomacy

Genuine

Openness

Authenticity

Calming

Friendly

KING OF CUPS

Intuitive

Perspective

Innovator

Imaginative

Far Reaching Insight

A Romantic

Straight Forward

Purposeful

Contemplative

Appreciative

Where the Major Arcana represent metaphysical, universal principles, the Minor Arcana are more grounded to our life experiences in the physical plane. Our everyday concerns and goals.

The Minor Arcana can represent the four basic functions of consciousness nicely. Thought (Swords), Emotion (Cups), Spirit (Wands), and the Physical (Pentacles). *Carl Jung, Isabel Myers, Kathryn Briggs* and other great thinkers of psychology have claimed that we are all born with one of these four basic functions of consciousness being our primary personality type. However all four aspects do affect us all to some degree. Some aspects in our lives will bring out one aspect more strongly than the other three. This will depend on who we are and how we think. I see the four suits of the Tarot representing this way of thinking very well.

Which Suit are you?

Where you are strong in one makes you weakest in its opposite type.
Cups and Swords are opposite personality types. So are Wands and Pentacles.
Note the five categories these personality types are viewed from:
• Being
• Trusting
• Yearning
• Seeking
• Prizing

The Suit of Pentacles

Pentacles are the suit of interaction and organization. They make good organizers and are vital for harmonous function in society. Pentacles enjoy having a sense of belonging to something bigger than themselves. Pentacles value tradition.
Pentacles make up approximately 40% of the population.

Suit of Pentacles
~ The Physical World ~

Pentacles value:
Being – concerned
Trusting – authority
Yearning for – belonging
Seeking – security
Prizing – gratitude

Suit of Wands
Wands value:
Being – excited
Trusting – impulse
Yearning for – impact
Seeking – stimulation
Prizing – generosity

Suit of Cups
Cups value:
Being – enthusiastic
Trusting – intuition
Yearning for – romance
Seeking – identity
Prizing – recognition

Suit of Swords
Swords value:
Being – calm
Trusting – reason
Yearning for – achievement
Seeking – knowledge
Prizing – deference

Minor Arcana
The Ace of Pentacles
~ New Concept ~

At a Glance
~ Newly Established
~ An Offer
~ Promising Start
~ Agreements
~ An Apprenticeship
~ New Involvement

~ Meaning ~
New involvement with skills and services. A move in the right direction. Improvement in a situation. Offering something to society. Your service will be recognized as sincere. Good company with new friendships. Identity is found.

Meaning from the past – 1980's
Card like a talisman that symbolizes success. Increase of money.
If placed near #21 **The World** it could mean "In general everything should go well."

Meaning from the past – 1960's
Material success by invoking aid from on high. A card of chance whose effects are delayed or hastened according to its place among the cards which surround it, for it is neutral and gives no information by itself.

Minor Arcana
The Ace of Pentacles
~ *Discovery* ~

—— Keyword Associations ——

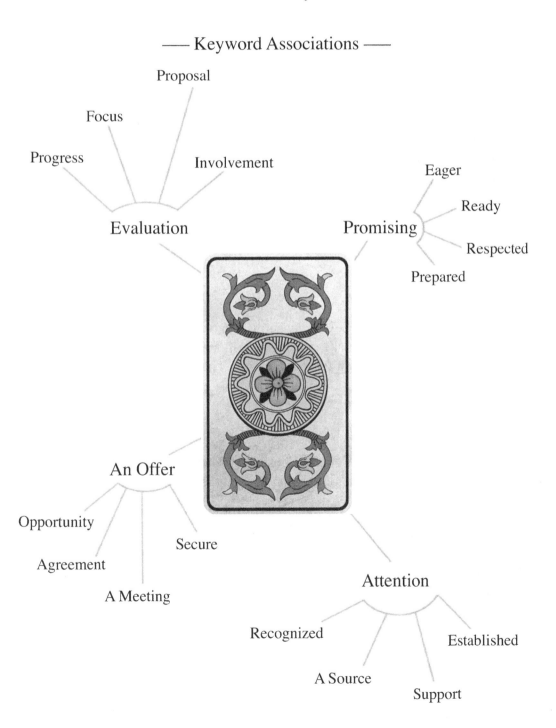

Proposal

Focus

Progress

Involvement

Evaluation

Promising

Eager

Ready

Respected

Prepared

An Offer

Opportunity

Agreement

Secure

A Meeting

Attention

Recognized

Established

A Source

Support

Minor Arcana
The Two of Pentacles

~ *Choice* ~

At a Glance
- *Keeping Options Open*
- *Time Will Tell*
- *New Direction*
- *Chosen Carefully*
- *A Difficult Choice*
- *Balanced Decision*

~ Meaning ~

A time to look for more insight before decisions can be made. The choice will be in your hands. A difficult time to make a decision. All is not yet seen clearly. More will be realized as time passes. Do not force a decision. The answers will come to you in time.

Meaning from the past – 1980's

Meanness and broken promises. Theft or possible dishonesty.
If placed near #10 **The Wheel** it could mean "Violent retaliation."

Meaning from the past – 1960's

Man can elevate himself by thought. His success on a physical plane will be subordinated to his actions on a psychic plane when these are in agreement with his conscience. Alliance in every sphere. Spiritual and physical riches.

Minor Arcana
The Two of Pentacles
~ *Response* ~

—— Keyword Associations ——

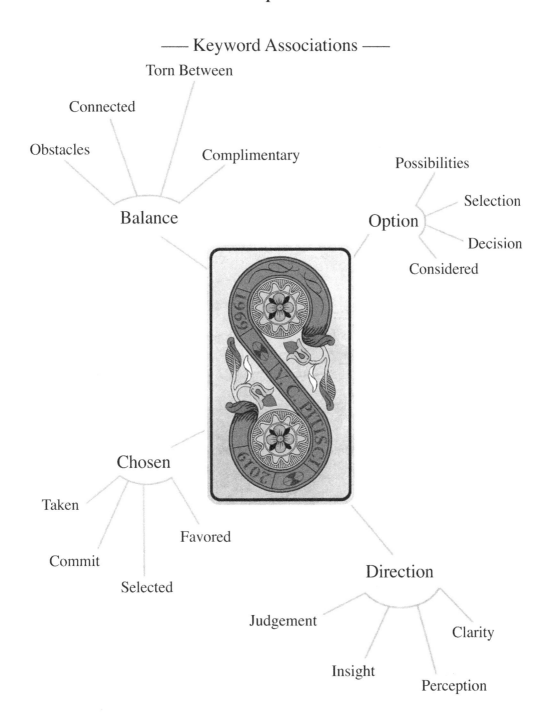

Torn Between

Connected

Obstacles

Complimentary

Possibilities

Selection

Balance

Option

Decision

Considered

Chosen

Taken

Favored

Commit

Selected

Direction

Judgement

Clarity

Insight

Perception

Minor Arcana
The Three of Pentacles
~ *Creativity* ~

At a Glance
~ *New Life*
~ *Opportunity*
~ *Manifestation*
~ *Taking Shape*
~ *Prosperity*
~ *Imagination*

~ Meaning ~
Newly established circumstances look positive. Happiness with your social status. Establishing security and well-being. Accomplished skills are created. A learning process works well and pays off. Efforts are rewarded. A time for creating new ideas.

Meaning from the past – 1980's
Luck and promotion. End of difficulties.
If placed near #20 *Judgement* it could mean "Efforts are rewarded."

Meaning from the past – 1960's
Forces taken from the occult to obtain realizations in the physical world. Equilibrium which is only relative.

Minor Arcana
The Three of Pentacles
~ *Variation* ~

—— Keyword Associations ——

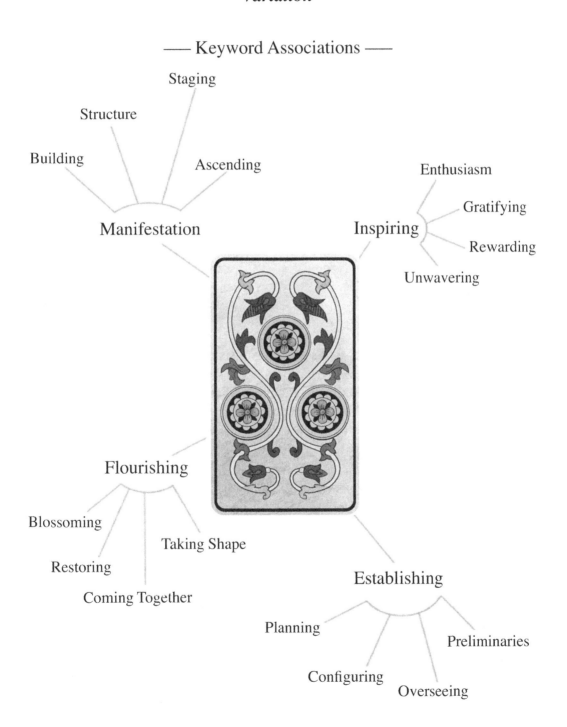

Staging

Structure

Building

Ascending

Enthusiasm

Gratifying

Manifestation

Inspiring

Rewarding

Unwavering

Flourishing

Blossoming

Taking Shape

Restoring

Establishing

Coming Together

Planning

Preliminaries

Configuring

Overseeing

Minor Arcana
The Four of Pentacles
~ Stability ~

At a Glance
~ Structured
~ Established
~ Secure
~ Conforming
~ Routine
~ Reliable

~ Meaning ~

A safe and secure environment.

A time to enjoy reliable routines and settings. Consistency with no changes. A good place to be for now.

A focus on material concerns. A time to focus on what you have. Change might come later.

Meaning from the past – 1980's

Pleasant change. Love comes into your life again and money too.

If placed near #20 **Judgement** it could mean "A present will be given to you. Fulfilled ambition."

Meaning from the past – 1960's

A card which stands for the expansion of the psychic and equilibrium between different planes. Halt, plan brought to a halt by contingencies which hold it fast. When it is modified by the cards around it, it no longer means abrupt halt but rather a great reversal.

Minor Arcana
The Four of Pentacles
~ *Grounded* ~

—— Keyword Associations ——

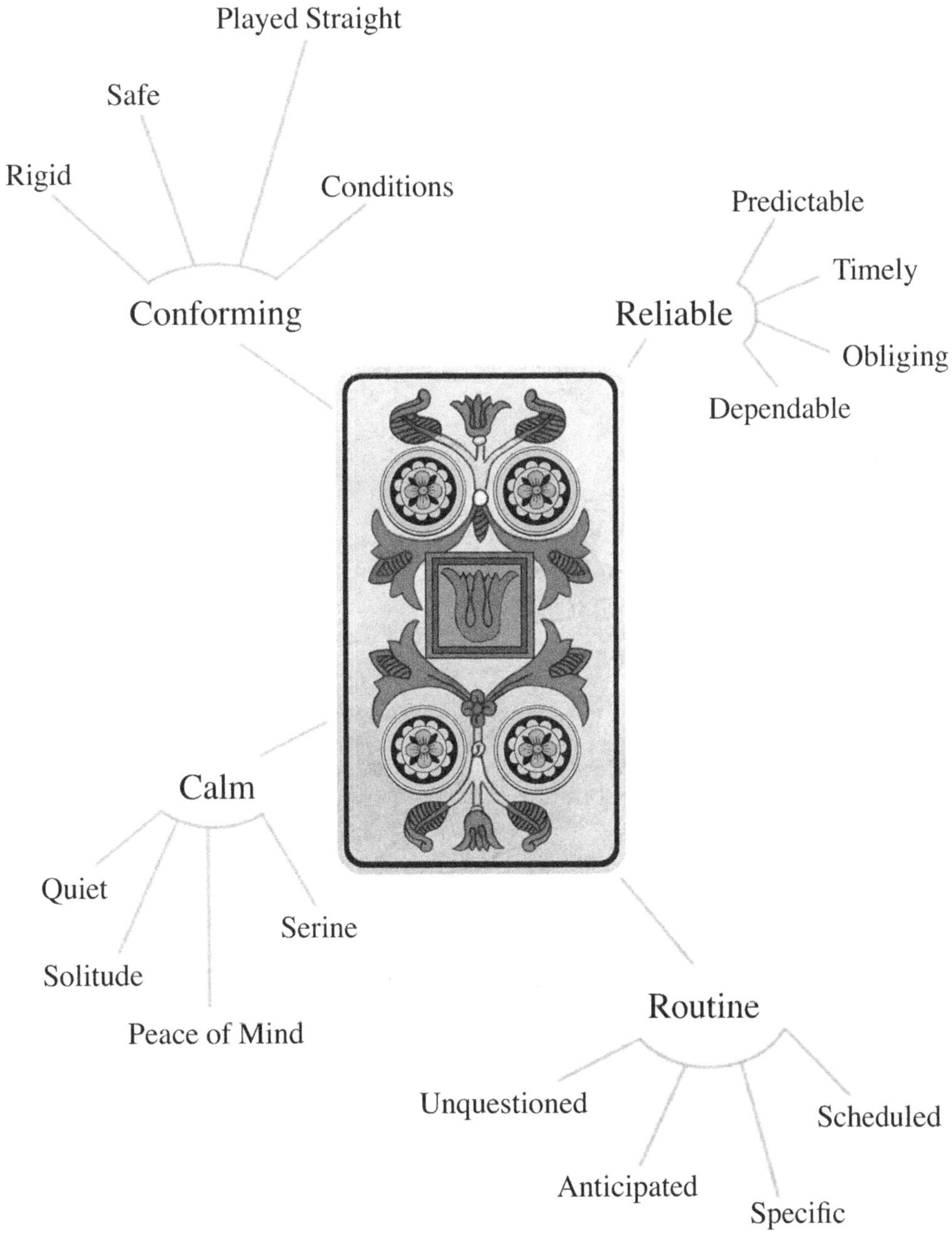

Played Straight

Safe

Rigid

Conditions

Conforming

Predictable

Timely

Reliable

Obliging

Dependable

Calm

Quiet

Serine

Solitude

Peace of Mind

Routine

Unquestioned

Scheduled

Anticipated

Specific

Minor Arcana
The Five of Pentacles
~ *Change* ~

At a Glance
- *Setback*
- *Slow Progress*
- *An Inconvenient Turn*
- *Hard Journey*
- *Unrest*
- *Stressful Situation*

~ Meaning ~
A challenging turn of events. Staying strong is key. Things will turn in your favor at a later time. Luck has turned a blind eye. Move forward and the light will come. Positive thinking will get you through tough times.

Meaning from the past – 1980's
Venal love or adultery. The lover (or the mistress) is the cause of ruin.
If placed near #20 **Judgement** it could mean "Improvement in your moral and physical conditions."

Meaning from the past – 1960's
This card means that the human reason should be able to come to terms with immaterial knowledge. Attack on the physical life of the individual. Collective but haphazard movement, or an uncertain period becomes settled. This card is essentially malleable and open to influence by the surrounding cards.

Minor Arcana
The Five of Pentacles
~ *Shifting* ~

—— Keyword Associations ——

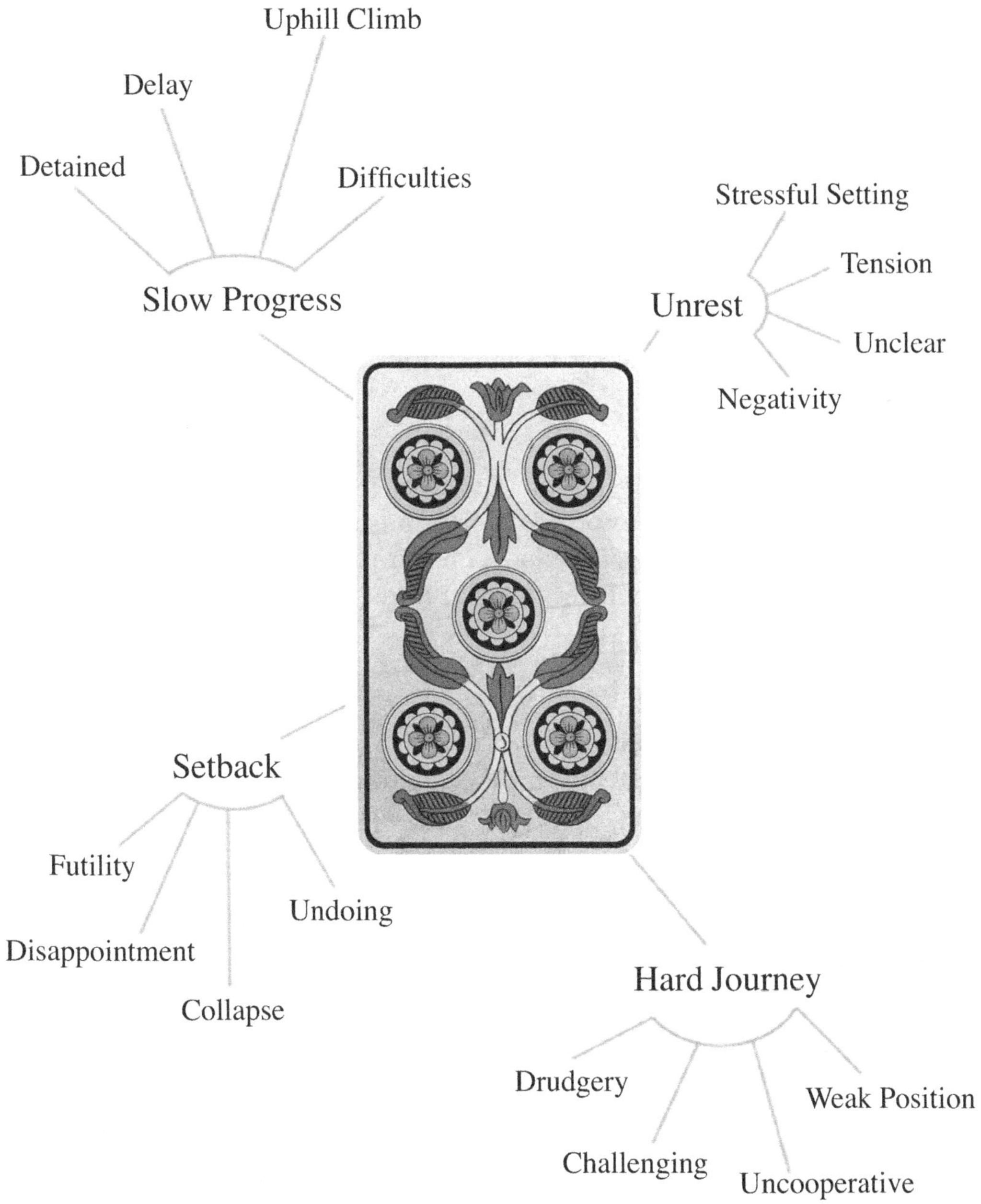

Uphill Climb

Delay

Detained

Difficulties

Stressful Setting

Tension

Slow Progress

Unrest

Unclear

Negativity

Setback

Futility

Undoing

Disappointment

Collapse

Hard Journey

Drudgery

Weak Position

Challenging

Uncooperative

Minor Arcana
The Six of Pentacles
~ *Perseverance* ~

At a Glance
- *A Positive Outlook*
- *Careful Planning*
- *Counsel*
- *Better Circumstances*
- *Comfort*
- *Improved Outlook*

~ Meaning ~

Meeting the challenge will be rewarded. Your efforts are making progress. Good moves. Staying on course will get results. A time to show how you can make things happen. Your resourcefulness will get you far. Efforts work quickly in your favor.

Meaning from the past – 1980's

Meanness. Beware of speculations.
If placed near #20 ***Judgement*** it could mean "Improvement on the way."

Meaning from the past – 1960's

Psychic force exerting its authority over the elements. Success in undertakings. Sure judgement in decisions. Stabilization in the midst of uncertainty.

Minor Arcana
The Six of Pentacles
~ *Unwavering* ~

—— Keyword Associations ——

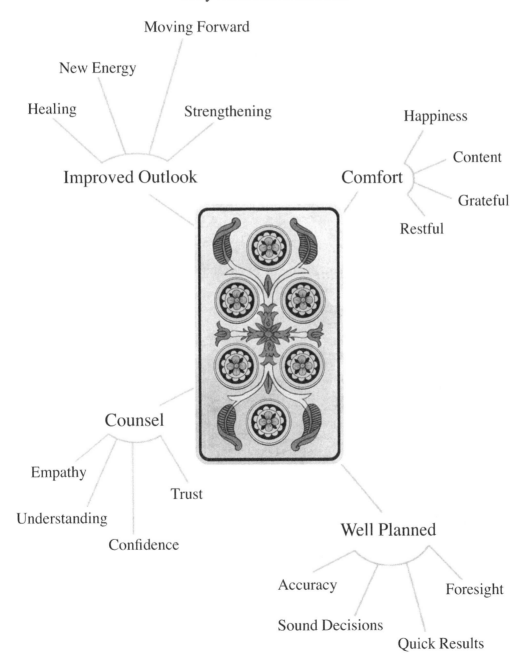

Moving Forward

New Energy

Healing

Strengthening

Improved Outlook

Happiness

Content

Comfort

Grateful

Restful

Counsel

Empathy

Trust

Understanding

Confidence

Well Planned

Accuracy

Foresight

Sound Decisions

Quick Results

Minor Arcana
The Seven of Pentacles
~ Confidence ~

At a Glance
~ Strong Position
~ Speedy Progress
~ Self-Made
~ Evaluation
~ Accomplished
~ Clear Progress

~ Meaning ~ Clear success is seen. Time to re-evaluate progress and potential. Hard earned efforts pay off nicely. Seeing full potential in a specific goal. Acting from a positive position with promising results. Right decisions have flourished into substantial benefits and rewards.

Meaning from the past – 1980's
Business man. Increase of wealth.
If placed near #20 ***Judgement*** it could mean "The consultant must take the initiative."

Meaning from the past – 1960's
Cosmic harmony. Equilibrium between matter and the psychic. Indecision, lack of precision, difficulty. It is a card which influences those around it rather than being influenced by them.

Minor Arcana
The Seven of Pentacles
~ *Absolute* ~

—— Keyword Associations ——

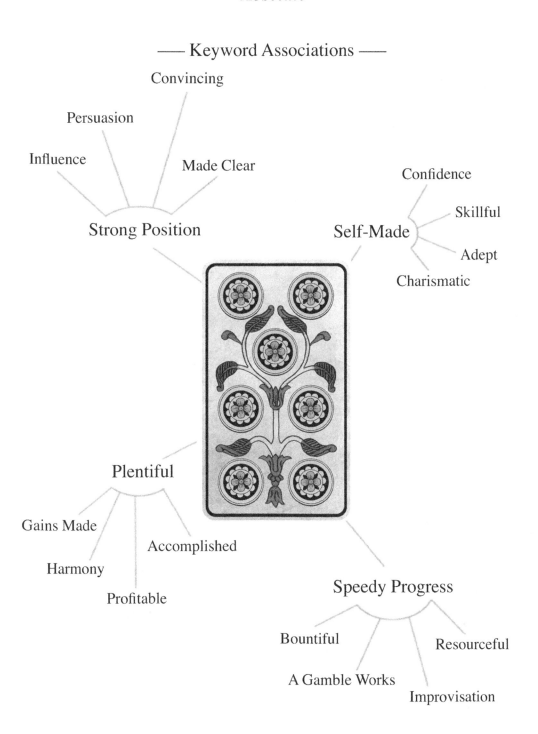

Convincing

Persuasion

Influence

Made Clear

Strong Position

Confidence

Skillful

Self-Made

Adept

Charismatic

Plentiful

Gains Made

Accomplished

Harmony

Profitable

Speedy Progress

Bountiful

Resourceful

A Gamble Works

Improvisation

Minor Arcana
The Eight of Pentacles
~ *Advancement* ~

At a Glance
- *Improvement*
- *Consistency*
- *Effective Action*
- *Carefully Planned*
- *Excellence*
- *Detailed Perception*

~ Meaning ~

Your experience is appreciated by others. Your efforts are well known and your reputation is respected. A time to focus on quality. Your capabilities will be reflected in your actions and final results. Progress is created through your ingenuity

Meaning from the past – 1980's

Betrayal and challenge. False promises. Risky speculations.
If placed near #20 *Judgement* it could mean "Improvement on all sides."

Meaning from the past – 1960's

Equilibrium of extremes in every realm. Harmony of the worlds. This card which has great strength in the abstract, loses much of its worth in the practical realm, for it is influenced by the cards around it. It can mean violent arrestation of an event, but equally well success of stability, according to the cards which surround it.

Minor Arcana
The Eight of Pentacles
~ *Unrestrained* ~

—— Keyword Associations ——

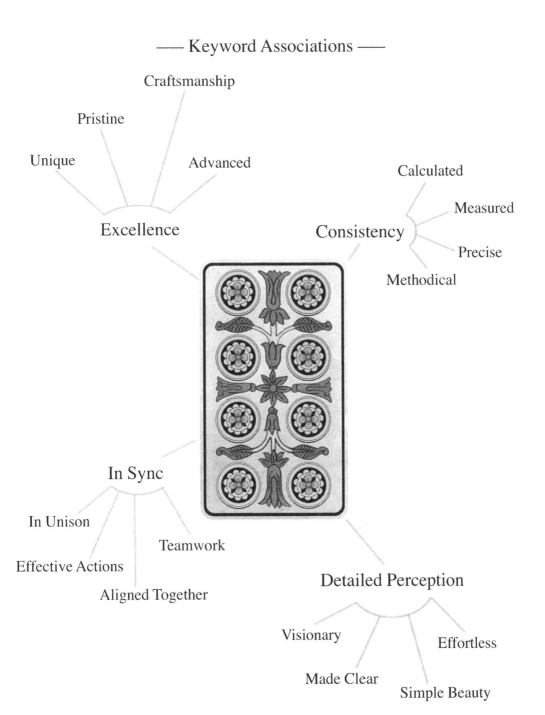

Craftsmanship

Pristine

Unique

Advanced

Excellence

Calculated

Measured

Consistency

Precise

Methodical

In Sync

In Unison

Teamwork

Effective Actions

Aligned Together

Detailed Perception

Visionary

Effortless

Made Clear

Simple Beauty

Minor Arcana
The Nine of Pentacles
~ Attainment ~

At a Glance
~ Worth
~ Proven Accomplishments
~ A Good Position
~ In your hands
~ Honor
~ Established Position

~ Meaning ~
Clear vision for the future. Inner wealth and abundance are yours.
A time to enjoy who you are and what you have. Acquiring what is rightfully yours.
Your contributions have paid off with rich rewards. A time to enjoy peace and harmony.

Meaning from the past – 1980's
Money. Beneficial to the consultant.
If placed near #20 **Judgement** it could mean "Highly remunerative work. Beneficial contract."

Meaning from the past – 1960's
Unattainable agreement between the spiritual and the material.
Difference of agreement, concealed, unknown and latent plans.

Minor Arcana
The Nine of Pentacles
~ *Possession* ~

—— Keyword Associations ——

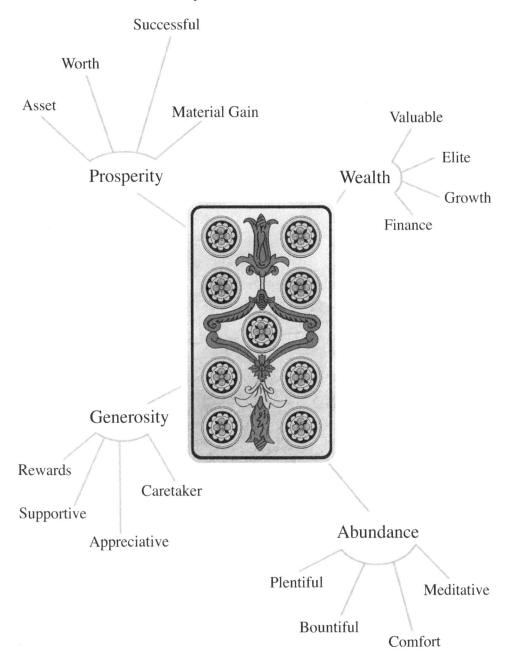

Successful

Worth

Asset

Material Gain

Valuable

Elite

Growth

Prosperity

Wealth

Finance

Generosity

Rewards

Caretaker

Supportive

Appreciative

Abundance

Plentiful

Meditative

Bountiful

Comfort

Minor Arcana
The Ten of Pentacles
~ *Completion* ~

At a Glance
- *A graduation*
- *A higher level*
- *A rich history*
- *Accomplishment*
- *A new understanding*
- *Tranquility*

~ Meaning ~
A time for celebration. Great achievements are made. All is realized as good. Peaceful harmony and joy. Hard earned accomplishments are celebrated and enjoyed by all. Looking back with joy. No regrets.

Meaning from the past – 1980's
Increase of wealth and property. A bold commercial deal is a success. Buy land and do business.

Meaning from the past – 1960's
Success, agreement, equilibrium. Satisfaction, complete joy.

Minor Arcana
The Ten of Pentacles
~ *Bliss* ~

—— Keyword Associations ——

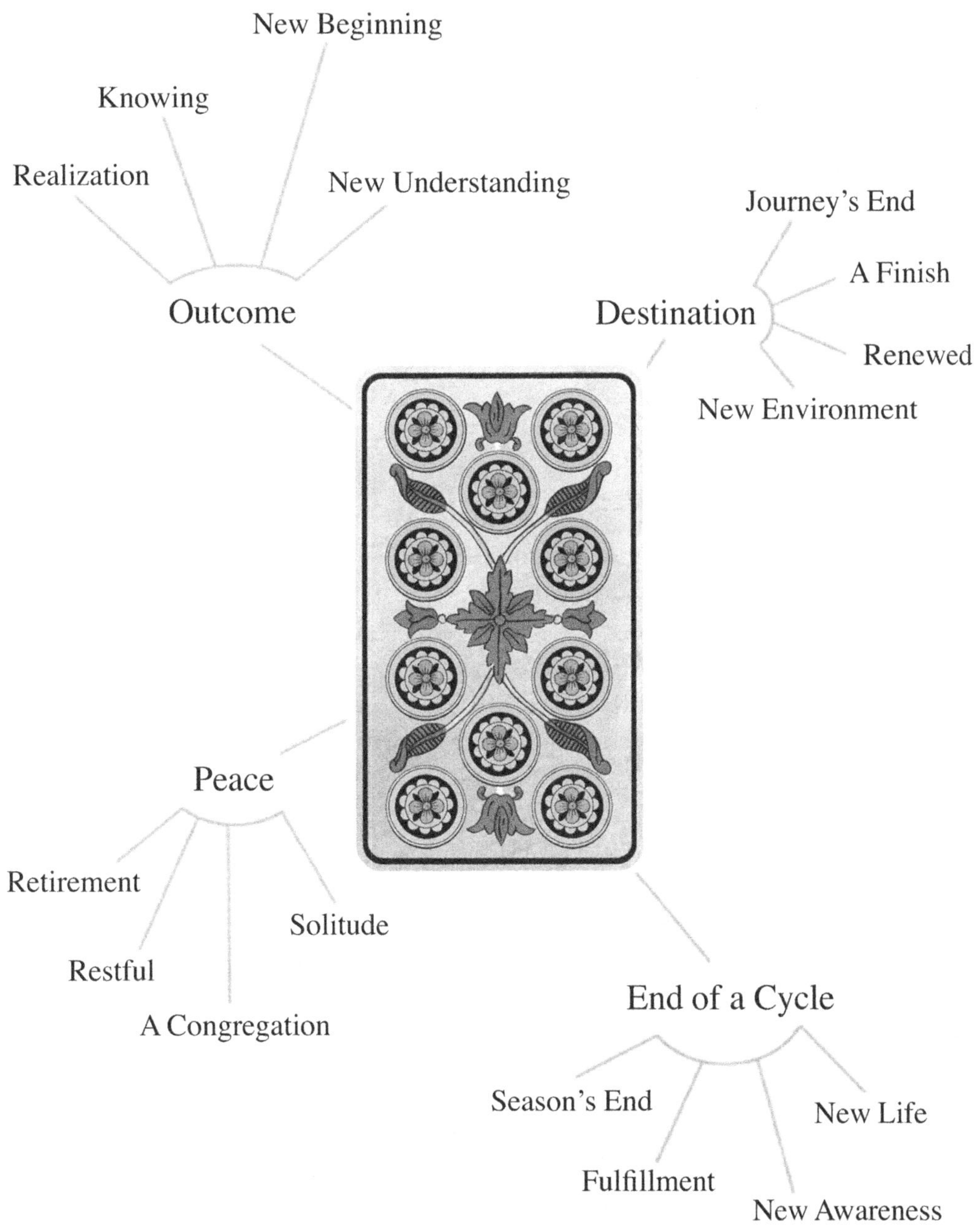

New Beginning

Knowing

Realization

New Understanding

Journey's End

A Finish

Outcome

Destination

Renewed

New Environment

Peace

Retirement

Restful

Solitude

A Congregation

End of a Cycle

Season's End

New Life

Fulfillment

New Awareness

Minor Arcana
The Page of Pentacles
~ New Path ~

At a Glance
- *New gateway*
- *A path is chosen*
- *A new endeavor*
- *Fresh start*
- *Plans for change*
- *Change of heart*

~ Meaning ~
A new set of circumstances is seen and acted on. Moving into a new environment with excitement. Anticipating good outcome. Positive thinking is strong. A time for successful changes. Opportunity knocks.

Meaning from the past – 1980's
A dark-haired woman genuinely charitable but disorganised. Extravagant spending. Unpaid debts.
If placed near #20 *Judgement* it could mean "Unexpected luck".

Meaning from the past – 1960's
Material work to ensure existence. Disinterested work bringing riches as a reward.

Minor Arcana
The Page of Pentacles
~ *Initiation* ~

—— Keyword Associations ——

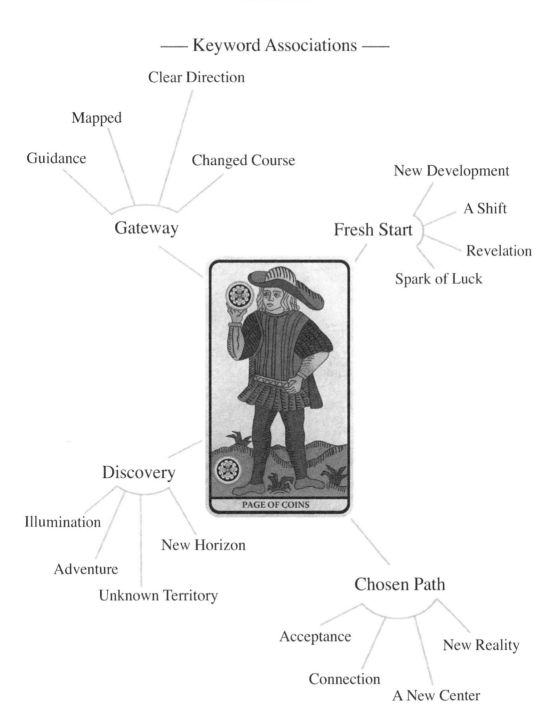

Clear Direction

Mapped

Guidance

Changed Course

New Development

A Shift

Fresh Start

Revelation

Gateway

Spark of Luck

Discovery

Illumination

New Horizon

Adventure

Unknown Territory

Chosen Path

Acceptance

New Reality

Connection

A New Center

PAGE OF COINS

Minor Arcana
The Knight of Pentacles
~ *Action* ~

At a Glance
~ *Initiative*
~ *Material gain*
~ *New career*
~ *Promotion*
~ *New responsibility*
~ *New challenges*

~ Meaning ~

Another level is taken to your advantage. Your progress is determined by your desires. Measured skill is yours for others to see. Much can be accomplished on your behalf with new authority. Pride and gratification are yours for the taking.

Meaning from the past – 1980's

Realistic and scheming person. Favors gambling, lotteries, speculation and share-market.

If placed near #20 ***Judgement*** it could mean "Success depends on you.".

Meaning from the past – 1960's

Fortune or attainment cannot come from laziness. Success do to force, perseverance and will.

Minor Arcana
The Knight of Pentacles
~ Involvement ~

—— Keyword Associations ——

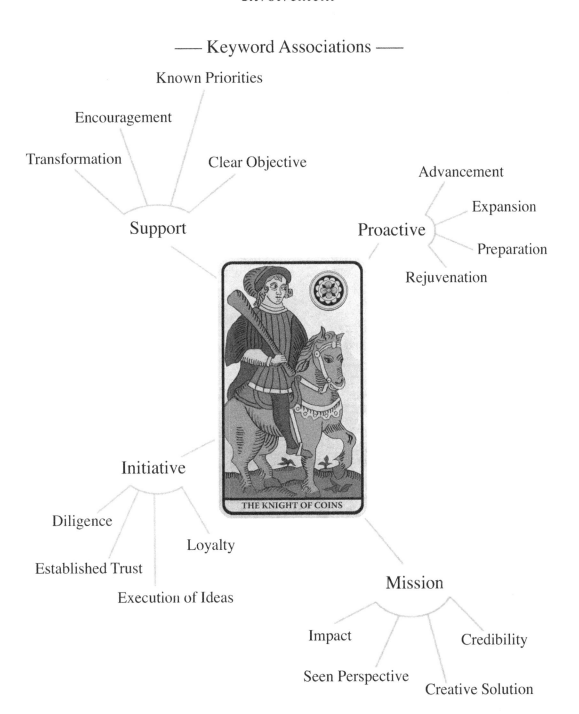

Known Priorities

Encouragement

Transformation

Clear Objective

Support

Advancement

Expansion

Proactive

Preparation

Rejuvenation

Initiative

Diligence

Loyalty

Established Trust

Execution of Ideas

Mission

Impact

Credibility

Seen Perspective

Creative Solution

THE KNIGHT OF COINS

Minor Arcana
The Queen of Pentacles
~ *Patience* ~

QUEEN OF COINS

At a Glance
- *Elegant strength*
- *Respected position*
- *A respected history*
- *Influence over peers*
- *Honest integrity*
- *A graceful influence*

~ Meaning ~
A clear focus. A time to move forward with thoughts and goals. Your present influence is high. Your ideas are true.

A time to take advantage of your status. Others will follow. Your persuasion is strong.

Meaning from the past – 1980's
Rich but mean woman, sensuous but understood by nobody. Is carried away by her imagination. Suffers from imaginary troubles.

If placed near #20 *Judgement* it could mean "Finds real love.".

Meaning from the past – 1960's
Struggle to acquire and difficulty in keeping that which is acquired. Disappointment in a given situation due to lack of wisdom.

Minor Arcana
The Queen of Pentacles
~ *Distinction* ~

—— Keyword Associations ——

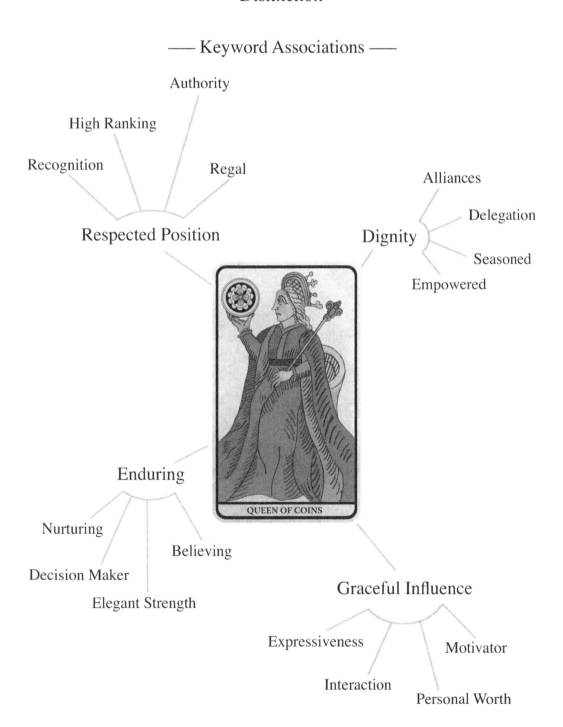

Authority

High Ranking

Recognition

Regal

Respected Position

Dignity

Alliances

Delegation

Seasoned

Empowered

Enduring

Nurturing

Believing

Decision Maker

Elegant Strength

QUEEN OF COINS

Graceful Influence

Expressiveness

Motivator

Interaction

Personal Worth

Minor Arcana
The King of Pentacles
~ *Knowledge* ~

At a Glance
- *Power*
- *Wisdom*
- *Fair judgment*
- *Order is in place*
- *A good authority*
- *Decisions are made*

~ Meaning ~
Things are seen correctly by the right people. Those who count are aware of transitions. Bide your time and things will come to pass as they should. All will right itself without your assistance. Wheels are in motion. Your insight is key.

Meaning from the past – 1980's
Rich powerful man, either in trade or industry. Encourages meanness and intolerance. If placed near #20 ***Judgement*** it could mean "Helps to attain one's aims."

Meaning from the past – 1960's
The occult and fatal action of the cosmic forces. Possessions in a precarious state.

Minor Arcana
The King of Pentacles
~ *Rulership* ~

—— Keyword Associations ——

Logical Consequences

Explicit

Authenticity

Analytical

Fair Judgment

Clearly Understood

Specified

Order

Factual

Cooperative

THE KING OF COINS

Wisdom

Mature

Committed

Accountability

Experienced

Establishment

Principles

Unifying

Bureaucratic

Desired Resources

Where the Major Arcana represent metaphysical, universal principles, the Minor Arcana are more grounded to our life experiences in the physical plane. Our everyday concerns and goals.

The Minor Arcana can represent the four basic functions of consciousness nicely. Thought (Swords), Emotion (Cups), Spirit (Wands), and the Physical (Pentacles). *Carl Jung, Isabel Myers, Kathryn Briggs* and other great thinkers of psychology have claimed that we are all born with one of these four basic functions of consciousness being our primary personality type. However all four aspects do affect us all to some degree. Some aspects in our lives will bring out one aspect more strongly than the other three. This will depend on who we are and how we think. I see the four suits of the Tarot representing this way of thinking very well.

Which Suit are you?

Where you are strong in one makes you weakest in its opposite type.
Cups and Swords are opposite personality types. So are Wands and Pentacles.
Note the five categories these personality types are viewed from:
• Being
• Trusting
• Yearning
• Seeking
• Prizing

The Suit of Swords
Swords are the suit of reason. Clear thinking. Intellect. This suit is ruled by the mind. The Sword personality is a very rational energy. They make most decisions based on clear thinking and the facts. They represent about 10% of the population.

Suit of Swords
~ The Mind ~

Swords value:
Being – calm
Trusting – reason
Yearning for – achievement
Seeking – knowledge
Prizing – deference

Suit of Cups
Cups value:
Being – enthusiastic
Trusting – intuition
Yearning for – romance
Seeking – identity
Prizing – recognition

Suit of Pentacles
Pentacles value:
Being – concerned
Trusting – authority
Yearning for – belonging
Seeking – security
Prizing – gratitude

Suit of Wands
Wands value:
Being – excited
Trusting – impulse
Yearning for – impact
Seeking – stimulation
Prizing – generosity

Minor Arcana
The Ace of Swords
~ New Concept ~

At a Glance
- *Awakening*
- *Revelation*
- *Challenging news*
- *Carefully planned*
- *New strategy*
- *Illumination*

~ Meaning ~
A breakthrough is seen. A means to an end. Good intentions bring success. Good news to a challenge is made clear. A turn for the good on an unpleasant situation. Things will improve if action is taken.

Meaning from the past – 1980's
Virility. Self-confidence. Courage brings a well-deserved victory.
If placed near #10 **The Wheel** it could mean "Recovery or end of an ordeal."

Meaning from the past – 1960's
Man must by his own strength penetrate and overcome the course of events. He is forced to struggle. Strong action with victory bringing advantage.

Minor Arcana
The Ace of Swords
~ Innovation ~

—— Keyword Associations ——

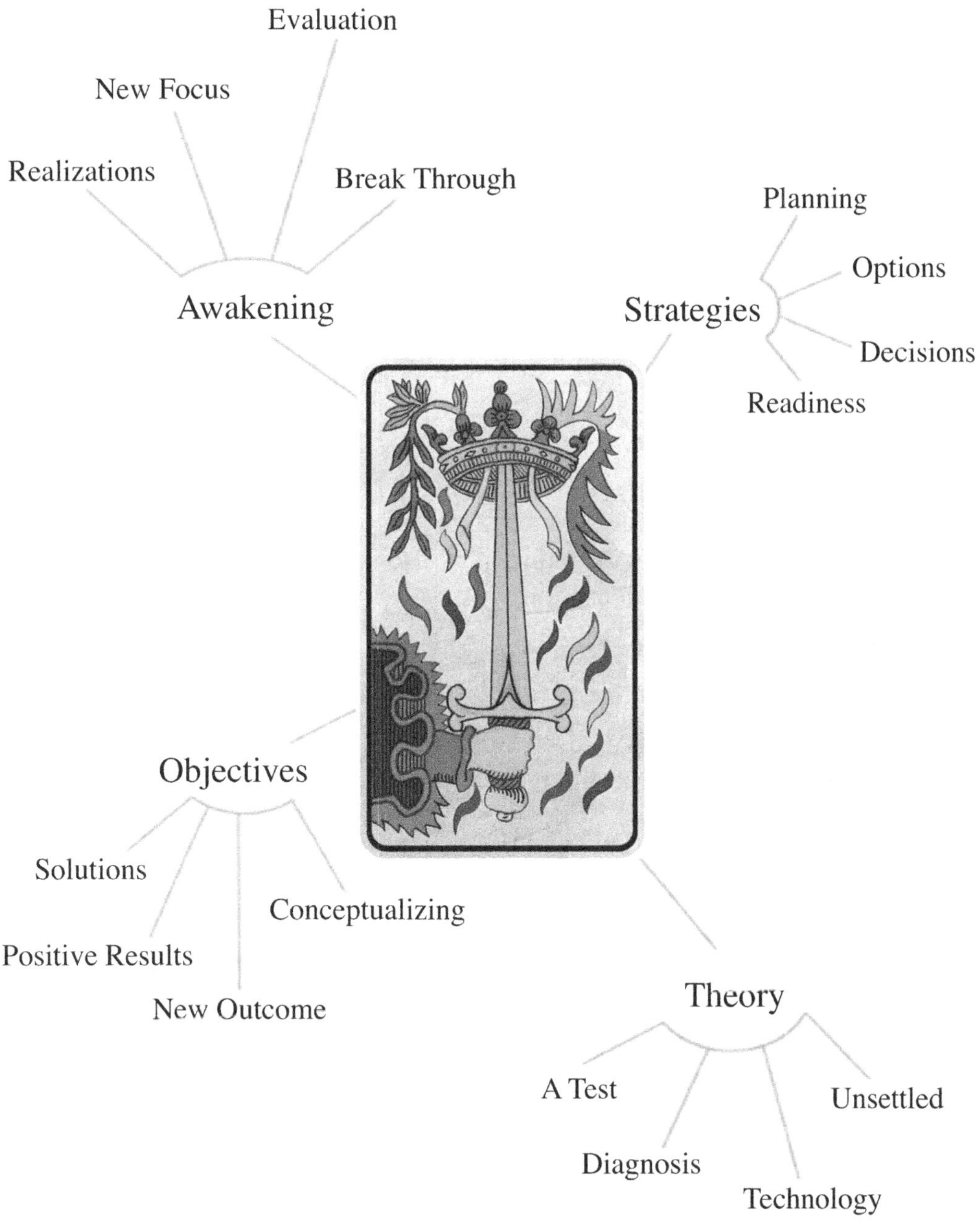

Evaluation

New Focus

Realizations

Break Through

Planning

Options

Decisions

Awakening

Strategies

Readiness

Objectives

Solutions

Positive Results

Conceptualizing

New Outcome

Theory

A Test

Unsettled

Diagnosis

Technology

Minor Arcana
The Two of Swords
~ Choice ~

At a Glance
- *Stalemate*
- *Confusing decision*
- *Delicate balance*
- *Unsure direction*
- *Slow progress*
- *A stand still*

~ Meaning ~

A need to know more before action can be taken. Facts aren't clear. A lack of information. A good time to focus on clear thinking. Know where you are headed before you proceed. Move forward with caution.

Meaning from the past – 1980's

Contradiction and hostility. This card often indicates hostility or sudden illness. If placed near #10 *The Wheel* it could mean "Violent retaliation."

Meaning from the past – 1960's

Harmony. Victory without conflict or battle. Passive success.

Minor Arcana
The Two of Swords
~ *Equilibrium* ~

—— Keyword Associations ——

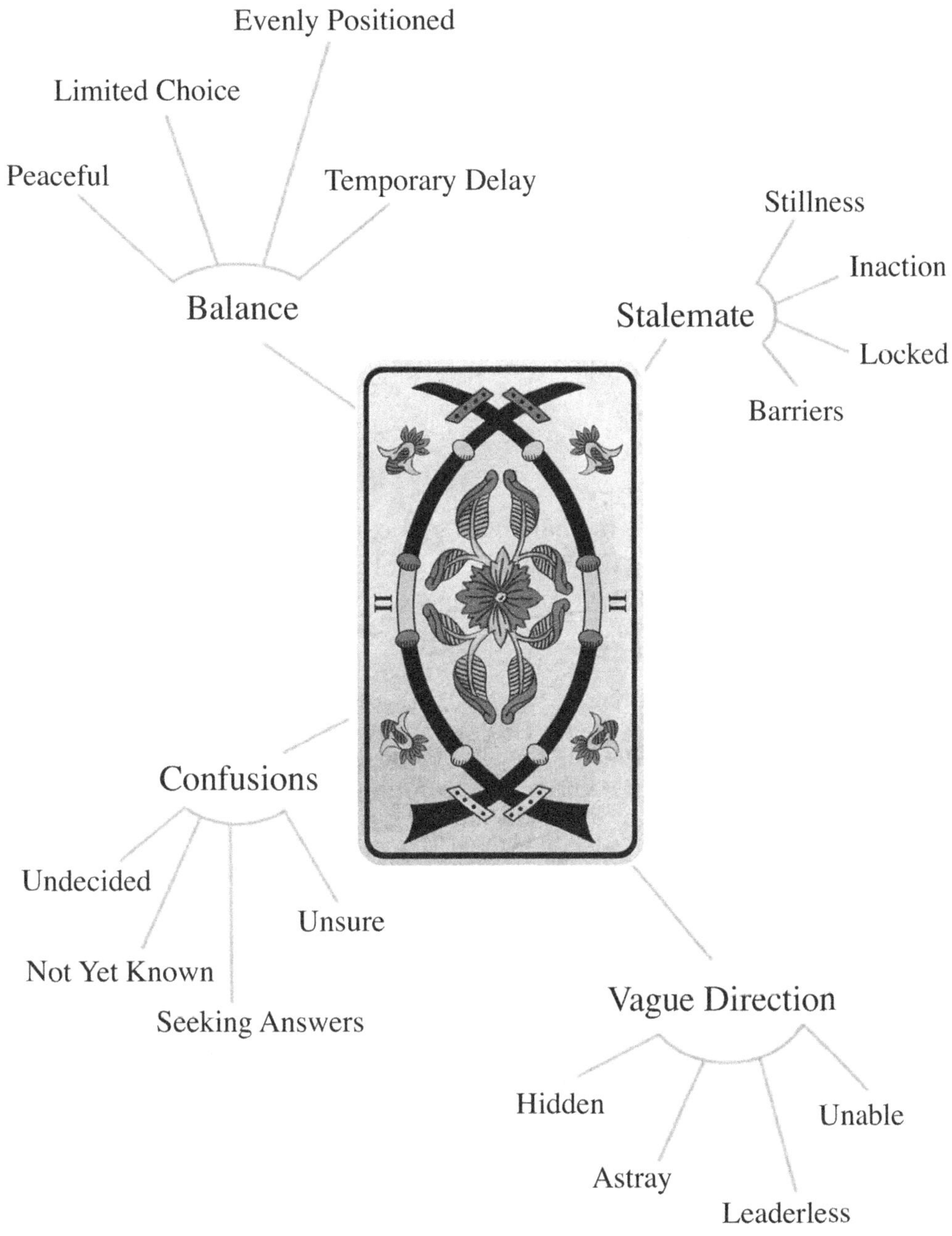

Evenly Positioned

Limited Choice

Peaceful

Temporary Delay

Balance

Stillness

Inaction

Stalemate

Locked

Barriers

Confusions

Undecided

Unsure

Not Yet Known

Seeking Answers

Vague Direction

Hidden

Astray

Unable

Leaderless

Minor Arcana
The Three of Swords
~ *Creativity* ~

At a Glance
- *Originality*
- *Fresh insight*
- *Vision*
- *Exploring options*
- *Fresh news*
- *Unlimited awareness*

~ Meaning ~

Fresh insight based on adversity or challenges. An awareness of a sad truth brings change for the better. A clearing of negative energy. Facing the core of an unpleasant situation brings new light and better circumstances.

Meaning from the past – 1980's

Repetitive errors. Love and friendship endangered or perhaps even destroyed. If placed near #20 ***Judgement*** it could mean "Nothing can alter destiny."

Meaning from the past – 1960's

Struggle upheld by mental strength, ensuring victory over the physical. Gain by force or by battle.

Minor Arcana
The Three of Swords
~ *Manifest* ~

—— Keyword Associations ——

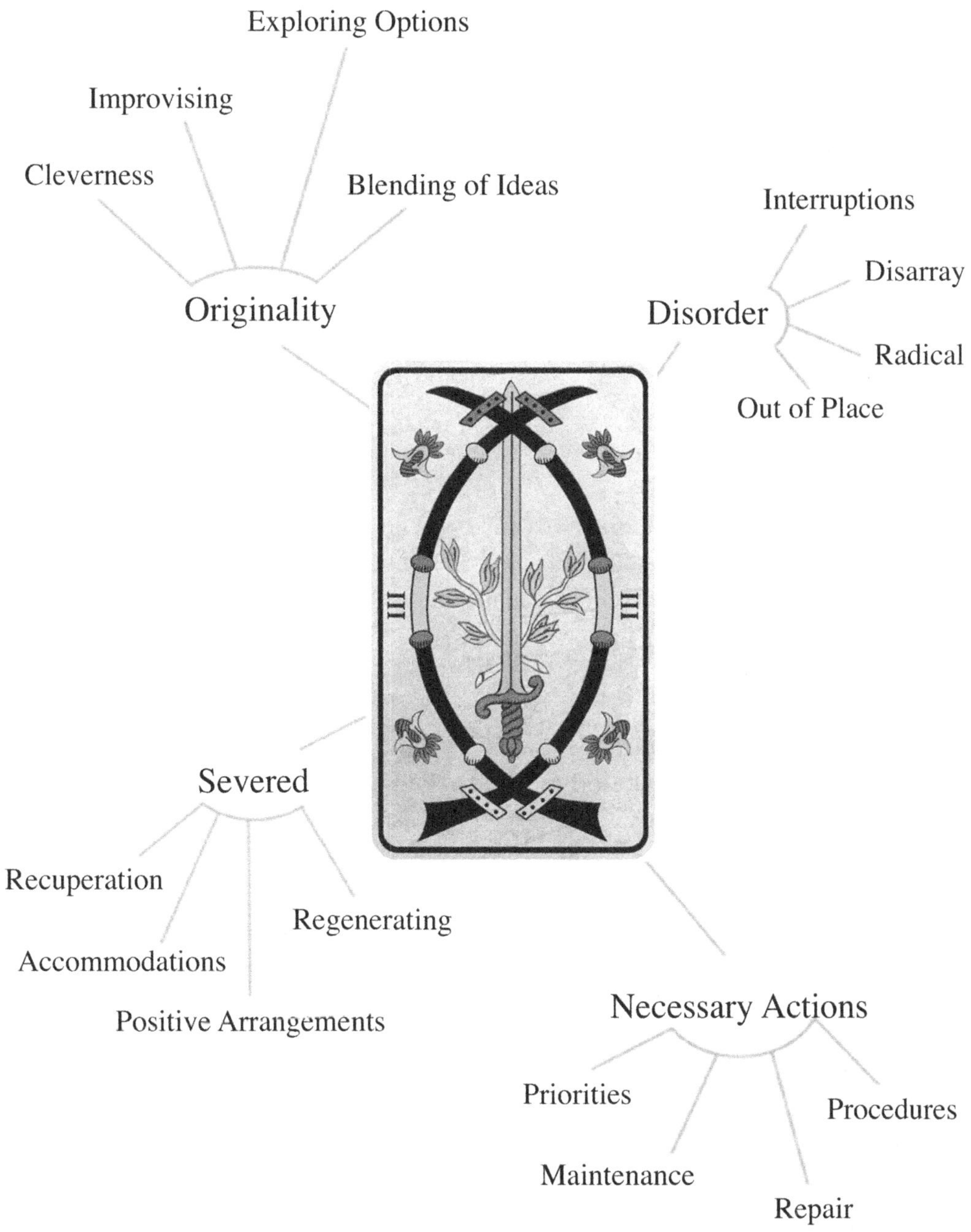

Exploring Options

Improvising

Cleverness

Blending of Ideas

Originality

Interruptions

Disarray

Disorder

Radical

Out of Place

Severed

Recuperation

Accommodations

Regenerating

Positive Arrangements

Necessary Actions

Priorities

Procedures

Maintenance

Repair

Minor Arcana
The Four of Swords
~ *Stability* ~

At a Glance
- *Predictable*
- *Planned arrangements*
- *Expected outcome*
- *An assumption*
- *Pre-determined procedures*
- *Scheduled action*

~ Meaning ~
Things remain on course but no quick advances in the near future. Progress is slow but issues are recognized with a need for improvement. Patience for now is best. Not a time for action. Things are understood clearly enough and change will come in time.

Meaning from the past – 1980's
Loneliness. Hurt feelings. Absence, death, disappointment.
If placed near #10 *The Wheel* it could mean "Unstable love. Poor health."

Meaning from the past – 1960's
After the struggle, a tendency towards mysticism, growing understanding of the ideal. Beginning of a plan, slow flowering of a realization.

Minor Arcana
The Four of Swords
~ *Belonging* ~

—— Keyword Associations ——

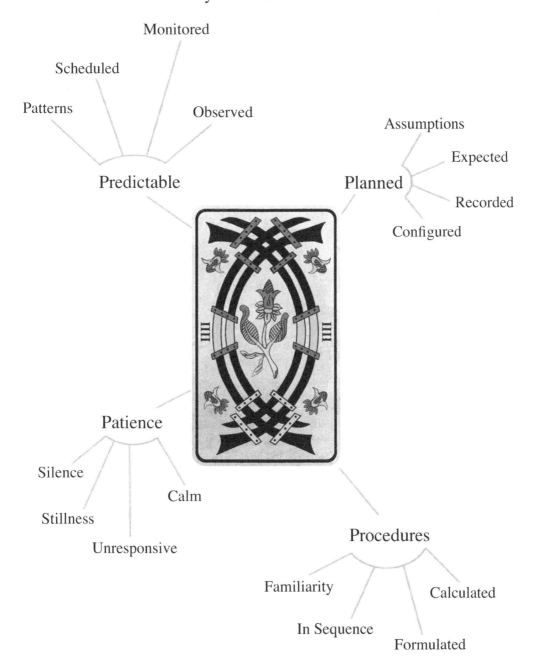

Monitored

Scheduled

Patterns

Observed

Predictable

Assumptions

Expected

Planned

Recorded

Configured

Patience

Silence

Calm

Stillness

Unresponsive

Procedures

Familiarity

Calculated

In Sequence

Formulated

Minor Arcana
The Five of Swords
~ Change ~

At a Glance
- *Disruption*
- *A challenge*
- *Unexpected situation*
- *A change in plans*
- *Bad timing*
- *Opposition awaits*

~ Meaning ~

An opportunity to clear the air. This is a time to meet on differences of opinions. A time to settle disagreements.

Tension in the air can be cleared away if faced with good intentions. Seeing both sides of the coin is key. A time of compromise.

Meaning from the past – 1980's

Jealousy and fear. The consultant must fight against bad influences.

If placed near #10 *The Wheel* it could mean "Any change would be beneficial."

Meaning from the past – 1960's

Fierce struggle to penetrate to higher planes. Wish to destroy the body in favour of the mind. Defeat, struggle without result.

Minor Arcana
The Five of Swords
~ *Adjustment* ~

—— Keyword Associations ——

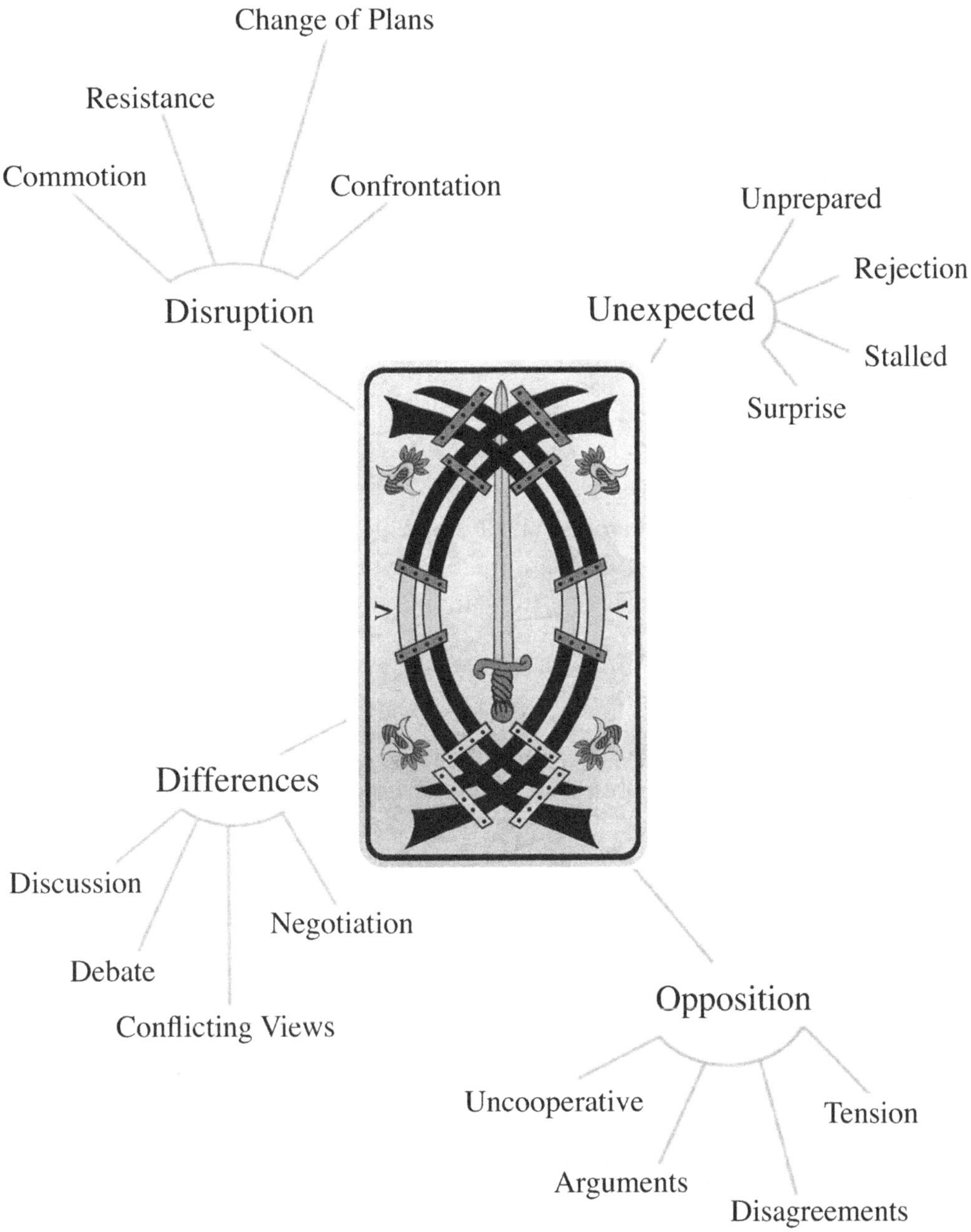

Change of Plans

Resistance

Commotion

Confrontation

Unprepared

Rejection

Disruption

Unexpected

Stalled

Surprise

Differences

Discussion

Negotiation

Debate

Conflicting Views

Opposition

Uncooperative

Tension

Arguments

Disagreements

Minor Arcana
The Six of Swords
~ *Perseverance* ~

At a Glance
- *Strategy*
- *Successful planning*
- *Facing conflict*
- *Evaluation*
- *Confronting issues*
- *An objective is seen*

~ Meaning ~
Answers are seen clearly. You have the ability to achieve a goal. A good position to make improvements. The resources are there for you. The situation turns in your favor. Opportunity created from your efforts are made available.

Meaning from the past – 1980's
Worries and obstacles. The consultant must stand firm.
If placed near #10 **The Wheel** it could mean "New contacts would be beneficial."

Meaning from the past – 1960's
The liberation of matter. Force or security.

Minor Arcana
The Six of Swords
~ *Resolution* ~

—— Keyword Associations ——

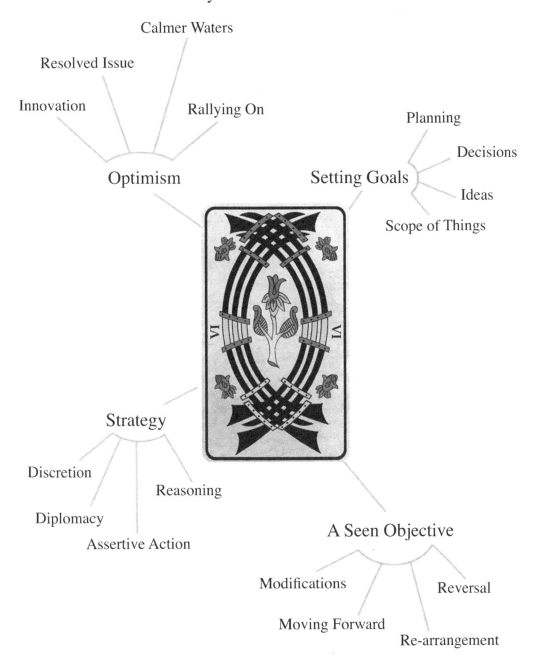

Calmer Waters

Resolved Issue

Innovation

Rallying On

Optimism

Planning

Decisions

Setting Goals

Ideas

Scope of Things

Strategy

Discretion

Reasoning

Diplomacy

Assertive Action

A Seen Objective

Modifications

Moving Forward

Reversal

Re-arrangement

Minor Arcana
The Seven of Swords
~ *Confidence* ~

At a Glance
- *Self awareness*
- *Improvising*
- *Chances are taken*
- *Answers are found*
- *Insightful situation*
- *Confident action*

~ Meaning ~

A solid understanding of a situation brings success. Talents and assets will create good progress. A surprise to others as things are seen clearly. A time to show your ability. Initiate incentives towards the challenge at hand.

Meaning from the past – 1980's

Moral and physical courage. Claims accepted.
If placed near #10 **The Wheel** it could mean "Prosperity comes easily."

Meaning from the past – 1960's

A wish to destroy, not only by material means such as armaments, but also by mental ones, e.g. acts of magic. Ephemeral realizations. Disappointment in a family or amongst several people having a common interest.

Minor Arcana
The Seven of Swords
~ *Spirit* ~

—— Keyword Associations ——

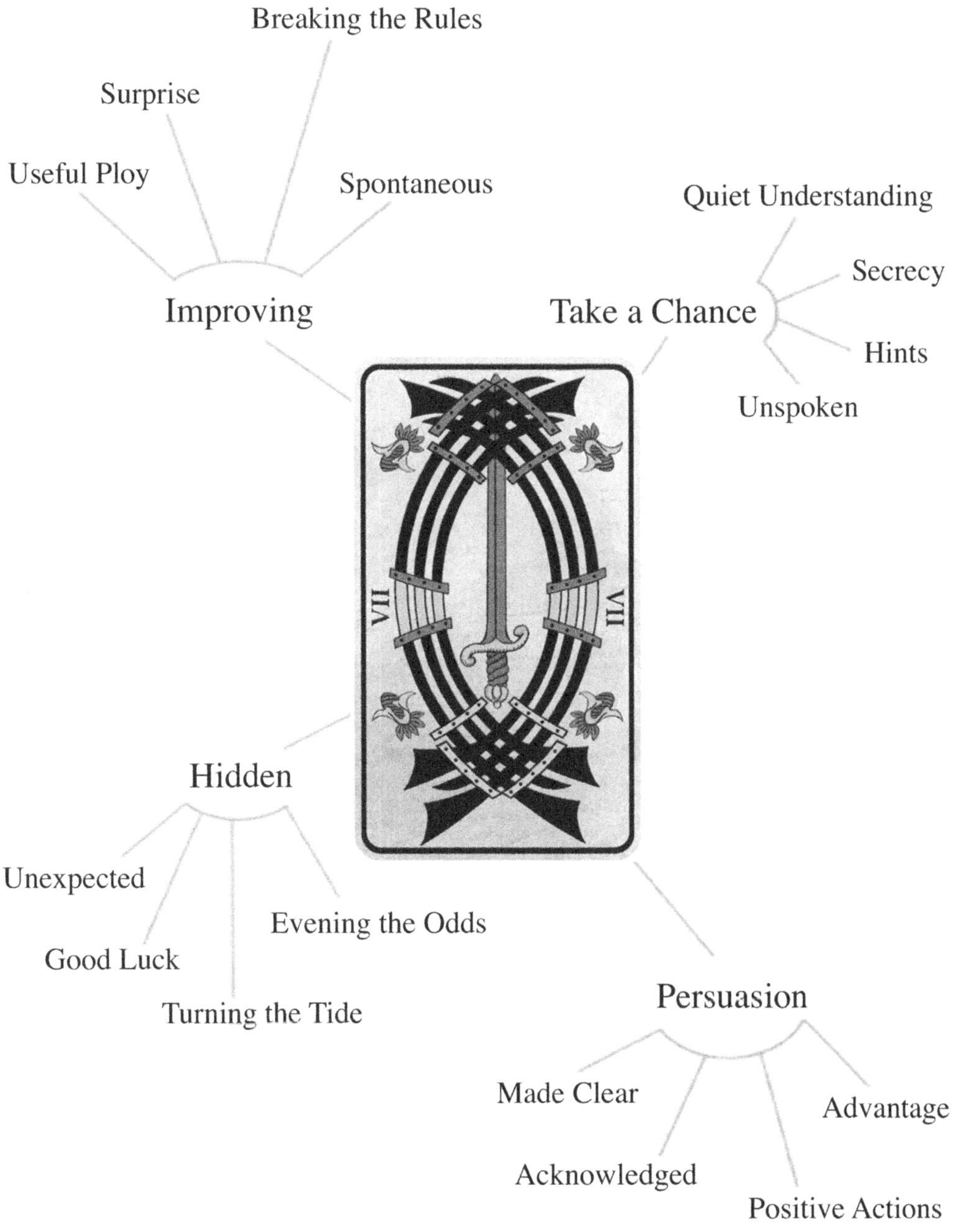

Breaking the Rules

Surprise

Useful Ploy

Spontaneous

Quiet Understanding

Improving

Take a Chance

Secrecy

Hints

Unspoken

Hidden

Unexpected

Evening the Odds

Good Luck

Turning the Tide

Persuasion

Made Clear

Advantage

Acknowledged

Positive Actions

Minor Arcana
The Eight of Swords
~ *Advancement* ~

At a Glance
- *Self limitations*
- *To see clearly*
- *Sharp focus*
- *Tempered strength*
- *Breaking through*
- *Limits are lifted*

~ Meaning ~
New understanding of predicaments bring freedom of movement and actions. Bonds are broken. An ability to create what you know and understand. Answers are found from within. A need to let go of restrictions.

Meaning from the past – 1980's
Uncertainty and lethargy. Tiredness. More care required regarding health.
If placed near #10 ***The Wheel*** it could mean "Inevitable complications."

Meaning from the past – 1960's
This card has powerful undercurrents and possesses no meaning in the abstract sense. Heavy and overpowering, it marks despair because of the evil undercurrents that it attracts.

Minor Arcana
The Eight of Swords
~ *Betterment* ~

—— Keyword Associations ——

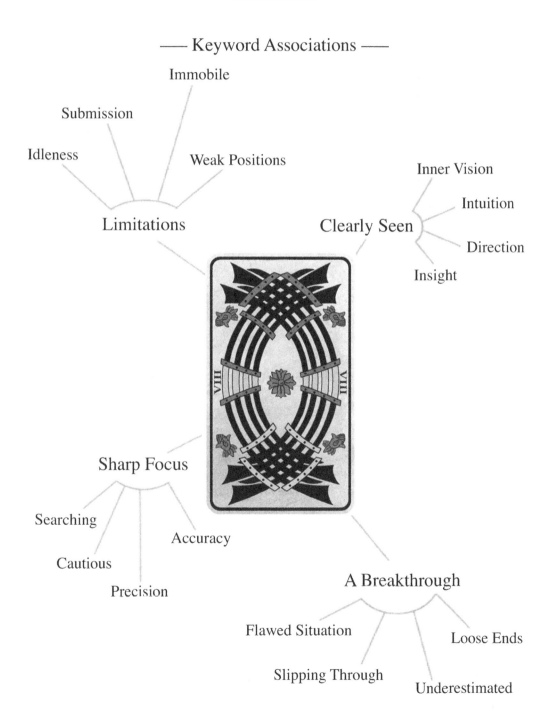

Immobile

Submission

Idleness

Weak Positions

Limitations

Inner Vision

Intuition

Clearly Seen

Direction

Insight

Sharp Focus

Searching

Accuracy

Cautious

Precision

A Breakthrough

Flawed Situation

Loose Ends

Slipping Through

Underestimated

Minor Arcana
The Nine of Swords
~ *Attainment* ~

At a Glance
- *Realization*
- *Complete understanding*
- *Belief in self*
- *An epiphany*
- *Coming to terms*
- *An awareness*

~ Meaning ~

Answers are clearly undeniable. The truth is seen clearly. Questions are answered. Progress can now be achieved.

A good position to correct old problems. Firm action is yours to take. The road to happiness is clearly shown.

Meaning from the past – 1980's

Fatal card. Always indicates a delay in any plan.

If placed near #10 ***The Wheel*** it could mean "Wounded pride. Illness or death of a person close to you."

Meaning from the past – 1960's

The struggle of matter working towards evolution. The struggle of all living things. The aspirations of matter towards a greater effort towards liberation. Desire to succeed.

Minor Arcana
The Nine of Swords
~ *Realization* ~

—— Keyword Associations ——

Responsibility

Communication

Interaction

Courage

Intervention

Perseverance

Steadiness

Resolve

Faith

Clear Focus

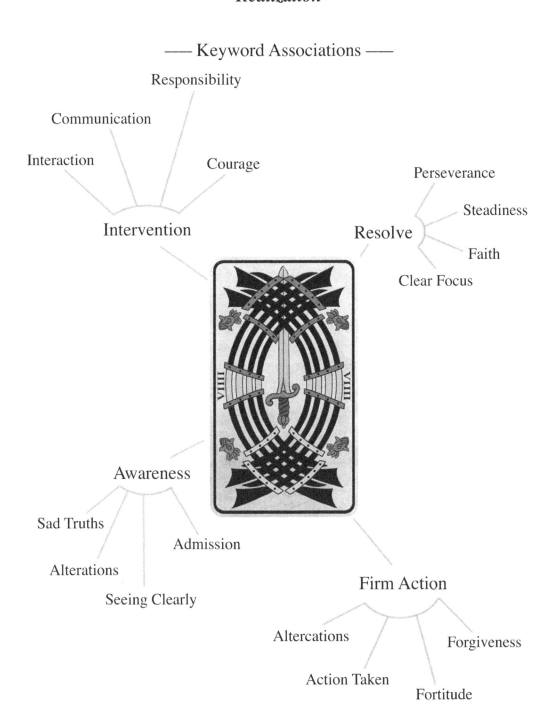

Awareness

Sad Truths

Admission

Alterations

Seeing Clearly

Firm Action

Altercations

Forgiveness

Action Taken

Fortitude

Minor Arcana
The Ten of Swords
~ *Completion* ~

At a Glance
- *A closure*
- *Ending negative energies*
- *Totality*
- *End of a cycle*
- *Obstacles are stopped*
- *The witch is dead*

~ Meaning ~
The end of a cycle and the beginning of another. Making way for better things. A clearing of the way. Cleaning house. The start of something new. Renewal makes way for prosperity and happiness. A respectful ending is near.

Meaning from the past – 1980's
Worry and misfortune. Useless and expensive journeys.
If placed near #10 **The Wheel** it could mean "Failure of a plan through bad luck."

Meaning from the past – 1960's
The beginning of harmony between evolved matter and the things of the mind. Agreement, equilibrium, understanding.

Minor Arcana
The Ten of Swords
~ *Closure* ~

—— Keyword Associations ——

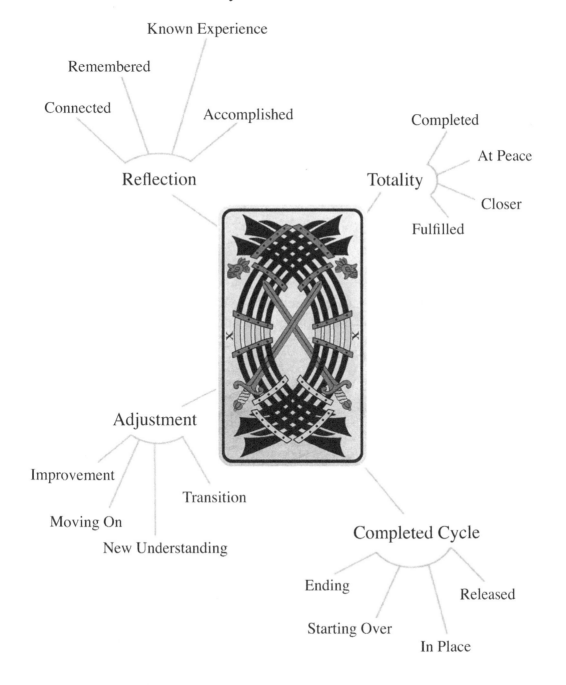

Known Experience

Remembered

Connected

Accomplished

Reflection

Completed

At Peace

Closer

Fulfilled

Totality

Adjustment

Improvement

Moving On

Transition

New Understanding

Completed Cycle

Ending

Starting Over

Released

In Place

Minor Arcana
The Page of Swords
~ New Path ~

At a Glance
- *Originality*
- *Worthwhile challenge*
- *Thought out efforts*
- *Admirable intentions*
- *Recognized efforts*
- *Sound judgment*

~ Meaning ~

Stand firm on your ideas but keep an open mind. Knowledge makes up for lack of support. Confidence is strong. A belief in self will be recognized by others. A time to advance on a goal. All is in good order to move ahead. Good progress is seen as you proceed.

Meaning from the past – 1980's

Ungrateful and hypocritical person (it may be a child). Upsets a plan; brings disappointment.

If placed near #10 *The Wheel* it could mean "False witness in a lawsuit; dishonest policeman; blackmail."

Meaning from the past – 1960's

Each Page implies the obligation of effort and work. Defensive and agile intellect triumphing without violence over matter. Defence against the blows of fate.

Minor Arcana
The Page of Swords
~ *Scholarship* ~

—— Keyword Associations ——

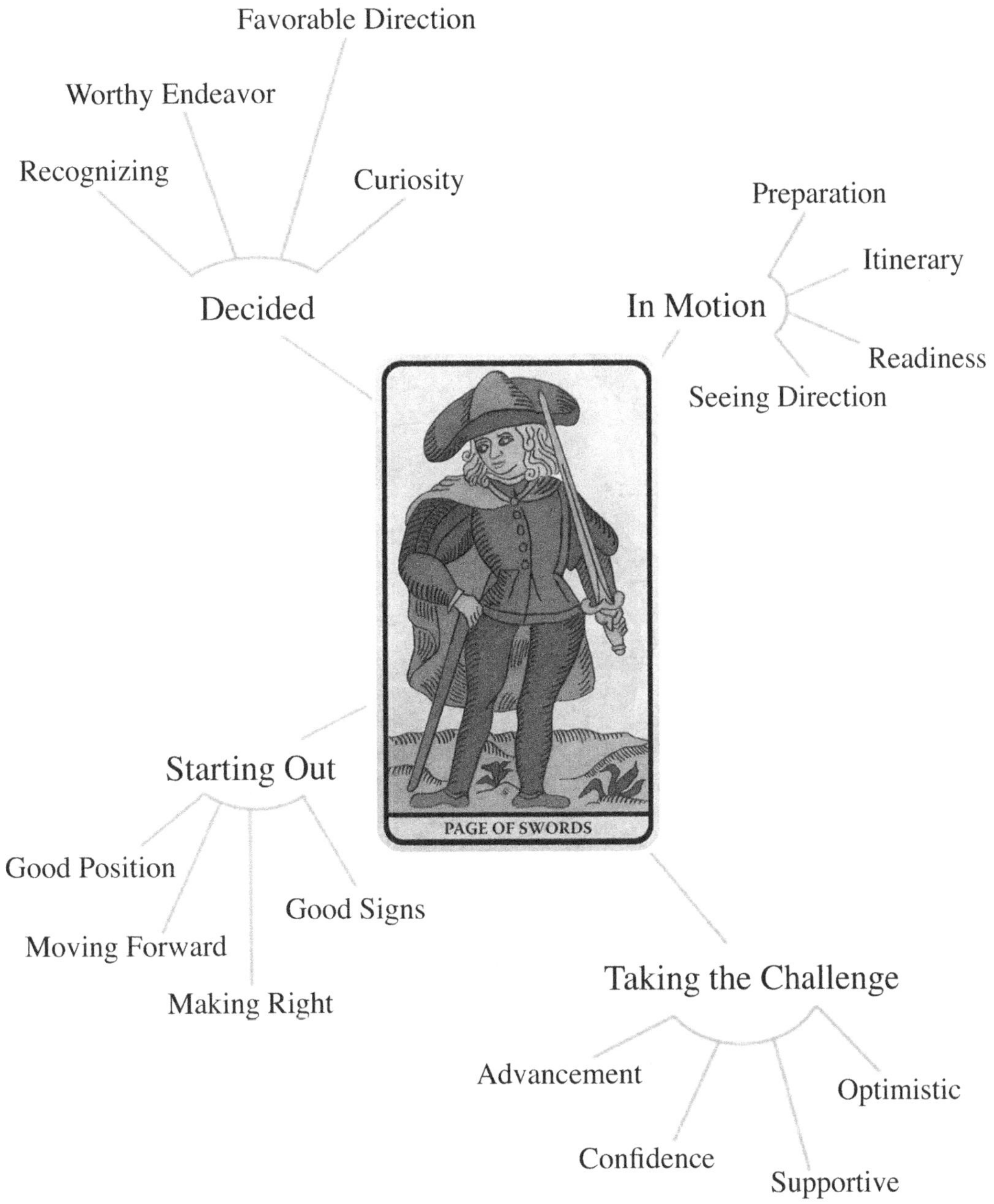

Favorable Direction

Worthy Endeavor

Recognizing

Curiosity

Preparation

Itinerary

Decided

In Motion

Readiness

Seeing Direction

Starting Out

Good Position

Good Signs

Moving Forward

Making Right

Taking the Challenge

Advancement

Optimistic

Confidence

Supportive

PAGE OF SWORDS

Minor Arcana
The Knight of Swords
~ Action ~

KNIGHT OF SWORDS

At a Glance
- *Rational action*
- *Advancement in progress*
- *Things taken in order*
- *Carried out specifically*
- *Sure footed advancement*
- *A strong start*

~ Meaning ~
A time to move on the issue. Fast progress if the opportunity is taken.
Timing is in your favor to act. Swift but planned action. Confidence is good. Positions are taken. Objectives can be made.

Meaning from the past – 1980's
Helpful and enterprising person. Indicates help, gain or unexpected support.
If placed near #10 **The Wheel** it could mean "Disappointed hope."

Meaning from the past – 1960's
Each Knight indicates activity to escape from chaos in order to evolve. What appears bad is good, events which seem troublesome take a turn for the better. Good news.

Minor Arcana
The Knight of Swords
~ *Movement* ~

—— Keyword Associations ——

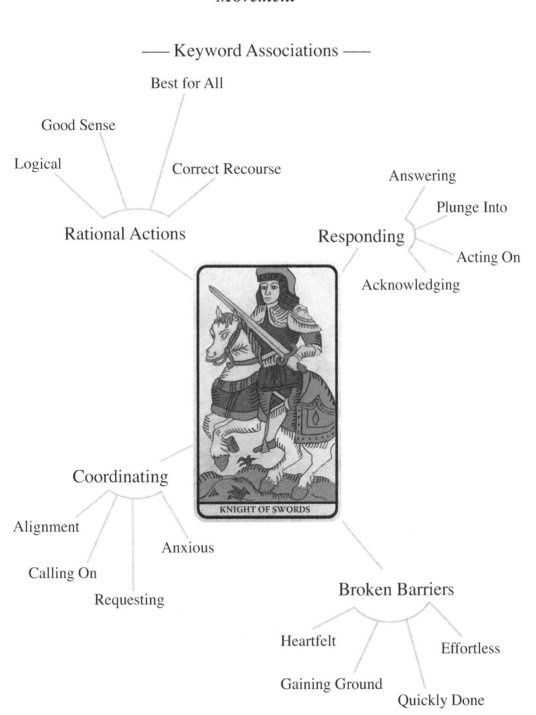

Best for All

Good Sense

Logical

Correct Recourse

Rational Actions

Answering

Plunge Into

Responding

Acting On

Acknowledging

KNIGHT OF SWORDS

Coordinating

Alignment

Anxious

Calling On

Requesting

Broken Barriers

Heartfelt

Effortless

Gaining Ground

Quickly Done

Minor Arcana
The Queen of Swords
~ Patience ~

At a Glance
- *Status*
- *Sound sincerity*
- *Compassionate judgment*
- *Fair evaluation*
- *A final decision*
- *Graceful authority*

~ Meaning ~
Decisions are made with compassion and fairness. The good of others is taken into consideration. The big picture is seen and finalized. Seeing things from all sides. Circumstances are acknowledged before decisions are made. A fair and just solution is found.

Meaning from the past – 1980's
Authoritive woman morbidly obsessed by other people's opinions. Poisons the life of people surrounding her.
If placed near #10 **The Wheel** it could mean "Things get better if the consultant goes away on a journey."

Meaning from the past – 1960's
Each Queen indicates the spoken word, good and bad advice, temperance. Calumnious will. Unpleasant advice, slander, evil words.

Minor Arcana
The Queen of Swords
~ *Tolerance* ~

—— Keyword Associations ——

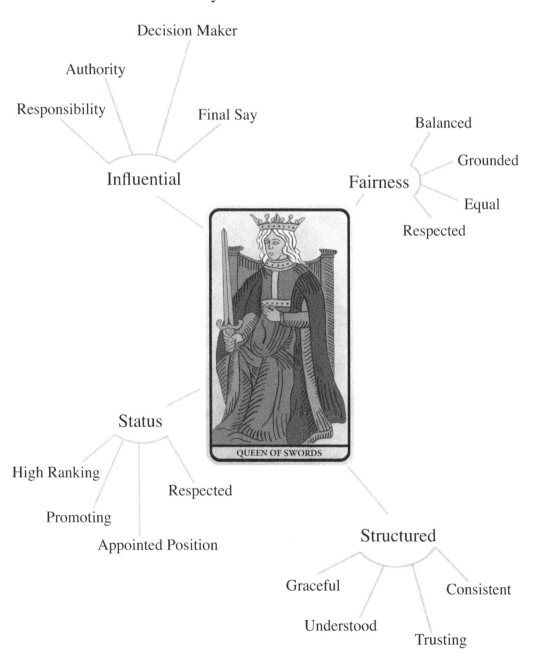

Decision Maker

Authority

Responsibility

Final Say

Influential

Balanced

Grounded

Fairness

Equal

Respected

Status

High Ranking

Respected

Promoting

Appointed Position

Structured

Graceful

Consistent

Understood

Trusting

QUEEN OF SWORDS

Minor Arcana
The King of Swords
~ *Knowledge* ~

At a Glance
- *Order*
- *Discipline*
- *Power*
- *Respected position*
- *Fair judgment*
- *Sound procedures*

~ Meaning ~

An influence of high authority. All is defined to be clearly seen. Opportunities present themselves through reputable sources. Things are seen clearly. Efforts and intentions have been recognized. Actions taken based on principle. An authority on your issue of concern is near.

Meaning from the past – 1980's

Meticulous man, who weighs his decisions. Represents repression (Police, Justice, The Law).

If placed near #10 *The Wheel* it could mean "Sometimes a protector but mostly harmful especially if the consultant is a man."

Meaning from the past – 1960's

Each King signifies the power of temporal domination. Supremacy. Sanctions taken by force can only be controlled by force. Alteration of events by force, threat of conflict. Justice is enforced by the sword. Matters are only settled by war.

Minor Arcana
The King of Swords
~ *Proficiency* ~

—— Keyword Associations ——

Bureaucratic

For the Good

Well Being

Impartial

Assertiveness

Challenging

Order

Power

Confident

All Seeing

KING OF SWORDS

Disciplined

Hard Truths

Logical

Unwavering

Rational

Judgement

Fairness

Regulated

Upholding

Systematic

Where the Major Arcana represent metaphysical, universal principles, the Minor Arcana are more grounded to our life experiences in the physical plane. Our everyday concerns and goals.

The Minor Arcana can represent the four basic functions of consciousness nicely. Thought (Swords), Emotion (Cups), Spirit (Wands), and the Physical (Pentacles). *Carl Jung, Isabel Myers, Kathryn Briggs* and other great thinkers of psychology have claimed that we are all born with one of these four basic functions of consciousness being our primary personality type. However all four aspects do affect us all to some degree. Some aspects in our lives will bring out one aspect more strongly than the other three. This will depend on who we are and how we think. I see the four suits of the Tarot representing this way of thinking very well.

Which Suit are you?

Where you are strong in one makes you weakest in its opposite type.
Cups and Swords are opposite personality types. So are Wands and Pentacles.
Note the five categories these personality types are viewed from:
• Being
• Trusting
• Yearning
• Seeking
• Prizing

The Suit of Wands

The suit of Wands shows adventure and always searching for new experiences. Excitement and living life to the fullest. Wands have a passion for life and desire to experience all realms of it. The passion for life is strongest in this suit. Wands make up approximately 40% of the population.

Suit of Wands
~ The Spirit ~

Wands value:
Being – excited
Trusting – impulse
Yearning for – impact
Seeking – stimulation
Prizing – generosity

Suit of Pentacles
Pentacles value:
Being – concerned
Trusting – authority
Yearning for – belonging
Seeking – security
Prizing – gratitude

Suit of Swords
Swords value:
Being – calm
Trusting – reason
Yearning for – achievement
Seeking – knowledge
Prizing – deference

Suit of Cups
Cups value:
Being – enthusiastic
Trusting – intuition
Yearning for – romance
Seeking – identity
Prizing – recognition

Minor Arcana
The Ace of Wands
~ New Concept ~

At a Glance
- *A high point*
- *New ground*
- *A turn in the road*
- *A plan is made*
- *Alteration*
- *Surprise turn of events*

~ Meaning ~

Following your spirit. Breaking away from the crowd. Following your own path. A fulfilling experience. Finding your center. Following your bliss. An inspiration will be followed through. A new endeavor is realized.

Meaning from the past – 1980's

Creation and domination. Ambitious and domineering consultant who is often the winner.

If placed near #5 ***The Hierophant*** it could mean "Financial situation is picking up. Success in love.."

If placed near #21 ***The World*** it could mean "Exceptional destiny."

Meaning from the past – 1960's

The power of man over matter. Success due to force.

Minor Arcana
The Ace of Wands
~ Revelation ~

—— Keyword Associations ——

Better Positioned

Well Planned

Readiness

Leverage

Advancement

Adjustments

New Ground

Gains

Progress

Promotion

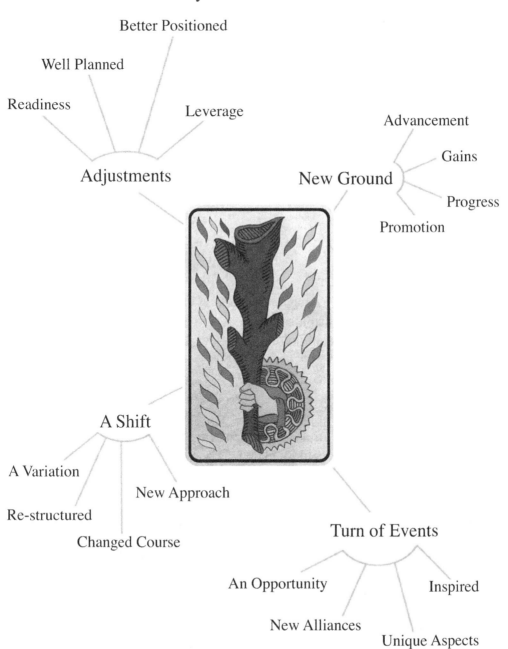

A Shift

A Variation

New Approach

Re-structured

Changed Course

Turn of Events

An Opportunity

Inspired

New Alliances

Unique Aspects

Minor Arcana
The Two of Wands
~ *Choice* ~

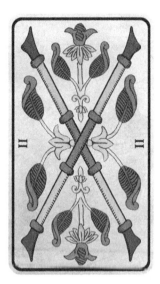

At a Glance
- *A personal preference*
- *Following your heart*
- *An offering is made*
- *Duality*
- *Sincere choice*
- *Fulfillment*

~ Meaning ~

A sincere offer.

Both sides are seen clearly and a decision is made. A careful weighing out before a choice is made. Two clashing attributes are measured and decided upon. Hard choice but all works well in the end for all involved.

Meaning from the past – 1980's

Arguments. Incompatibility. Poor health. No communication.

If placed near #5 ***The Hierophant*** it could mean "Better prospects."

If placed near #21 ***The World*** it could mean "Harmony restored to the relationship."

Meaning from the past – 1960's

Occult knowledge. Unfavorable influence, for in physical matters this card holds an evil power. It destroys the kindly influences of the cards around it.

Minor Arcana
The Two of Wands
~ Embraces ~

—— Keyword Associations ——

Good Arrangement

Selected

Desired

Compatible

Personal Preference

Sincerity

A Gift

An Offering

A Truce

Compromise

Pursuits

Speculation

Inspirational

Enriching

Soulful Experience

A Proposition

A Proposal

A Pact

Reaching Out

A Settlement

Minor Arcana
The Three of Wands
~ *Creativity* ~

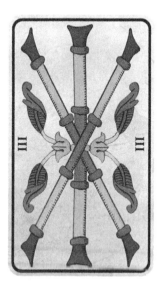

At a Glance
- *Discovery*
- *Stimulating experience*
- *Wonder*
- *Imagination*
- *Piercing energy*
- *Uncovered*

~ Meaning ~

The grand scale of things is understood. Creative energy is strong. A time to see things in a different light. A new perception. A relationship of unlimited potential. Original insight will bring positive results.

Meaning from the past – 1980's

Ideas and knowledge. Business is picking up. The mind becomes more alert.
If placed near #5 **The Hierophant** it could mean "The consultant could benefit from other people's mistakes."
If placed near #21 **The World** it could mean "Life is worth living."

Meaning from the past – 1960's

A card of departure, beginning groping advance, research. Success in an undertaking. It is not a master card. It is not easily interpreted in isolation as it is influenced by those around it.

Minor Arcana
The Three of Wands
~ *Substance* ~

—— Keyword Associations ——

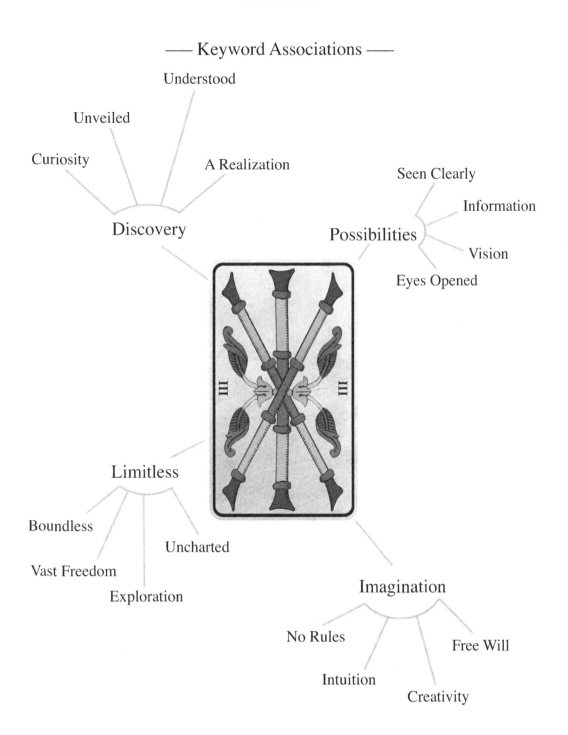

Understood

Unveiled

Curiosity

A Realization

Discovery

Seen Clearly

Information

Possibilities

Vision

Eyes Opened

Limitless

Boundless

Uncharted

Vast Freedom

Exploration

Imagination

No Rules

Free Will

Intuition

Creativity

Minor Arcana
The Four of Wands
~ Stability ~

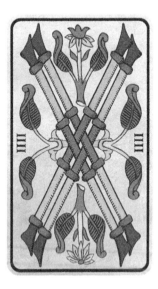

At a Glance
- *Calm*
- *Safe*
- *Unmoving*
- *Needed change*
- *A planned adjustment*
- *Stillness*

~ Meaning ~

A stable spirit and a clear mind are yours. Safe and secure situation remains in tact. A time of joy and celebration. Support is there for you. The time is right to remain as is. Moving would be challenging right now. A time of inaction is best for now.

Meaning from the past – 1980's

Change and good contacts. Conducive to a practical marriage and property transactions.
If placed near #5 **The Hierophant** it could mean "Good advice leads to desired success."
If placed near #21 **The World** it could mean "You will soon enjoy the best things in life."

Meaning from the past – 1960's

Tendency towards psychic equilibrium. Solid bias, agreement in a durable enterprise yielding a fruitful result. This is more of a master card than the others, for its presence can destroy or neutralise unfavorable cards around it.

Minor Arcana
The Four of Wands
~ *Procedures* ~

—— Keyword Associations ——

Strong Foundation

Structured

Calculated

Ritualized

Measured

Enjoyed

Well Established

Organized

Calm

Counted On

All in Place

Planned

Routine

Inspection

Readiness

Aligned

Anchored

Inaction

Interlocked

Fitting Together

Minor Arcana
The Five of Wands
~ *Change* ~

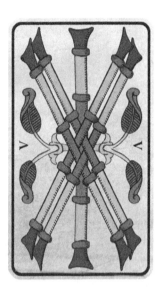

At a Glance
- *Confusing situation*
- *Inner conflict*
- *Clashing ideas*
- *Heated discussions*
- *Emotional situation*
- *Scattered energy*

~ Meaning ~
A time of tense feelings can bring disruption easily. Time to keep calm. Confusion and misunderstandings can fan a fire. Scattered energy causes confusing circumstances. Staying calm is key for now. A better time to act is near.

Meaning from the past – 1980's
Generous heart and mind. You will be on the right road if you persevere.
If placed near #5 ***The Hierophant*** it could mean "A deserved success. Happiness in love.."
If placed near #21 ***The World*** it could mean "Joy of being together."

Meaning from the past – 1960's
A wish to understand and penetrate mysteries without however, impeding material life. An indeterminate card. Plan, whose outcome cannot be determined.

Minor Arcana
The Five of Wands
~ *Stimulation* ~

—— Keyword Associations ——

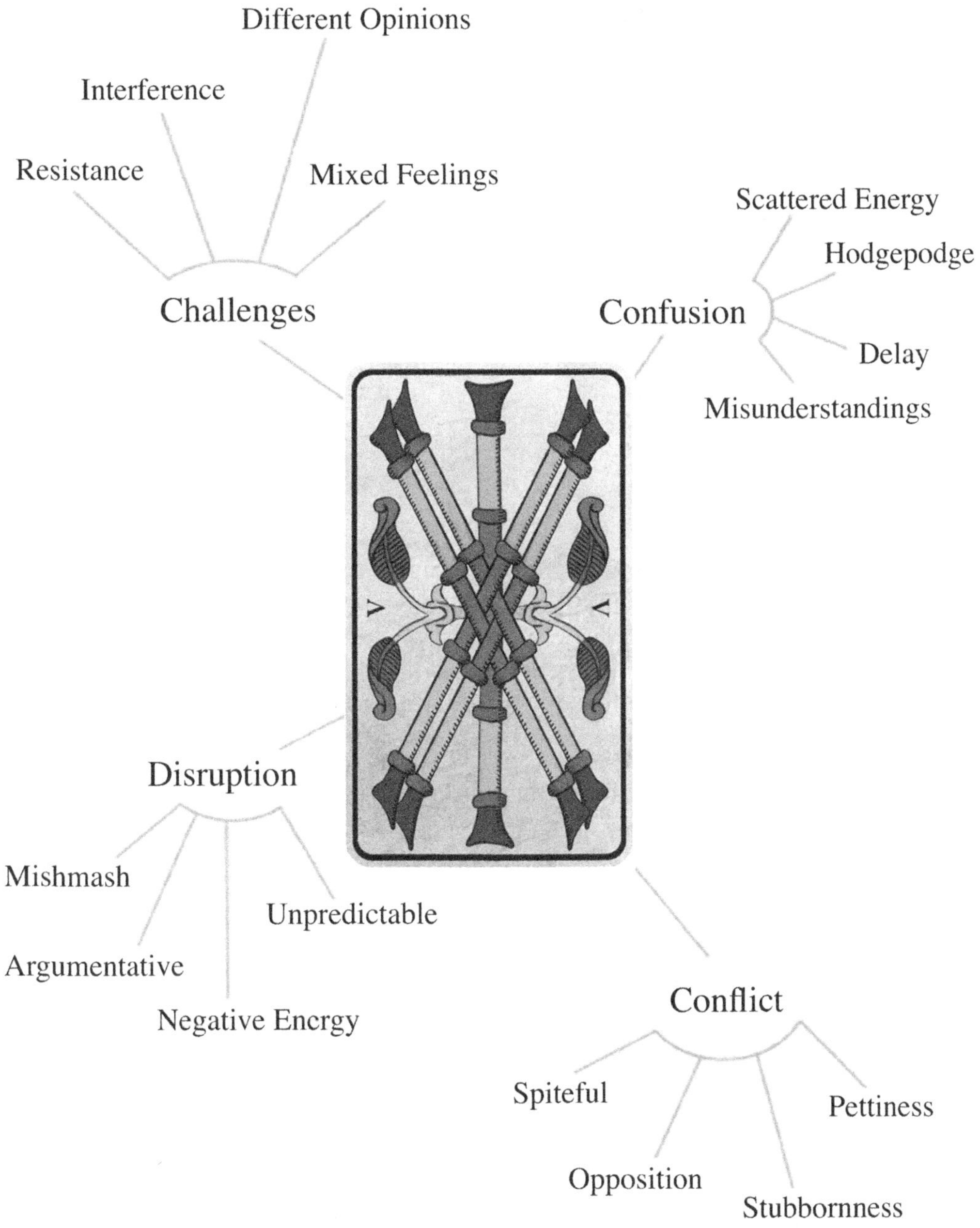

Different Opinions

Interference

Resistance

Mixed Feelings

Challenges

Scattered Energy

Hodgepodge

Confusion

Delay

Misunderstandings

Disruption

Mishmash

Unpredictable

Argumentative

Negative Energy

Conflict

Spiteful

Pettiness

Opposition

Stubbornness

Minor Arcana
The Six of Wands
~ *Perseverance* ~

At a Glance
- *Moving on*
- *Self awareness*
- *Courage*
- *Selfless action*
- *Re-evaluation*
- *Compassion*

~ Meaning ~
Celebrated accomplishments.
Coming together. Working well with good communication. Things will start to smooth out soon. The worse is behind you. You have gotten through a stormy time. Congratulations on your perseverance. Succeeding on your goal is now in sight.

Meaning from the past – 1980's
Hesitation and inferiority. More losses than profit.
If placed near #5 ***The Hierophant*** it could mean "Less unhappiness."
If placed near #21 ***The World*** it could mean "Influential people help the consultant."

Meaning from the past – 1960's
Halt in the evolution of things to allow something to be brought to perfection. Victory, but only on an earthly plane, in practical matters. A firm, stable card.

Minor Arcana
The Six of Wands
~ Established ~

—— Keyword Associations ——

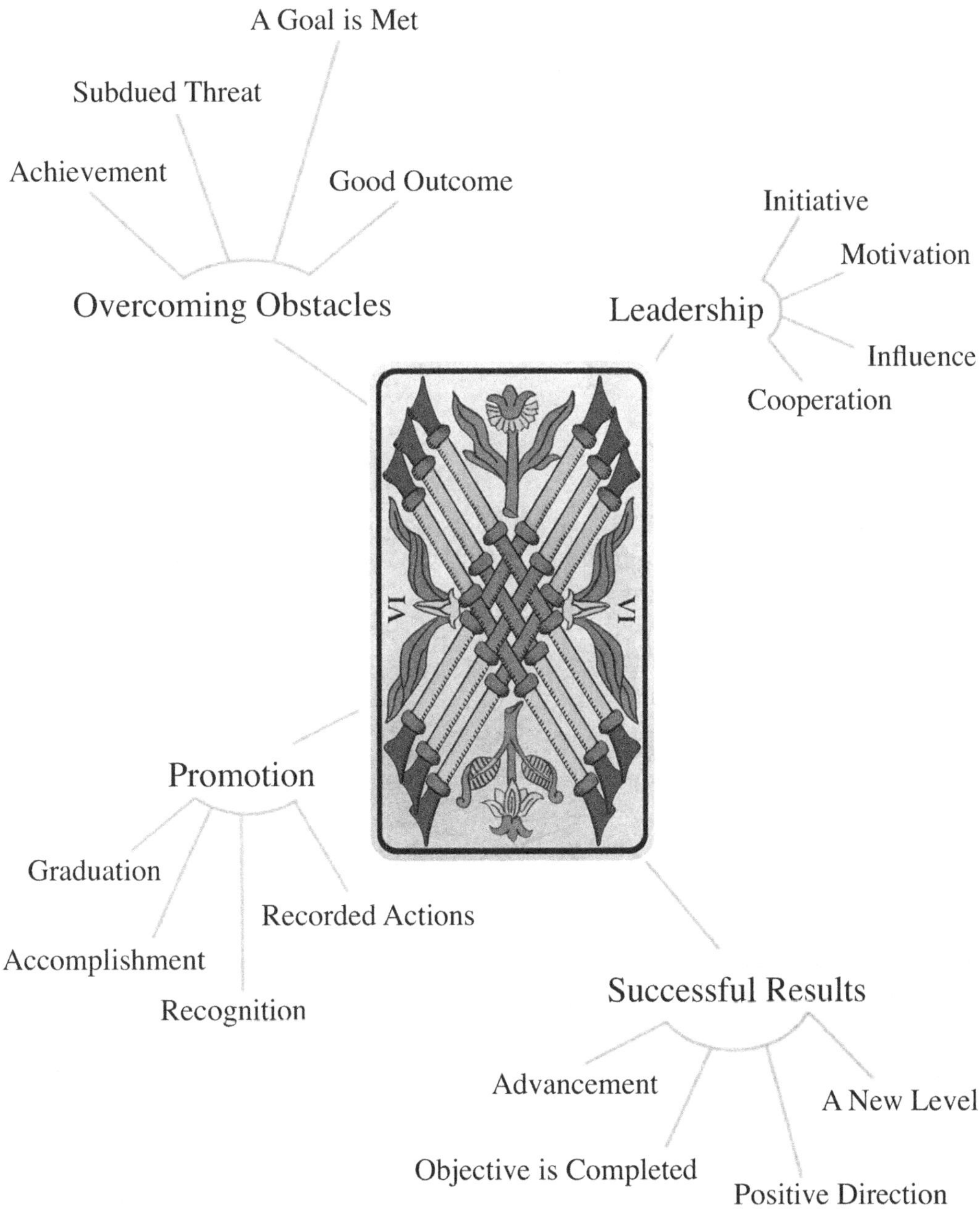

A Goal is Met

Subdued Threat

Achievement

Good Outcome

Overcoming Obstacles

Initiative

Motivation

Leadership

Influence

Cooperation

Promotion

Graduation

Recorded Actions

Accomplishment

Recognition

Successful Results

Advancement

A New Level

Objective is Completed

Positive Direction

Minor Arcana
The Seven of Wands
~ Confidence ~

At a Glance
- *Freedom*
- *Unbound*
- *Independent*
- *Clear purpose*
- *Unyielding*
- *Determination*

~ Meaning ~
Successful enterprise. Achieving goals. Much is done in positive ways. Things fall into place. Successful outcome. Progress is on the way. You will be happy with a final solution. A strong spirit is rewarded.

Meaning from the past – 1980's
Successful intellectual results. Good ideas. Surprising initiative.
If placed near #5 **The Hierophant** it could mean "Honours and glory brought about by a journey."
If placed near #21 **The World** it could mean "Security, comfort, money."

Meaning from the past – 1960's
This card does not have its basis in the universal, therefore its action is not unalterable, but variable. Violence, violent break, conflict because its balance seems to be upset by an event which abruptly breaks it, and by all whose nature it is to disrupt matter or sensation.

Minor Arcana
The Seven of Wands
~ *Intense* ~

—— Keyword Associations ——

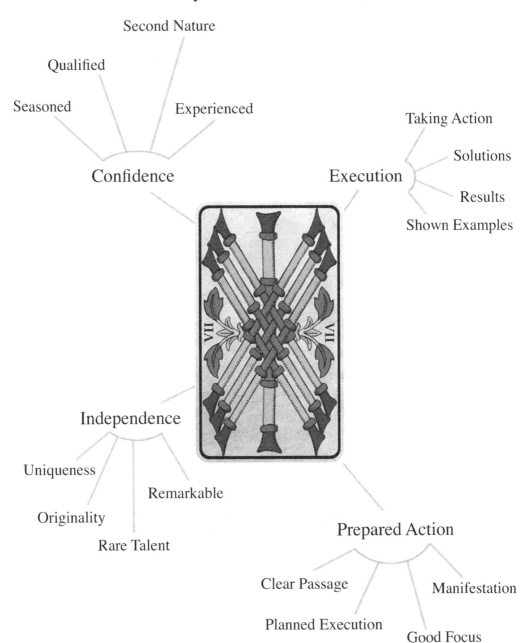

Second Nature

Qualified

Seasoned

Experienced

Confidence

Taking Action

Solutions

Results

Execution

Shown Examples

Independence

Uniqueness

Remarkable

Originality

Rare Talent

Prepared Action

Clear Passage

Manifestation

Planned Execution

Good Focus

Minor Arcana
The Eight of Wands
~ *Advancement* ~

At a Glance
• *No resistance*
• *Clarity*
• *Clear sailing*
• *Self made destiny*
• *Positive action*
• *A good direction*

~ Meaning ~
A good outcome of what the situation involves. Clear direction and instruction is carried out well. A time to take advantage of your skills in a matter of concern. Good viewpoint and the ability to move things forward is yours.

Meaning from the past – 1980's
Doubt and worry. The wheel is turning. The consultant gives up his/her plan.
If placed near #5 ***The Hierophant*** it could mean "Follow your inspiration."
If placed near #21 ***The World*** it could mean "You must learn to say No."

Meaning from the past – 1960's
Card of transition between life and death. It means a fresh beginning, birth or new life, or according to its surroundings, separation, break or death.

Minor Arcana
The Eight of Wands
~ *Undeviating* ~

—— Keyword Associations ——

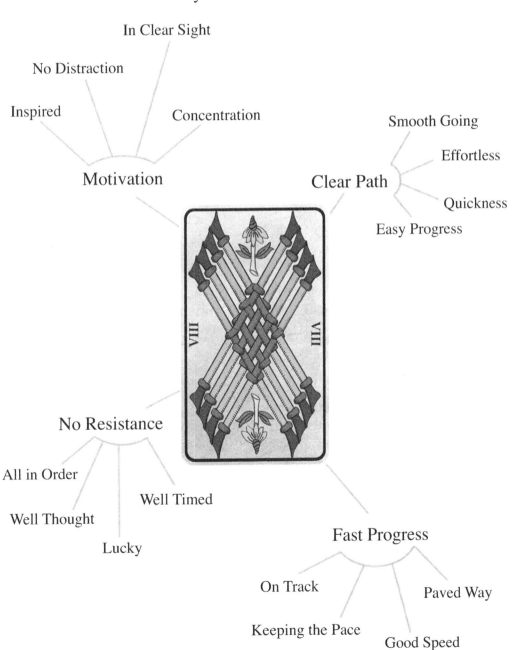

In Clear Sight

No Distraction

Inspired

Concentration

Smooth Going

Motivation

Clear Path

Effortless

Quickness

Easy Progress

No Resistance

All in Order

Well Timed

Well Thought

Fast Progress

Lucky

On Track

Paved Way

Keeping the Pace

Good Speed

Minor Arcana
The Nine of Wands
~ *Attainment* ~

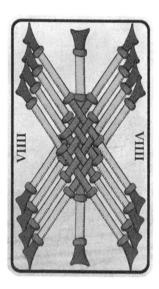

At a Glance
- *Steadfast position*
- *Untamed reality*
- *Realized potential*
- *Seasoned background*
- *Unlimited possibilities*
- *In control*

~ Meaning ~

Your efforts allow you to move forward on your goal. Your position is secure. The ability to hold back negative influence. A strong spirit holds true. On higher ground than before.

Meaning from the past – 1980's

Represents caution, thought. Circumstances force you to think; it is a good thing. If placed near #5 **The Hierophant** it could mean "Wait before making a decision." If placed near #21 **The World** it could mean "Change in your profession that may prove hazardous."

Meaning from the past – 1960's

Desire to attain the regions of the psychic, going beyond the bounds of physical safety. The card signifies the abstract or physical sciences.

Minor Arcana
The Nine of Wands
~ *Extending* ~

—— Keyword Associations ——

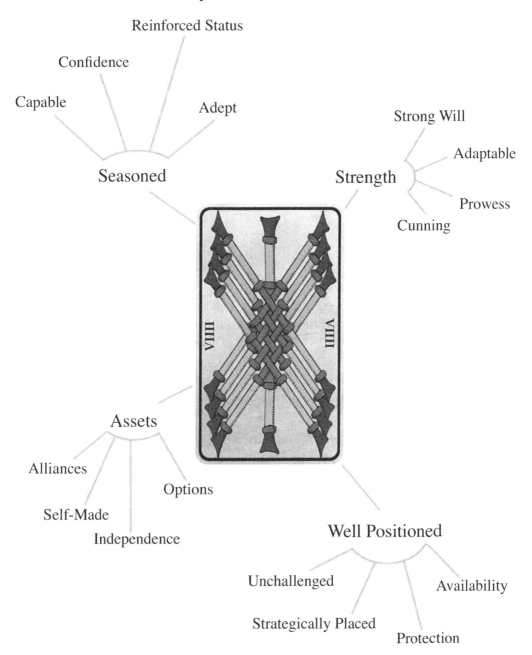

Reinforced Status

Confidence

Capable

Adept

Seasoned

Strong Will

Adaptable

Strength

Prowess

Cunning

Assets

Alliances

Self-Made

Options

Independence

Well Positioned

Unchallenged

Availability

Strategically Placed

Protection

Minor Arcana
The Ten of Wands
~ *Completion* ~

At a Glance
- *Journey's end*
- *Encompassing*
- *A good return*
- *Harvest*
- *Old ways ended*
- *New horizons*

~ Meaning ~

A time to take hold of what has been accomplished. The fruits of your labor is enjoyed. A gathering of all that's been done. Work at this level is complete. Time to move to another challenge. Inspiration will keep things moving well.

Meaning from the past – 1980's

Beneficial card for business. The consultant must change his tactics if he wants success.

If placed near #5 ***The Hierophant*** it could mean "Expected results achieved."

If placed near #21 ***The World*** it could mean "Better health. Prosperity. Luck."

Meaning from the past – 1960's

Temporary power in the realm of the psychic. Difficulties, plans which do not succeed or only do so with difficulty. With other cards it indicates halt, sterility.

Minor Arcana
The Ten of Wands
~ *Adeptship* ~

—— Keyword Associations ——

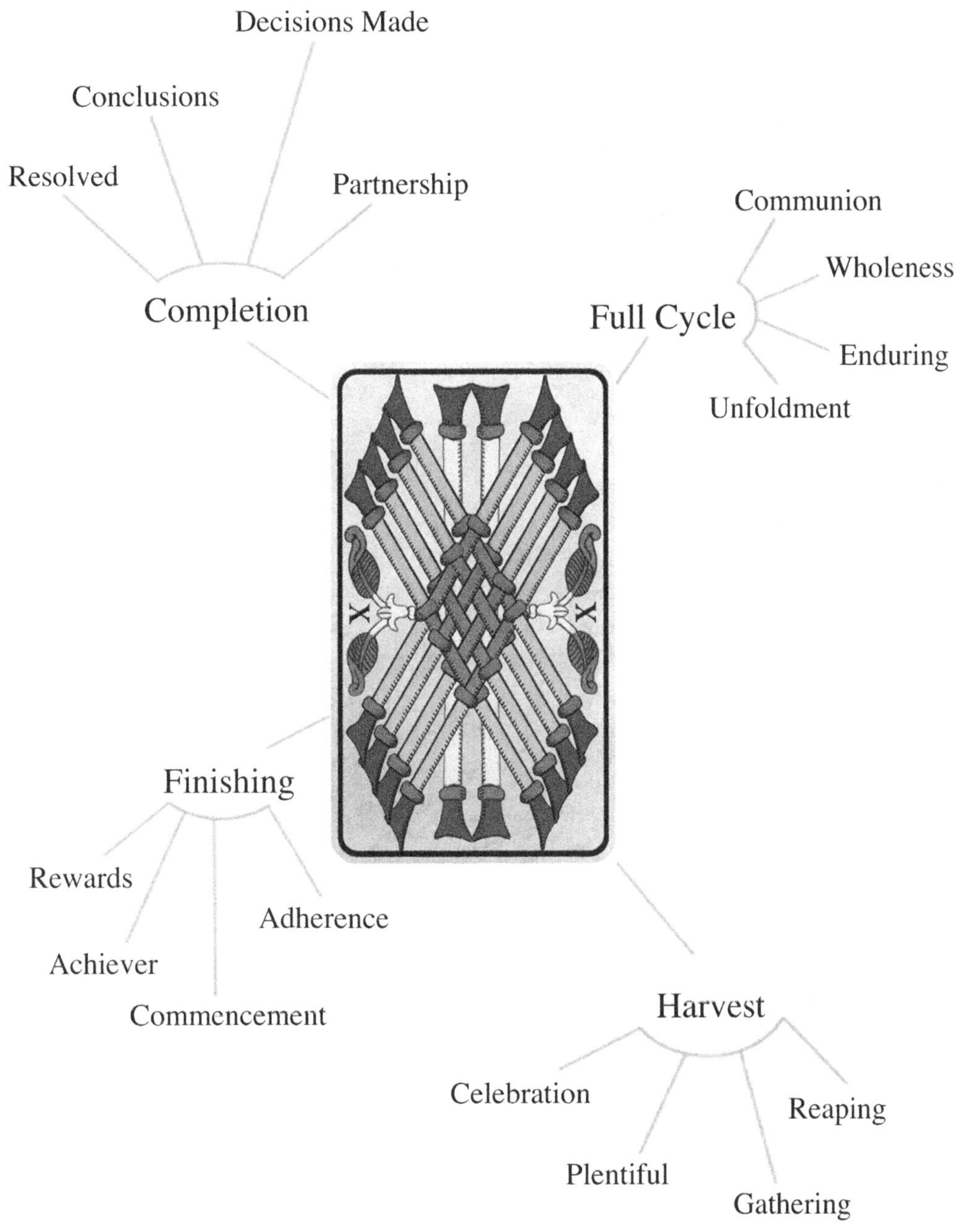

Decisions Made

Conclusions

Resolved

Partnership

Communion

Wholeness

Completion

Full Cycle

Enduring

Unfoldment

Finishing

Rewards

Adherence

Achiever

Commencement

Harvest

Celebration

Reaping

Plentiful

Gathering

Minor Arcana
The Page of Wands
~ New Path ~

At a Glance
- *A new inspiration*
- *Unknown environment*
- *New insight*
- *New direction*
- *Beginning of a journey*
- *Following experience*

~ Meaning ~
Finding what you truly seek.

The start of a new journey. Excitement and experience will be yours if you act. Timing is good to start something new. Something from the spirit needs to be quenched. Your path will bring much reward.

Meaning from the past – 1980's
Ambitious, hardworking person, always grateful. Gives hope for a better job.

If placed near #5 **The Hierophant** it could mean "If the consultant is a child he will have a successful life."

If placed near #20 **Judgement** it could mean "Lasting and beneficial association."

Meaning from the past – 1960's
Man faced by difficulty becoming aware of his forces and who can prevail or stagnate according to his abilities. Hard work with chances of success.

Minor Arcana
The Page of Wands
~ *Phases* ~

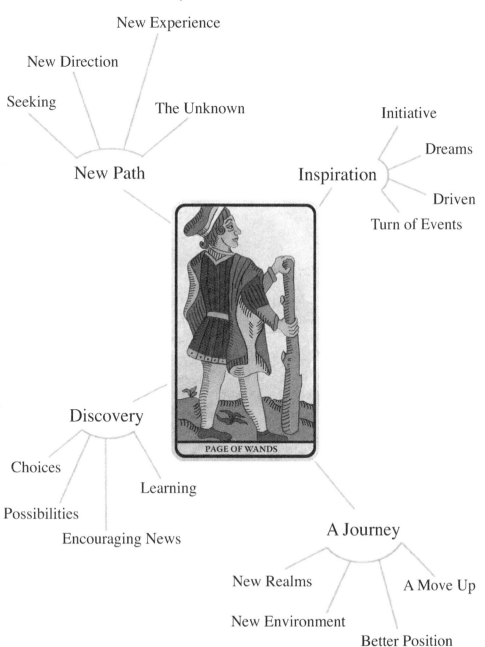

—— Keyword Associations ——

New Experience

New Direction

Seeking

The Unknown

New Path

Initiative

Dreams

Driven

Turn of Events

Inspiration

Discovery

Choices

Learning

Possibilities

Encouraging News

A Journey

New Realms

A Move Up

New Environment

Better Position

PAGE OF WANDS

Minor Arcana
The Knight of Wands
~ Action ~

At a Glance
- *A strong belief*
- *Unshakable desire*
- *Passionate fulfillment*
- *Moving forward*
- *Positive attitude*
- *Winning situation*

~ Meaning ~

Quick and direct results.

Your energy is strong right now. Moving forward at this time is best. Progress will be swift. A seen change in the situation brings action. Good results. Much ground is covered.

Meaning from the past – 1980's

Friendly person, honest go-between. Predicts a pleasant event.

If placed near #5 **The Hierophant** it could mean "Material success brought about by a journey."

If placed near #21 **The World** it could mean "Beneficial to work, plans and love affairs."

Meaning from the past – 1960's

Providential aid. Support is given in everything. Protection, support and strength brought by the unknown.

Minor Arcana
The Knight of Wands
~ *Integrity* ~

—— Keyword Associations ——

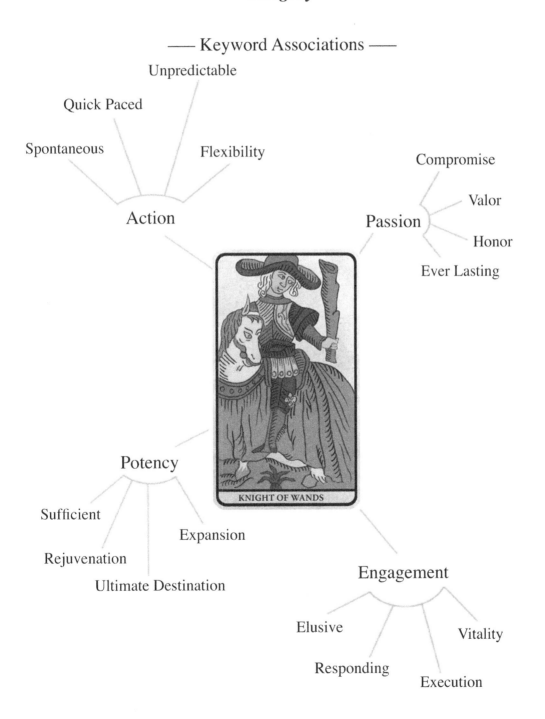

Unpredictable

Quick Paced

Spontaneous

Flexibility

Action

Compromise

Valor

Passion

Honor

Ever Lasting

Potency

Sufficient

Expansion

Rejuvenation

Ultimate Destination

Engagement

Elusive

Responding

Vitality

Execution

KNIGHT OF WANDS

Minor Arcana
The Queen of Wands
~ *Patience* ~

At a Glance
- *A quiet strength*
- *Understanding perception*
- *Predetermined action*
- *Sincere motive*
- *Things seen clearly*
- *Loving concern*

~ Meaning ~

Things are seen clearly. Good judgment. Sound decisions are made based on merit. Rewards from the right place. A positive energy is contagious. Inspiring leadership is recognized by others. Graceful diplomacy will reap rewards.

Meaning from the past – 1980's

Independent and fickle woman. Dangerous rival for other women.
If placed near #5 **The Hierophant** it could mean "Earns more respect."
If placed near #21 **The World** it could mean "Helps towards an appreciation of all that is beautiful, truthful and stable."

Meaning from the past – 1960's

Fatality prevails in all domains. Defence by means of brutality. Passionate anger. Stubbornness, efforts to avoid the blows of fate.

Minor Arcana
The Queen of Wands
~ *Ambition* ~

—— Keyword Associations ——

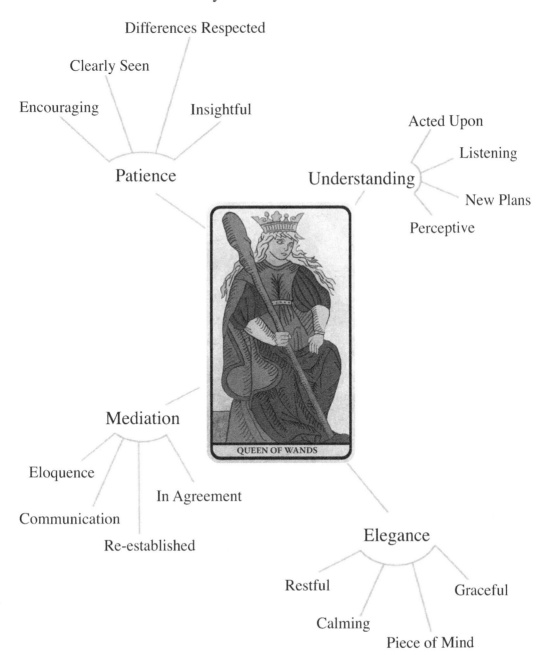

Differences Respected

Clearly Seen

Encouraging

Insightful

Acted Upon

Listening

Patience

Understanding

New Plans

Perceptive

QUEEN OF WANDS

Mediation

Eloquence

In Agreement

Communication

Re-established

Elegance

Restful

Graceful

Calming

Piece of Mind

Minor Arcana
The King of Wands
~ *Knowledge* ~

At a Glance
- *A wise authority*
- *Sound decisions*
- *Good advice*
- *Clear planning*
- *Constructive action*
- *New opportunity*

~ Meaning ~

In a position to make sound choices. No opposition. Your position is strong. Things moving in the right direction. Smart decisions are paying off. Success through proper preparation is yours. Your strength is in your knowledge of the situation.

Meaning from the past – 1980's

Clever man of high rank. Try your luck. You might succeed.
If placed near #5 *The Hierophant* it could mean "Sign of wealth and enthusiasm."
If placed near #21 *The World* it could mean "Triumph over all obstacles."

Meaning from the past – 1960's

Spiritual force brings mediation in discussions. Moral support.

Minor Arcana
The King of Wands
~ *Influence* ~

—— Keyword Associations ——

Profound

Experienced

Seasoned

Qualified

High Ranking

Authority

Knowledge

Empowered

Certified

Licensed

KING OF WANDS

Integrity

Reputation

Righteous

Distinction

Strong Principles

Responsibility

Following Through

Judgmental

Lawful

Carefully Planned

4. Card Spread Anatomy & Instruction

What is a card spread? Card spreads are a collection of issues that pertain to the question being looked into. This collection of issues are set up as a template of topics meant to be useful to any question asked of it. So they are general, not specific but considered important regardless.

Can we change those positions to more useful topics to look into? Of course. I have done that over time with my Celtic Cross card spread. In this chapter I will be showing both a traditional Celtic Cross as well as my Celtic Cross with what I feel are more meaningful positions. You are more than welcome to use either one.

The card spread is a key component to the whole application. Understanding why card spreads work will bring more clarity into your readings.

In Chapter 2 we learned why this centuries old system works and that we can now improve the process. I feel this will be a major breakthrough in our understanding and use of the Tarot.

First I will show the classic traditional Celtic Cross. I have used Eden Grays term of this spread from her book The Complete Guide to the Tarot Copyright © 1970. At that time she called this "The Ancient Keltic Method."

NOTE: In the following sample of The Ancient Keltic Method, Eden Gray implies in her wording that the cards put into play represent the position they are placed with. I feel today a clearer approach is to think of the card spread positions as segments of the question itself and the cards placed into those positions as the answer to those questions. Two separate parts of the application.

The Ancient Keltic Method

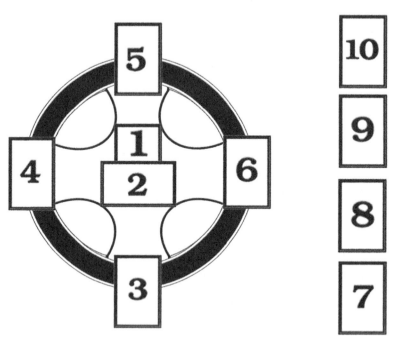

The numbering pattern varies from one source to another with this spread.
In this classic version the cards are read clockwise around the center.

Position #1 – This Covers Him
This card represents the general atmosphere of the situation. The influences at work.

Position #2 – This Crosses Him
This card is always laid across position #1 and is always read right side up. This card shows opposing forces to the situation. Both good and evil.

Position #3 – This is Beneath Him
This card represents what has already happened. Something that is already a part of the issue at hand.

Position #4 – This is Behind Him
This card shows influences that have recently happened and are now passing away.

Position #5 – This Crowns Him
This card represents something that may come to pass in the future.

Position #6 – This is Before Him
This card shows what will come to pass in the future.

Position #7 – What the Querent Fears
This card represents the negative fears the client has about this issue.

Position #8 – Family Opinion
This card represents opinions and influence family and friends have on this question.

Position #9 – The Client's Hopes
This card represents what the client hopes to achieve in this quest.

Position #10 – Final Outcome
This last cards tells what the final outcome will be. It should also take into consideration all the cards that have been laid out on the table.

Now let's take a deeper look into these positions.

The Ancient Keltic Method

Positions of a card spread are never seen on the table. Only the cards placed into them are noticed. But the positions are aspects of the question. Each position is a segment of the question being looked into.

The cards placed into those positions are meant to give us answers to those aspects of the question being asked. They are meant to spark ideas for answers intuitively, metaphorically, imaginatively or even logically and rationally. They allow us to see answers we didn't see before about a question being looked into.

Position #1 – This Covers Him

This position addresses the general atmosphere of the situation. The influences at work.

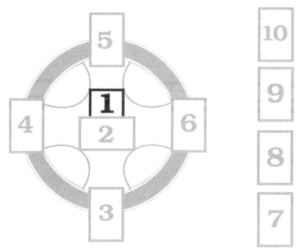

Position #1 allows us to look into what outside influences are affecting the situation. It allows us to make adjustments to our advantage in some way. To improve our predicament. The card helps us see new ideas for ways to help alter and adjust things in our favor.

It can also show us what challenges we can avoid. What to stay away from that are close to us now. It makes us look at the situation overall and what is affecting it. A card here can show us new ideas on how to deal with something that is influencing things against us or it can show us things that are around us that will help us if we can adjust them or notice them in some way.

What insight is the card showing you that can help the general atmosphere of the question?

Position #2 – This Crosses Him

This card is always laid across position #1 and is always read right side up. This position addresses opposing forces to the situation. Both good and evil.

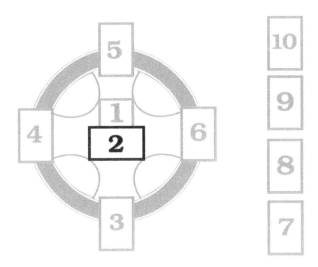

Position #2 allows us to look at things working against the issue. If the question is some type of negative obstacle then these can be seen as favorable aspects working against that negativity. Things in your favor to consider. If the question is a positive issue then this position can show things working against you that need to be resolved.

A card placed here can show ideas for assets that are there to help you move forward. It can also show forces that are working against you and need to be carefully handled. A card here has the opportunity of showing new insight into forces around you and how to grab them and handle them.

NOTE: Positions #1 & #2 are commonly seen as working together to create a close look at the question itself. To see what is surrounding the question and what the general situation is. I feel this is why they are the only two cards in contact with each other in the lay out pattern. They work together. These two cards address the issue being looked into.

Position #3 – This is Beneath Him

This position addresses what has already happened. Something that is already a part of the issue at hand.

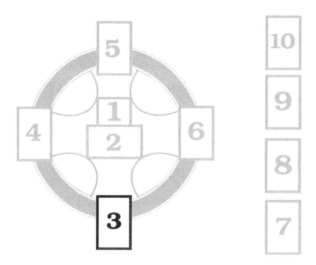

Position #3 allows us to take a look at what has already become manifest. Many times this is the core of the issue. What happened? What is the set of circumstances? This can be a useful aspect of the question. What occurred? How did it all come together? Was there some misunderstanding? Confusion?

If we look at what has happened we might be able to reverse it's result. Undo the past. Resolve it. Looking at what happened allows us to seek solutions. The card placed here might give us new ideas for ways to resolve the issue. To undo what has been done. If it is something that cannot be undone it allows us to look for ways to heal the situation. To smooth it out and move forward the best way possible.

Sometimes things that have happened are opportunities to create something amazing. Something great can come out of a challenging situation. A card placed here might show us something we didn't see before to do just that.

Position #3 is the root of the matter at hand. A card placed here might show us solutions we didn't see before.

Position #4 – This is Behind Him

This position addresses influences that have recently happened and are now passing away.

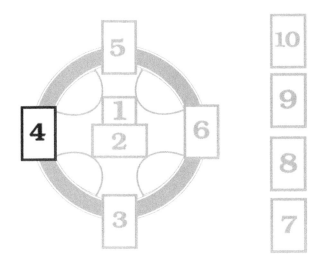

Position #4 allows us to look into the result of what has happened. The repercussions of the situation. What kind of circumstances has the actions of position #3 put the client in?

A card placed in this position allows us to look at the recent results of this issue with a new set of eyes. Is the result of this issue causing a challenge? Has it put us in a different set of circumstances?

A card placed here can show us new ways of adjusting things in our favor. Putting us in a better space. Or strengthening a space that is already favorable to the client if Position #3 was a favorable occurrence.

Position #4 can be seen as the effect created from the cause of Position #3. A card placed here might show us new insight in ways to adjust this situation in our favor.

Position #5 – This Crowns Him
This position represents something that may come to pass in the future.

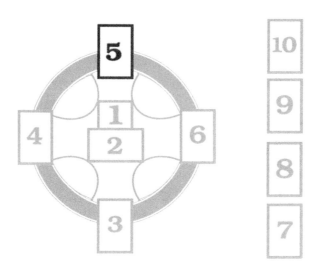

Position #5 allows us to look for opportunities to put things in favor for the client. We have opportunities every day. We just don't notice them. A card placed here can give us a peek at opportunity that may be coming. One to keep an eye out for. If we're looking for it, we will see it when it appears and then we can grab it.

I feel this position significantly taps into our intuitive side.
A card placed here can open up our intuition clearly. It lets us look for possibilities. The card will show us those possibilities that we didn't see before.

I find it interesting that this position states "What May Happen" while position #6 will be stating "What Will Happen" What will happen implies what is seen rationally. The facts. But Position #5 shows us possibilities that might be attained seen from our intuitive side.

Your dreams may come true if you seek them out.

Position #6 – This is Before Him
This card shows what will come to pass in the future.

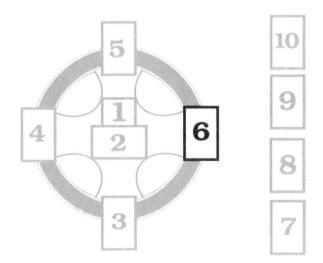

Position #6 makes a strong statement. "What will come to pass." This hints of some higher source knowing what will happen through these cards. The centuries old mystery of the Tarot knowing your future is strongly stated in this position. The random card placed here shows us what will be. But only if the reader interprets it correctly.

Although facts might be seen clearly on where this is headed our intuition can be key in finding new choices and options. What feelings do we have about this card? How do we see it as it pertains to the question and it's path? Where are we headed?

This position shows something significant that will happen related to the issue being looked into. This could be a challenge or it could be an advantage. A card placed in this position allows us to anticipate things we didn't consider. It allows us to prepare ourselves for something unexpected. Something to be ready for.

Although this position implies what will come to pass it should not be confused with the end result or answer to the reading. That is shown in position #10. The final outcome in this classic spread.

Position #7 – What the Querent Fears

This position represents the negative fears the client has about this issue.

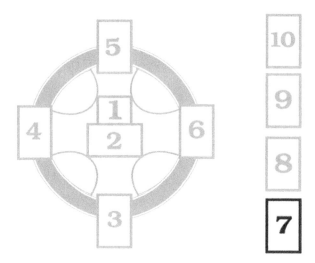

Position #7 allows us to look into what the querent hopes to avoid. This position can show the weaknesses the client feels they might have. Where they are vulnerable What they are trying to protect against happening.

A card here can help us find ways to safeguard against threatening results the client is worried could happen. It can show us how the client can strengthen their situation to eliminate those fears and anxiety. Living in fear is not helpful although caution is always wise. Finding that balance between the two is helpful.

How can the client find ways to safely weaken what she fears without putting other things in jeopardy that are well placed. A constructive outlook on the challenge can eliminate much of these fears. A card placed here might be able to show us how to resolve those fearful concerns and strengthen the clients position, which in turn can eliminate those fears the client feels.

Position #8 – Family Opinion

This card represents opinions and influence family and friends have on this question.

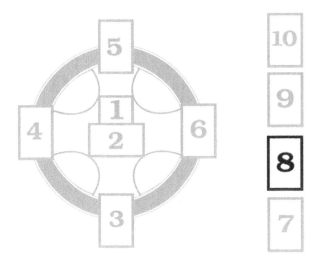

Position #8 allows us to look at the support and the resistance from others close to us. Ultimately we want support but this isn't always the case. Here we have an opportunity to see how to sway others to see our side of things.

If support is weak a card here might show us ways to strengthen that support. How can this card show us how we can influence others around us to agree with our wants. Our desires. A card here might show compromise being the answer. It might show that having patience with others will help sway them to come around to our thinking in time.

It might show we need to fine tune what we are trying to accomplish in some manner. Maybe their support is not really as necessary as originally thought. What are our options of getting by without it? A card placed here will give us ideas of possible options to consider.

Position #9 – The Client's Hopes

This position represents what the client hopes to achieve in this quest.

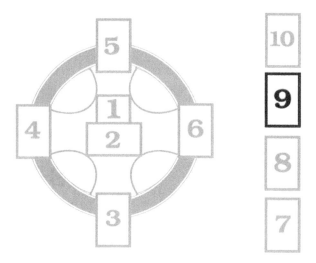

Position #9 allows us to look at the whole reason for this question. The purpose of this goal the client is hoping to accomplish. This position allows us to focus on what the client really wants out of all this effort.
What are they ultimately looking for?

A card placed here can help confirm an issue or open up the bigger picture of what the client really seeks. Here we can question the path this client is on. Is it really going to be the right way to move forward to where they want to end up?

Many times people can stray from the right path. Here we can call attention to their ultimate goal. Will this question bring them closer or put more distance between them and that goal.

Position #10 – Final Outcome

This last position tells what the final outcome will be. It should also take into consideration all the cards that have been laid out on the table.

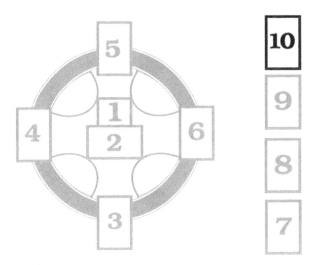

Position #10 allows us to see the final outcome of this question. It is important to blend in the rest of the cards interpretations into this final outcome as well. The other 9 positions have important variables to consider.

This position might be able to show us that if we pay attention to the other cards in play we can have different outcomes based on how those other cards influence the reading.

Final outcome is a strong statement to make and I feel what this position is meant to say is to consider the reading as a whole and then see how this card can sway various final outcomes from there. But you can interpret final outcome literally if you choose. I leave that up to you.

This classic card spread has seen many wonderful readings with the Tarot cards over time. It is a classic for sure. But over time I fine tuned this classic to work better for me personally. What follows is what I consider a Celtic Cross that works with more direction and clarity. It is what I've chosen to use for most of my life as a professional Tarot reader.

Pitisci's Celtic Cross

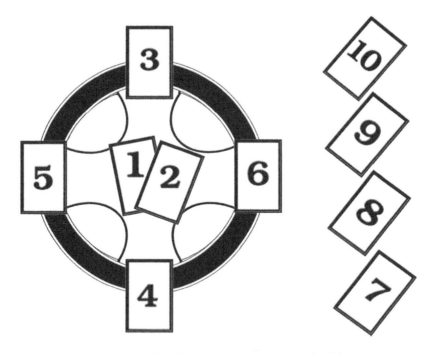

The meanings I have assigned to this version of the Celtic Cross are my own. Although I would say they can be seen as comparable to the classic version in some ways.

Over time and many readings my application of this classic spread shifted here and there. Gradually I adjusted position meanings to represent more meaningful aspects to any question asked. My approach focuses on four principles of a question. Those are "What, Why, How, & When." I've gently adjusted the 10 positions of this classic spread with those four principles in mind. *What is the real question? Why do you want this in your life? How are we going to attain this? When do we take action?*

If you can answer just one of those four basic principles to a question in a reading, your reading had value to the client. If you can answer 2 or 3 of these four elements, your reading can be highly significant. If you can accurately answer all four of these elements, your reading was amazing. It's as simple and as complicated as that.

Position #1 & #2 – A look at the question itself

These two positions working together allow us to use 2 cards to take a hard look at the question itself.

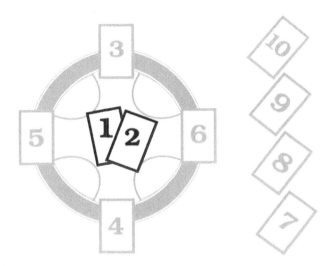

Positions #1&#2 working together allow us to look deeply into the question. Can the question be rephrased? Is there more to the question then what the client is asking? Is there a question behind the question? Is the client seeing their own question clearly? Is there more to the question than realized by the client? Is there a deeper question here that the client is not seeing clearly?

Two cards working together or even separately can allow us to see the question at different angles. Tilt it here and there and see it from different sides. A correct question is the most important part of the process. If anything, these two positions can confirm the client is seeing things clearly in what they seek to know or accomplish.

These two positions allow us to look at what we are really asking about?

These two positions are key to WHAT. What is the real issue and how can it be seen in other ways?

Position #3 – Client's current actions

This position allows us to look at what efforts the client is currently taking.

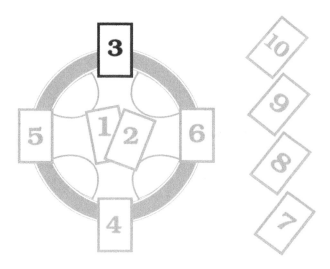

Position #3 allows us to focus on the current concerns the client has on this issue. Sometimes initial reactions are short-sighted and need to be rethought. This can also effect the immediate objectives the client is attempting to complete in position #4. Position #3 allows us to look at the immediate actions the client is taking at this time to achieve their goal. Are these actions the best to take? Could the actions being taken hurt their chances of success? Are they taking the best actions for success?

This position works hand-in-hand with position #4. Immediate goals.
If the immediate goals are misdirected then the actions the client is taking to achieve them are not wise choices.

A card placed in this position allows us to see new ideas for actions to be taken. New approaches. The client might be putting too much effort into actions that aren't necessarily going to help them. They might even be putting themselves further away from their goal.

Correct actions can only be achieved once we have effective initial goals in place. That is what we look for in positions #3 and #4. These two positions work well together in your reading.

This position is key to WHY. Are you sure this is really what you want to do?

Position #4 – Immediate Objectives

This position allows us to look at what the client feels is first and fore-most to be taken care of. The first priorities.

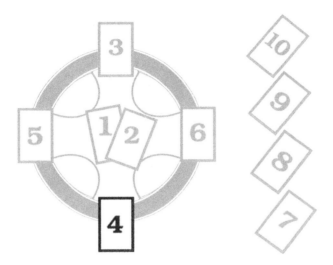

Position #4 allows us to look at what the client is trying to accomplish initially. Some fist step that the client feels is a priority to achieve. Many times a client will not see that other steps have to be in place before this step can happen.

This position allows us to question the client's priorities. Is the client missing some important aspect of this process? Do they need to adjust the actions they are taking in position #3?

Maybe some crucial step is not being considered that needs to be recognized. A card placed here might show us new insight into something that is missing that needs to be added. Maybe something needs to be adjusted just slightly.

Maybe something has to be eliminated or replaced with another objective that will be more useful to accomplishing this goal. Are there other more important goals that should be addressed first?

Positions #3 & #4 work well together to find or confirm direction. Why are they taking these actions. Why do they feel this immediate goal is key to their objective?

This position is key to WHY. Are you sure this is really what you want?

Position #5 – An Asset of the Client

This Position allows us to look at what the client has going for them. We all have strengths and weaknesses. Here we can look at strengths the client needs to use. And weaknesses the client needs to be aware of.

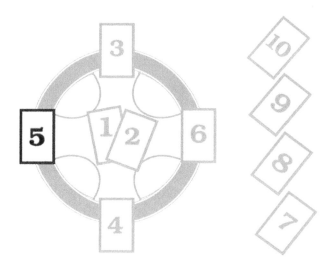

Position #5 allows us to look at attributes and strengths the client has that they might not be using right now. Maybe they don't realize they have them. A card placed here can show strengths the client might not have considered before. Or thought not to be important attributes on their quest.

How can these strengths help us to achieve what we are trying to accomplish? What are they? How will others respond if I utilize them?
What experience do you have that might help? Is there a history on this matter that makes you stand out to others.

This might also be a strength that is needed to be developed or learned in order to ac-complish what it is you seek.

This position shows things that can be used to make this goal possible. Or at least give you the best advantage to succeed.

This position allows us to remind the client of what they can do if they really choose to. It is a confidence building position that can help us prepare for Position #6. The opportunity.

This position is key to HOW. How are we going to accomplish this quest?

Position #6 – An Opportunity

This Position allows us to look at opportunities that will come to help the client achieve what they are striving for.

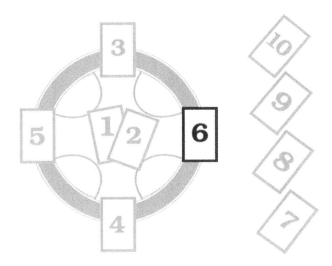

Position #6 allows us to look for an opportunity to come. We all have many opportunities every day. We just don't see them because we're not looking for them. Or we convince ourselves that they are not there. *"Seek and you shall find"*

This opportunity could be an event the client is aware of. Perhaps a meeting. Or they might not have a clue but should keep an eye out for it to come. Be aware and look. When it happens remember your asset from position #5 might be helpful now.

Opportunities come in many ways. A phone call. An epiphany comes to you. An old friend. A dream. An idea you think of as you walk down the street.

There could be more than one opportunity. A card placed in this position allows us to see what opportunities might be coming to the client. I give this a very general time period of within 3 months. It could come today. Or it could come 3 months from now. Or any time in between those times.

This position works well with position #5. The Asset might help when the Opportunity comes to the client.

This position is key to HOW. How are we going to accomplish this quest?

Position #7 – Client's perception of the question

This Position allows us to look at the clients' feelings about this question. We can question whether the client is seeing things clearly or misguided.

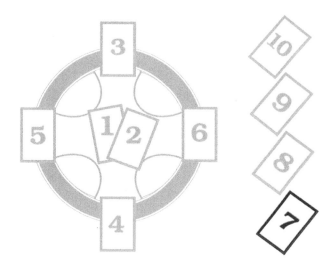

Position #7 allows us to question how the client is viewing this situation. Many times we see things in ways that might not be truly correct.
We can convince ourselves of something that might not be real. Other times we may see something in a negative way that really isn't the case.

Position #7 works well with Positions #1 &#2. The real question. The reality of the situation being looked into. Is the client seeing things as they really are? Or are they seeing an illusion. Placing a card in this position allows us to see aspects of the clients perception of what is real from Position #1 & #2.

If these three cards seem to flow nicely with each other or if there is a conflict between Position #7 and the center 2 cards, #1 & #2 we can question the clients own viewpoint on the question.

This position allows us to question the client about the good or bad aspects about what they are trying to accomplish.

This position is key to WHAT. What is the real issue and how is it perceived by the seeker?

Position #8 – The Timing

This Position allows us to look at when is the best time to act on this issue.

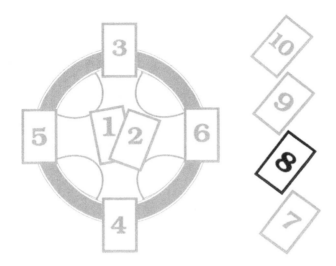

Position #8 allows us to look at when is the best time to move on this quest. Do we take action now? Or do we wait for a more opportune time.

Timing is everything and taking that into consideration can be beneficial for success. A card placed here allows us to see new ideas on when to move on this goal. It allows us to look closely at things that can make it easier if done at a certain time.

Maybe action needs to be taken now before opportunities are lost for good. Maybe it is best to wait for a more favorable time before we take action.

A card placed here may give us insight into when to make a move.

This position is key to WHEN. When and in what way do we proceed?

Position #9 – The Purpose

This Position allows us to look at the true purpose of the quest itself.

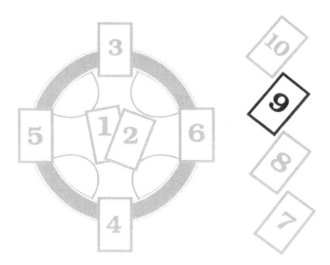

Position #9 allows us to look closely at the big picture. What is the true reason for this goal? Why do you want this to come to pass? What happiness do you feel it will bring you. Will it really bring you that happiness that you imagine it will?

Maybe this quest won't really bring what you ultimately want. Be careful. You might get what you wish for. Will this really bring you happiness? Will it really bring you what you think it will? This position works well with Position #4. The immediate goals of position #4 are done to bring the ultimate goal of position #9.

Many times we think we want something but don't stop to really think about what this all will encompass. We don't look at that. A card placed in this position allows us to see insight into what may come of this if accomplished. Is this what you thought it would be? What you hoped for?

This position is key to WHY. Are you sure this is really what you want?

Position #10 – Finer Details & Closing Thoughts

This Position allows us to wrap up the reading with closure and focus.

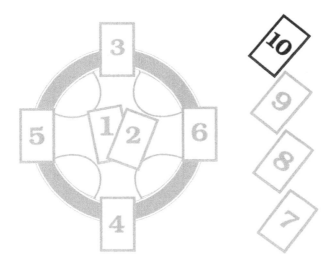

Position #10 allows us to come up with definite direction taking into consideration everything that has been discussed from the other positions. It is a position that can sum things up and come up with a plan.

Here we can weigh everything out that has been covered and make an evaluation on the matter. A strategy. Position #10 can also show small details of things not covered in the other positions. A second opportunity from Position #6 perhaps. Or maybe another factor to consider in the timing of Position #8.

It is an intuitive position allowing us to add freely to the reading. It can show a hunch. A feeling. This is like the free card position that can add spice to the reading.

Another option is blending the energy of the card placed into position #10 to each of the other positions for added insight and details. Maybe something else to watch for.

Honestly I can say I've changed this positions meaning many times over the years. You can do many things with this position but I would say it's key is all four areas.... What, Why, How & When.

So have fun using position #10 like a wild card and see what works best for you. You might use it differently over time on this journey as a reader.

I feel position #10 works mostly with the key of HOW. Other key details influencing the other positions that can help accomplish this quest?

Sample Reading
Pitisci's Celtic Cross

I thought it would be helpful to add a sample reading in this chapter. I decided not to use any specific question in this sample. Therefore it can be related to any situation. It is just an example to show how the cards can create meaning in a reading.

I would also like to suggest using this same card reading in a number of your own questions. Keeping the same cards in place used for different questions will show you how card meanings can shift from one reading to another. That shift is what expands your range of meaning as you use these cards on your Tarot journey.

So the Celtic Cross as I use it. It has given me amazing results for many years. Seeing if you can relate this sample reading to something going on with you at this time might also be an interesting exercise.

Sample Reading
Pitisci's Celtic Cross

Cards will be looked at individually as well as how they work with other cards in the spread. The cards drawn were:

Position 1) • 4 of Pentacles
Position 2) • The Empress
Position 3) • Ace of Cups

Position 4) • Knight of Swords
Position 5) • 8 of Swords
Position 6) • The Hanged Man

Position 7) • 9 of Wands
Position 8) • Page of Pentacles
Position 9) • The Chariot
Position10) • 2 of Swords

Positions 1 & 2
A look at the question

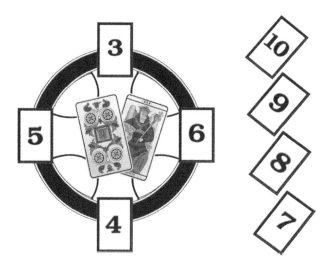

Position 1

4 of Pentacles
~ *Stability* ~

Read Together

Position 2

The Empress
~ *Creativity* ~

Positions #1 & #2 are combined for meaning to the question: An issue that needs to be stable in order to prosper. Structure is key for growth on this question. Solid planning is needed for success to flourish. How can we plan this issue in better ways?

Position 3
Current priorities of the client

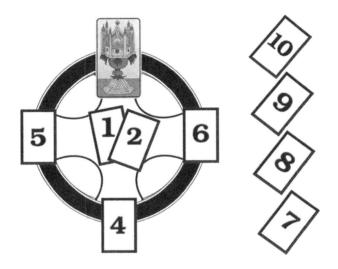

Position 3

Ace of Cups
~ The New Situation ~

Reading Position 3: The client is in a good position to create a new environment. Efforts being made by the client to start something new that will advance the issue forward.

Position 4
Immediate objectives

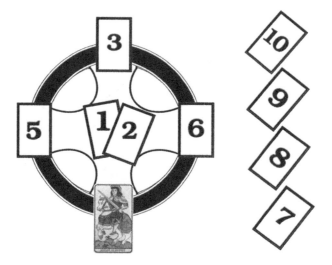

Position 4

Knight of Swords
~ Taking Action ~

Reading Position 4: The client wants to put themselves in a space were action can be taken soon. Looking at all the options of position 3 allows our client to see what actions should be taken and how to move on those actions once a plan is in place.

Position 5
Client's assets

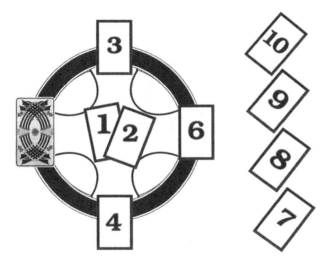

Position 5

Eight of Swords

~ Capable Advancement ~

Reading Position 5: The client is in a good position to advance on this quest. Resistance is not really a factor once it is addressed. Nothing holding the client back to move forward is seen here with the 8 of Swords. The client is in a good position to eliminate any obstacles that are holding them back if they take the initiative. Confronting any resistance now will pay off in their favor.

Position 6
An opportunity to come

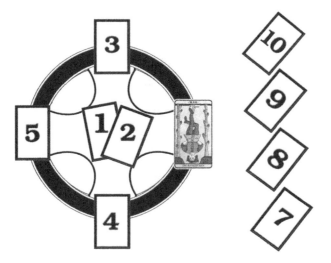

Position 6

The Hanged Man
~ Reversal ~

Reading Position 6: An opportunity to turns things around in the clients favor will be made available to them in the coming months. The client should be ready to grab this opportunity when it makes itself available.

Position 7
Client's viewpoint of this scenario

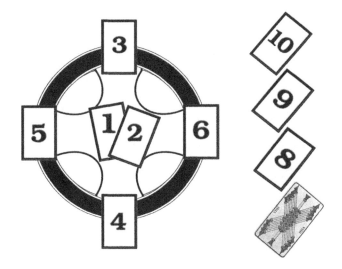

Position 7

Nine of Wands
~ *Promising Rewards* ~

Reading Position 7: The client is seeing this quest in a positive light. The seeker feels this issue will put them in a very nice situation once achieved. The client sees this as a positive opportunity if pursued.

Position 8
When & How to act on this issue?

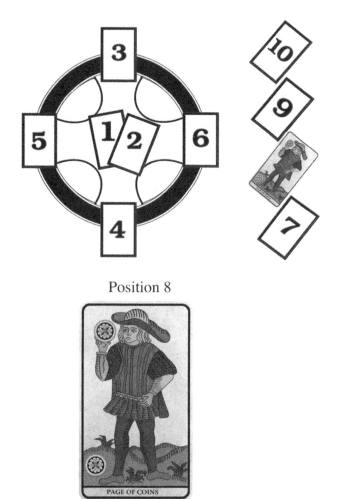

Position 8

Page of Pentacles
~ Seeking Your Quest ~

Reading Position 8: The timing is right for the client to move in new directions and take on new endeavors. This is especially seen if the question deals with business or finance with the suit of Pentacles. But the timing is good to act in any new direction with the main message being seen in the Page.

Position 9
What are you ultimately trying to accomplish?

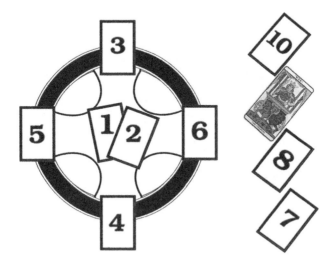

Position 9

The Chariot
~ Bold Advancement~

Reading Position 9: The Chariot in this position shows the client's purpose is to be recognized and respected in their accomplishments. Getting a high degree of credit for the efforts and accomplishments they have made and can make in the future. This can also be seen as the client seeking a sense of self-worth through this quest.

Position 10
Finer Details & Closing Thoughts

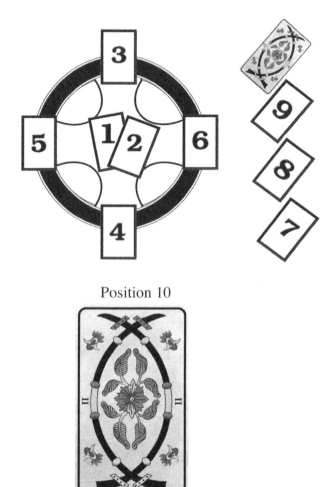

Position 10

Two of Swords
~ More Choices to Come ~

Reading Position 10: The 2 of Swords in this position may be showing us that as the client moves forward on this quest other hard decisions will have to be made. Progress will open up new doors of understanding not yet seen by the client.

Summary of the reading:

The question is seen as dealing with a promising situation that needs to be put in place with some feasible planning. The client is looking for those ideas now and anxious to take action swiftly. They are in a good position in life to move on a quest of this type if they can address some older blockage and iron out any problems that would put a stop to this quest.

Opportunity will come to really turn things around if they watch for the chances to improve the reality of this issue. The client is seeing this quest with much promise and the positive attitude they project to others is to their advantage. Everything is aligned for moving forward and nothing is holding the client back to lay the ground-work on this issue.

This endeavor will be a growing experience for the client and a life changing step in positive ways. It will also open up new understanding to many other issues and goals the client may have for further growth and happiness.

The cards can be seen in many different ways. This is just the way I happen to see these cards in this reading. What do you see? Have fun with it and remember there is no wrong way to see the cards giving you ideas.

NOTE:

A card spread is nothing more than a question broken apart into aspects to be looked into about a given subject. The cards placed into those aspects of the question are meant to spark new ideas for answers previously not seen before the card spread was put into place.

The random cards placed into these elements of our question force us to see those aspects of our question from an innovative and intuitive point of view. This can result in some very interesting and dynamic concepts that give the impression that the cards themselves have some type of unexplainable intelligence. The real mystery seems to be this creative and intuitive ability our own mind can develop.

The Classic 3 Card Spread

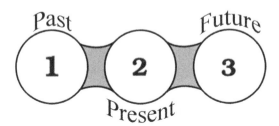

If there is a classic Tarot card spread this is it. The most basic card spread we have is the 3 card spread. I would say not too many readers use this spread. The reason being what we look into with it seems to be too simplistic.

OK, here is your past on this issue. Here is what is happening now, the present. Lastly here is what is going to happen in your future on this issue.

But now that we can see the importance of position meanings we can look deeper into those aspects for something more useful. If we just tilt this spread a little we can see there is much more to look into. The light starts to come through if we look at it from a different angle. Here is what's possible with this classic spread.

THE PAST: What is the reason we want to look at the past? The past holds our experience on this question. What have we learned in the past that can help us find answers to this question? What have we acquired that can give us an advantage on our quest? What assets have we attained from our past that could help us with this goal? Sorta like position #5 of my Celtic Cross. The Assets position.

A card placed here might help us see things we can use from our past challenges. What type of frame of mind did we have then? What position were we in then? What influences did we have when sharing our ideas with others? What can we take from our past that would be useful in our quest? What have we acquired or learned from our past that will help us on this goal? Something from our past that will be an asset to us.

Now we can see purpose to looking into "The Past"

THE PRESENT: Here is where we can look deeper into what we are doing at this time about this issue. How are we handling it? Do we need to calm down? Or maybe do we need to shake things up a little. Are the actions we're taking in the present useful or are they making things worse? A card placed here can give us fresh ideas on what we should be doing at this time on the matter at hand. Setting new priorities. Changing our approach.
Rearranging our strategy. Looking at what we're doing right now allows us to stop and think. Am I taking the right approach to this question?

This allows us to look at what needs to be done now. "The Present"

THE FUTURE: This position allows us to see what to look for that will be beneficial to our goal. What to anticipate. What to prepare for. What opportunities to grab when they come before us. A card placed here might show hints of what those opportunities will look like. This compares to position #6 of my Celtic Cross. The Opportunity. This is the position of prediction. Here is where logic and intuition blend together to see what may come. It allows the querent to be ready for it if it does come to pass.

Wrapping it up: Looking into the *Past* allows us to find things that we have learned or acquired that will help us with the question being looked into.

Looking into the *Present* we can take a close look at the things we are currently doing about this question. We can question the actions we are currently taking. We might find more effective actions to take.

The position of the *Future* allows us to see what to watch for. What to prepare for in our quest. It allows us to seek out specific opportunity not seen before.

Here is another approach to this spread that shows an expanded variation of the possibilities you can use to do readings with just three cards.

Advanced Methods of the 3-Card Spread.

Changing the positions meanings to something more useful can be very beneficial. Past, Present & Future is not etched in stone. We can look into other aspects that may be more useful to us. Here is an example of something that might be more effective.

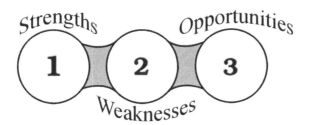

Here we can find ways to focus on our *Strengths* and improve our *Weaknesses* to a quest we seek to accomplish. We can also search for *Opportunities* to come.

Position #1 allows us to look for *Strengths* we have that have not been considered. It can help remind us to use these strengths as well. A card placed here might show us what strengths to focus on the most.

Position #2 helps us see our *Weaknesses*. Knowing our weaknesses allows us to protect against them being tested. It also allows us to try to strengthen those weaknesses if possible. A card here might show weaknesses that could delay progress in our goal if they are not addressed.

Position #3 allows us to keep an eye out for possible *Opportunities* to turn things in our favor in this quest. A card placed here might show us insight into a specific opportunity to watch for.

The position meanings that can be used in this spread are endless. They can also easily become custom factors to specific areas of concern.
See what ideas you might have for position meanings that would be helpful to use for the 3 card spread. The possibilities are many.

Here is another example of changing the positions.

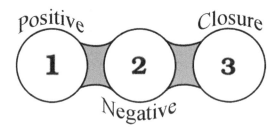

These position meanings allows us to look into *Positive* aspects about the question. *Negative* aspects about the question. And then the last position *Closure* allows us to weigh out the differences and make a decision. A card placed in these positions will allow us to find new ways of seeing all three of these aspects in a different light.

So you see that changing the positions meanings can be quite helpful to the substance of the reading. With this new knowledge you will find meanings that work very well for your readings. Now you can change them to whatever you feel works best for you.

Positions are aspects of a question we are looking into. The more substantial these aspects are the more valuable the information we see in the cards will be.

The position meanings can be endless. I really feel this gives the classic 3 card spread new life!

The Four Points

If you had to decide four factors that would be useful to any Tarot reading what would they be? I felt factors of "What,Why, How & When" can be useful subjects to look into with regard to any question asked.
Hence the Four Points.

Using three cards for each section allows us to blend cards together easily for each of the four factors. This would create a 12 card spread. It can easily be read as four 3-card spreads. Then the cards can be read in any other fashion the reader feels works well for them.

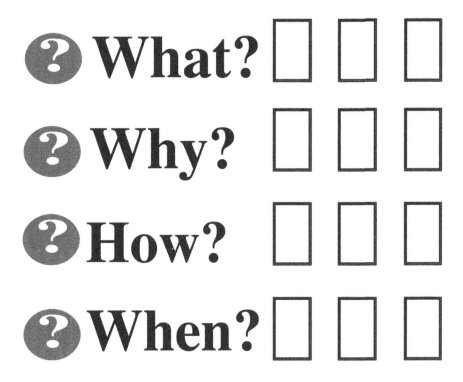

It is my feeling that if you can give new insight into any of these four factors in a reading the reading had value to the seeker.

Giving new insight into all four factors would make a very valuable reading! *What* is the real question? *Why* do you want this in your life? *How* are we going to achieve this goal? And *When* is the best time to act on this quest?

The Six Points

This is an extension of the Four Point spread adding *Who*, &*Where*.
I do not feel those two aspects are as important as the other four points
But it shows the flexibility you have in adding other elements if your choose to.

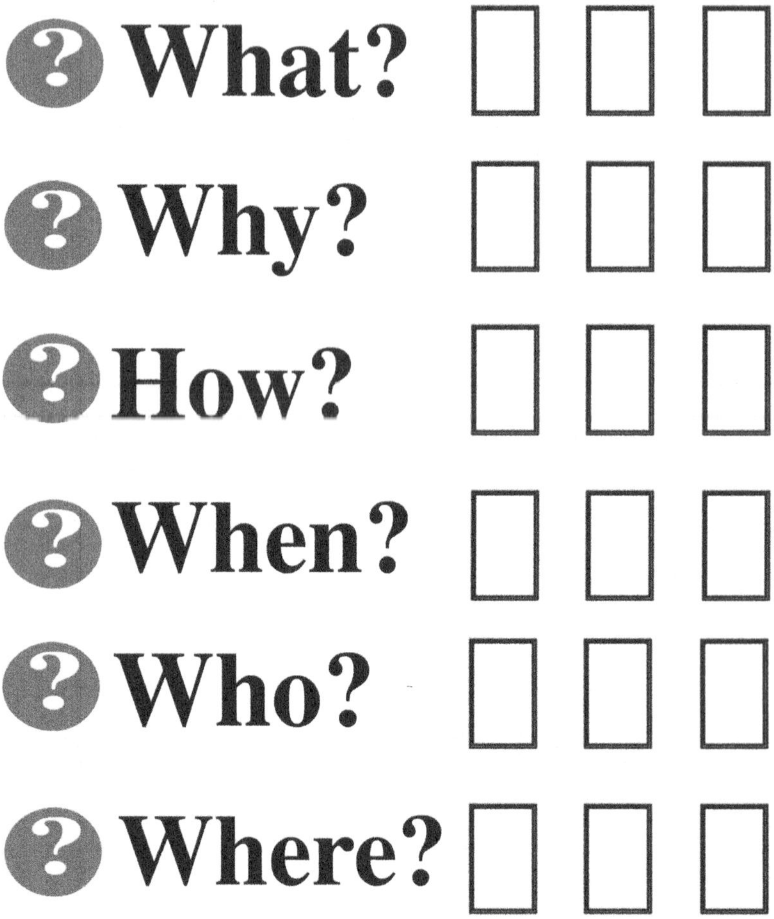

? What? ☐ ☐ ☐

? Why? ☐ ☐ ☐

? How? ☐ ☐ ☐

? When? ☐ ☐ ☐

? Who? ☐ ☐ ☐

? Where? ☐ ☐ ☐

The Horseshoe Spread

The Horseshoe spread is an easy one to adjust position meanings to your liking. Below is the traditional meanings of the 7 positions for this spread. Now that we know we can adjust and change these meanings, the possibilities become endless. This pattern is also easy to adjust the amount of positions as well. Going anywhere from 7 positions to less such as 3 positions without any real thought. It's your choice.

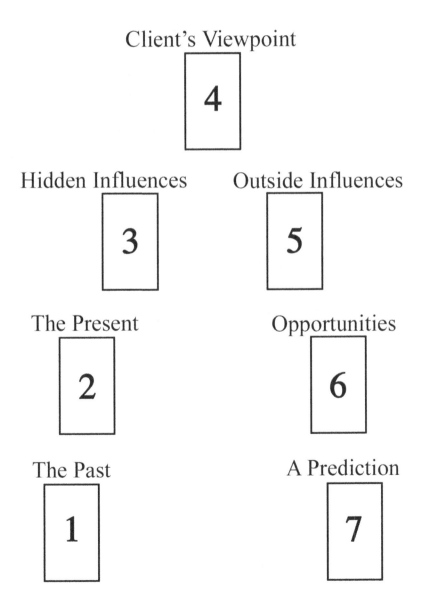

NOTE:

A card spread is aspects of what you feel would be useful to look into with most readings. This way you can use the same spread over and over. Now that we know that, we can see the pattern on the table and the order cards are laid down is not that important.

Position your spread in anyway that feels easy for you to map out a question. You can mix and match aspects from one spread with another as well. Position #5, from the Celtic Cross added to the Horseshoe spread is fine. Or visa-versa. Anything you feel would be useful! Have fun playing around with spread ideas. The main thing is to know you can change card spreads to make them work better for you.

The key to card spreads lie in the aspects being looked into in the reading. It has nothing to do with the numerical order of the pattern the spread appears in. It doesn't really have anything to do with the pattern itself. It's all about what is being addressed. Are the issues being looked into from those positions relevant to the reading? Questioning that helps us improve our layout and ultimately our readings become more insightful. More meaningful to our clients.

Ultimately having a card spread that has position meanings that are useful for looking into any question asked is golden! That is your quest. The perfect card spread.

On the next page is a list of topics I feel keeping in mind will help you create such a spread.

Have fun on that journey!

Key factors for adjusting and creating card spreads

Here are some significant issues that tend to be good key points for card spreads:

• A close look at the question itself. What is the real question?

• When is the best time to act on this issue?

• Why do you want this in your life? What do you feel it will bring you?

• Is there a better way to go about attaining this objective than what you're doing right now?

• Are you using all the assets you have available to their fullest potential?

• Are the efforts currently being made the best efforts to take or are there better options?

• What possible opportunities are out there that you can grab hold of when they become available?

• What influence do you have that might be getting overlooked?

• Will this objective truly make me happy if it is attained or am I chasing the wrong situation?

• Where will I find clear direction on this issue?

• What should be improved, strengthened before proceeding further?

• What drastic measures should be avoided? How should crucial measures be taken carefully?

• Is the frame of mind of the client clear? Calm?

• Visualize starting at the finished result and working your way back to the beginning. How did you get there? What happened along the way?
What were the steps taken? How did the finished result look? Is this what you wanted?

5. Positional Influence

Card positions influence what we see in the cards.

I felt it would be helpful to show the range of possibilities a card's meaning can have depending on the position in the card spread that card is placed into. These interpretations are only a glance at all the variables and meanings each card can bring to the table. The purpose is to show how card positions influence the card's meaning in our readings.

Looking through these differences will give you some insight of what the cards mean in ways that cannot be put into words but only felt by you personally. They are meant to give you basic thoughts into the many possibilities that can arise as you lay cards into each card position.

The meanings of the Tarot cards are infinite as they spark ideas that only you can interpret. See how the meanings can shift as they are placed into the various positions here in my version of the Celtic Cross. This will happen no matter what card spread you prefer to use in your readings.

The position meanings are a big factor in how we perceive the cards placed in a spread. Card spread positions are segments of a question being looked into. The cards placed unto the table represent insightful answers to the positions they are placed with.

Each position is asking a different aspect of a question. Therefore the card meaning shifts in it's interpretation to answer in a meaningful way.

~ Positional Influence ~

The Minor Arcana

The Aces

INSIGHT: The Aces allow us to see new energy in our quest. New situations, new people, new ideas or anything else new coming into our environment. Something new is key with the Aces.

~ The Aces ~
• New Concepts • New Options • New Situations •

Position #1 – The real question

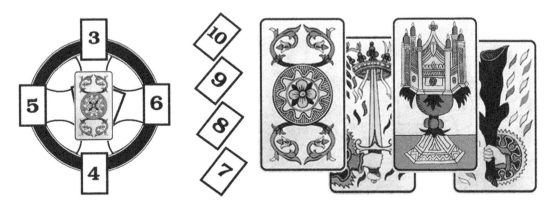

POSSIBLE INTERPRETATION: A new situation. New ideas, new challenges. New insight into the situation. New energy. A whole new endeavor.

The issue has many possibilities. New exciting situations can be exhilarating. Looking deeply into the possibilities is key. A new look at the situation. Something new approaches.

Position #2 – The real question cont'

Blended with Position #1: *This position is meant to compliment position 1. Position 1 & 2 are read together to see the question more in depth. Therefore the meaning remains the same as above and is blended together with a second card for a combined interpretation. These two cards read together allow us to see new possible ways to see our question. Or at least to confirm that things are being seen clearly by the client.*

The Aces
• New Concepts • New Options • New Situations •

Position #3 – Actions being taken

POSSIBLE INTERPRETATION: The client is searching for suggestions on the issue. Looking for guidance. A new direction is key to the seeker.
Consider other options before moving forward just to make sure you are heading down the right path before you begin.

Position #4 – Immediate Objectives

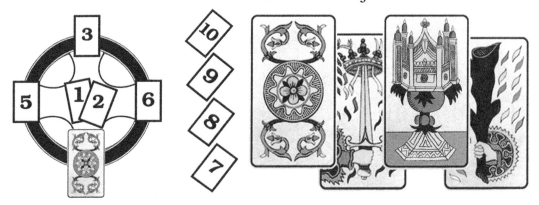

POSSIBLE INTERPRETATION: Establishing a new agreement with an outside influence before proceeding. Setting up a whole new situation. A new aspect being introduced works in a favorable way. Seeking a new approach. New ideas that need to be turned into realities is the goal of the seeker.

The Aces
• New Concepts • New Options • New Situations •

Position #5 – An asset to the client

POSSIBLE INTERPRETATION: You are in a good position to take on this new quest. You have the ability to add something new to the situation. What significant element can you add that would be helpful to your cause? Adding something will put new light on the subject.

Position #6 – An opportunity still to come

POSSIBLE INTERPRETATION: An opportunity to acquire new strategies will be available to you as you proceed. New alliances will be available as you build this endeavor. Be ready to persuade others to your side soon!

The Aces
• New Concepts • New Options • New Situations •

Position #7 – Client's viewpoint

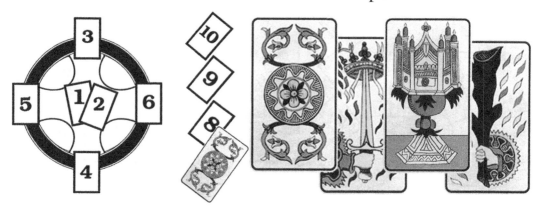

POSSIBLE INTERPRETATION: The client sees this as a new opportunity. A change from what was in the past. Usually this is seen as a promising change by the seeker but not always. Tread carefully in this new territory. A new situation that the seeker is not totally familiar with. The client is seeing this as a new scenario they are not totally familiar with.

Position #8 – When to take action

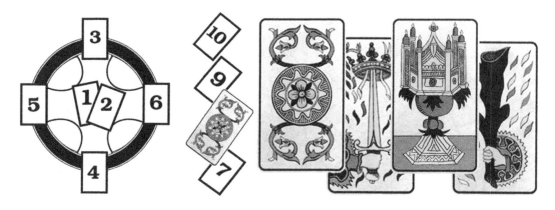

POSSIBLE INTERPRETATION: The time is now to look at other options for approaching this issue. A time to inject new ideas for consideration on this quest. A time to start something new.

The Aces
• New Concepts • New Options • New Situations •

Position #9 – The real purpose of this quest

POSSIBLE INTERPRETATION: A new and better way of action. A whole new beginning. Turning over a new leaf. Renovation to an old situation. Changing things in ways that will create a better quality of life. Changing things for the better in a big way on your quest. Rearranging things in some way to see if it has an advantage to attaining the big picture in your quest.

Position #10 – Closing remarks and finer details

POSSIBLE INTERPRETATION: An added strength will manifest itself. This issue will bring about new settings not yet seen. Unexpected new options to your goal will be presented to you allowing you to move further to a completion.

Be cautious about welcoming in new influences into your circle. They might not be in total agreement with your end plan.

~ Positional Influence ~

The Minor Arcana

The Twos

INSIGHT: The Twos give us the energy of direction. Direction can only be made once choices are decided on. Clear focus is achieved once the choices are made. Choice is key to the Twos.

~ The Twos ~
• Choice • Direction • Possibilities •

Position #1 – The real question

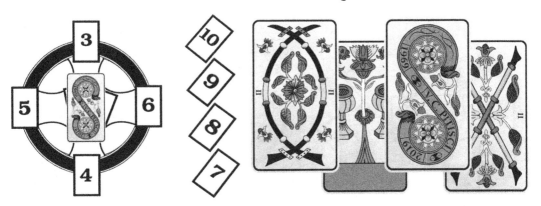

POSSIBLE INTERPRETATION: A major decision is key. A question of choices. Torn between two issues of concern. Fear challenges choosing one way or the other. Seeing both sides simultaneously causes inaction. Weighing out one path or the other. Duality is clear. Polarity. Opposites attract!

Position #2 – The real question cont'

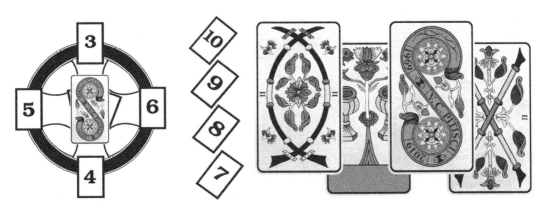

Blended with Position #1: *This position is meant to compliment position 1. Position 1 & 2 are read together to see the question more in depth. Therefore the meaning remains the same as above and is blended together with a second card for a combined interpretation. These two cards read together allow us to see new possible ways to see our question. Or at least to confirm that things are being seen clearly by the client.*

~ The Twos ~
• Choice • Direction • Possibilities •

Position #3 – Actions being taken

POSSIBLE INTERPRETATION:

The seeker is challenged in making a decision on this issue. The client needs to decide which way to move on the issue.

What new decision could be helpful in this quest?

Position #4 – Immediate Objectives

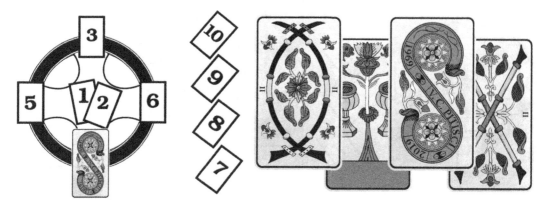

POSSIBLE INTERPRETATION: Key choices need to be thought out carefully on what is needed first. Correct choices on what immediate objectives are key before advancing forward.

~ The Twos ~
• Choice • Direction • Possibilities •

Position #5 – An asset to the client

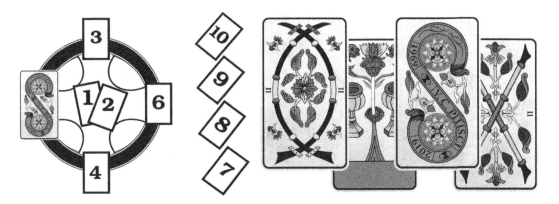

POSSIBLE INTERPRETATION: You are in a good position to make a choice. Decide on things that are in your control that will help your quest. Make decisions in ways that bring you closer to your goal. Sound decisions create a sound direction on your path.

Position #6 – An opportunity still to come

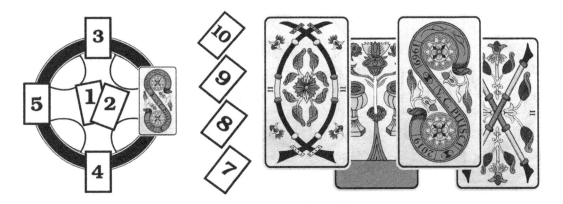

POSSIBLE INTERPRETATION: An opportunity will come that shows you the way. A key choice will be up to you in the future. Be prepared to make a decision based on new insight still to come.

~ The Twos ~
• Choice • Direction • Possibilities •

Position #7 – Client's viewpoint

POSSIBLE INTERPRETATION: The client sees this issue as a hard choice. It might be helpful to look at all the facts to finalize a choice.
The client sees both sides clearly with many options available. Time will show the client which way to move on this question.

Position #8 – When to take action

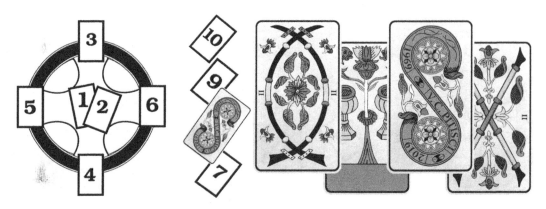

POSSIBLE INTERPRETATION: A time to think clearly, not a time to act. Don't chase after an answer. If the client is undecided on the issue, don't force it. The answer will come to you in time.

~ The Twos ~
• Choice • Direction • Possibilities •

Position #9 – The real purpose of this quest

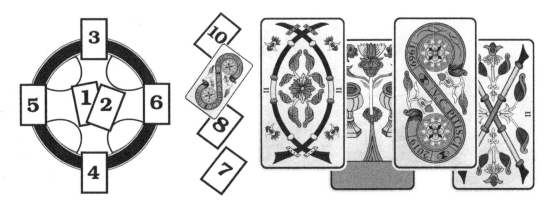

POSSIBLE INTERPRETATION: The client realizes that the direction they decide could have long term consequences. A right choice is made by the seeker.
Seeing all aspects of the goal clearly allows a direction to be made clear. Go back to the question and review the purpose of this quest. Are you making the right choices to get what you ultimately desire?

Position #10 – Closing remarks and finer details

POSSIBLE INTERPRETATION: Confidence in your ability to make decisions and stand by them will be your gain in the end. Your progress will bring about more choices and options as you proceed. The experience will create confidence in making decisions without need for verification from others. Confidence in your decisions made on this issue will be key for future endeavors.

~ Positional Influence ~

The Minor Arcana

The Threes

INSIGHT: The Threes show us the force of creativity. Creativity in situations, ideas and other influences are seen as a flourishing energy in our environment. New energy is key with the Threes.

~ The Threes ~
• Creativity • Abundance • Expansion •

Position #1 – The real question

POSSIBLE INTERPRETATION:

The question calls for a creative look at the situation.

New ideas not considered before now. Many possibilities to consider. A dreamlike situation. The seeker has many choices in this quest. A growing situation. A new idea is considered. A time to use your imagination for new ideas on this quest.

Position #2 – The real question cont'

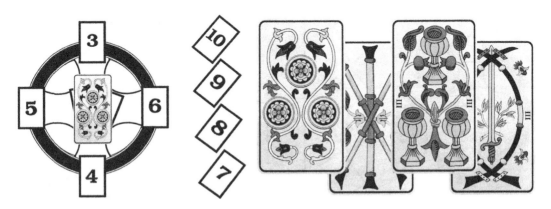

Blended with Position #1: *This position is meant to compliment position 1. Position 1 & 2 are read together to see the question more in depth. Therefore the meaning remains the same as above and is blended together with a second card for a combined interpretation. These two cards read together allow us to see new possible ways to see our question. Or at least to confirm that things are being seen clearly by the client.*

~ The Threes ~
• Creativity • Abundance • Expansion •

Position #3 – Actions being taken

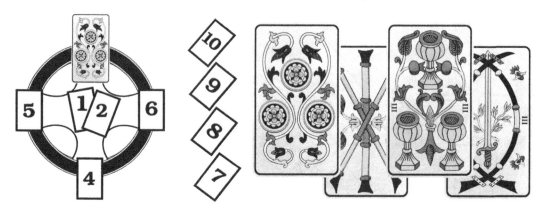

POSSIBLE INTERPRETATION: Getting creative with plans that will prove useful. A creative strategy for advancement needs to be put into place.
Open to new concepts for solutions. A gathering of minds. A healthy and nurturing situation is being created.

Position #4 – Immediate Objectives

POSSIBLE INTERPRETATION: Innovation and originality for initial plans will be an advantage. Something being introduced into the mix will be helpful.
A new approach to your goal will be useful in convincing others to your point of view.

~ The Threes ~
• Creativity • Abundance • Expansion •

Position #5 – An asset to the client

POSSIBLE INTERPRETATION: You have a good imagination. You have the ability to be innovative with this question. Plant ideas like seeds that will grow in the mind of others. Remember that seeds take time to grow. Patience is key.

Position #6 – An opportunity still to come

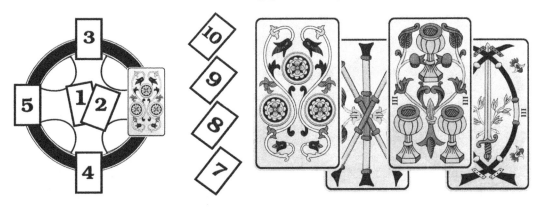

POSSIBLE INTERPRETATION: An opportunity to create a new situation helpful to your goal is near. New opportunity will blossom as you proceed on your quest.

~ The Threes ~
• Creativity • Abundance • Expansion •

Position #7 – Client's viewpoint

POSSIBLE INTERPRETATION: The client has original ideas towards achieving the goal at hand. The seeker might be seeing many confusing possibilities on this issue. A mystical and intuitive quest by the seeker. Following your heart closely at this time could be a strong force to be cautious with.

Position #8 – When to take action

POSSIBLE INTERPRETATION: The time is good to consider the issue in new and original ways. The time is now to consider something not thought of before! Originality and innovation is key.

~ The Threes ~
• Creativity • Abundance • Expansion •

Position #9 – The real purpose of this quest

POSSIBLE INTERPRETATION: A new approach to something that the client feels will make a difference is realized. New concepts to old scenarios will be attained. Gaining innovative and creative ideas on this quest will help on the path to success. Something not considered before will make itself available to you.

Position #10 – Closing remarks and finer details

POSSIBLE INTERPRETATION: The opening up of new growth will come as you proceed. This quest can flourish and bring rewarding experiences to the seeker in ways not yet realized. The final destination will open up new doors of understanding not yet seen.

~ Positional Influence ~

The Minor Arcana

The Fours

INSIGHT: The energy of the Fours show us an unmoving and stable situation. They can also show us stubbornness and unwillingness to make adjustments. The Fours show us a predictable scenario as being key.

~ The Fours ~
• Stability • Unchanging • Routine •

Position #1 – The real question

POSSIBLE INTERPRETATION: A persistent concern. Seeking a stable situation. Getting a firm grip on this quest would be helpful. A calming environment. Something that can be counted on and dependable is key to the question. Being stuck in a situation difficult to escape from. Boredom is setting in on a particular situation.

Position #2 – The real question cont'

Blended with Position #1: *This position is meant to compliment position 1. Position 1 & 2 are read together to see the question more in depth. Therefore the meaning remains the same as above and is blended together with a second card for a combined interpretation. These two cards read together allow us to see new possible ways to see our question. Or at least to confirm that things are being seen clearly by the client.*

~ The Fours ~
• Stability • Unchanging • Routine •

Position #3 – Actions being taken

POSSIBLE INTERPRETATION: An attempt to stabilize the current situation. Trying to organize what is needed to be done. A need for predictability. Trying to figure what is to come.

Position #4 – Immediate Objectives

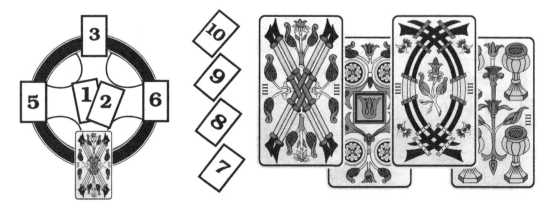

POSSIBLE INTERPRETATION: Getting everyone involved thinking along the same lines. Seeking cooperation and teamwork helps stabilize initial objectives. Assistance is needed by other key players to move forward in an organized fashion. Efficiency will help make the end goal more predictable.

~ The Fours ~
• Stability • Unchanging • Routine •

Position #5 – An asset to the client

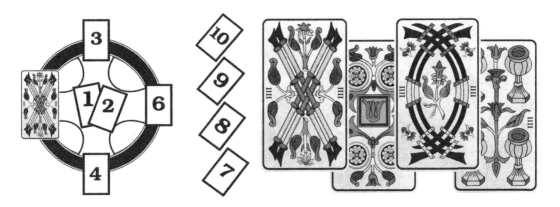

POSSIBLE INTERPRETATION: You have the ability to stabilize the situation. You are in a good position to tie up loose ends on the matter. Structure and sound strategy are key elements that work to your advantage.

Position #6 – An opportunity still to come

POSSIBLE INTERPRETATION: An opportunity to organize all aspects of your quest. Other influences become easily structured into play in a positive way. Things start to fall into place soon.

~ The Fours ~
• Stability • Unchanging • Routine •

Position #7 – Client's viewpoint

POSSIBLE INTERPRETATION: The client wants to tie up loose ends on a given subject in question. There might be an urge to stabilize and secure the quest in question. The seeker may be seeing this situation as stuck in the middle with no where to move to. Searching for clear cut insight on the issue at hand.

Position #8 – When to take action

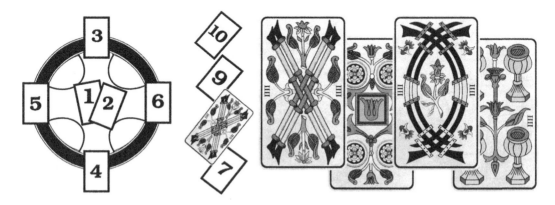

POSSIBLE INTERPRETATION: A time of inaction. Staying stable with no changes at this time seems wise. A time to plan. Not a time for action. Inaction until a structured strategy is well in place.

~ The Fours ~
• Stability • Unchanging • Routine •

Position #9 – The real purpose of this quest

POSSIBLE INTERPRETATION: A better situation than before. A workable situation. Not hidden and vague. A dependable and stable environment. A safe and satisfying situation. A well protected and lasting environment that can be counted on. A very stable, predictable accomplishment of importance for the seeker.

Position #10 – Closing remarks and finer details

POSSIBLE INTERPRETATION: Last minute delays are possible. Be prepared to move them along if they occur. Inaction could put delays on progress. Perseverance is key. A very stable outcome manifest's itself as predicted.

~ Positional Influence ~

The Minor Arcana

The Fives

INSIGHT: The Fives can represent an energy of change. Shifts in a situation good or bad. Adjustment and transition. Commotion and movement. It is common for Fives to be seen as disruptive to a good situation or as a welcomed change to a challenging situation.

~ The Fives ~
• Change • Disruption • Adjustment •

Position #1 – The real question

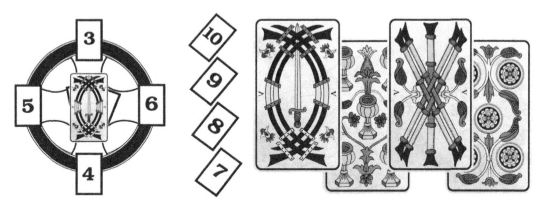

POSSIBLE INTERPRETATION: A change in a situation that concerns the seeker. The seeker is wanting something to change. How can this change be handled to the seeker's advantage? A change means some new situation. How can this change be advantageous to the seeker? Changes can be exciting and they can also be troublesome. How does the client see this change?

Position #2 – The real question cont'

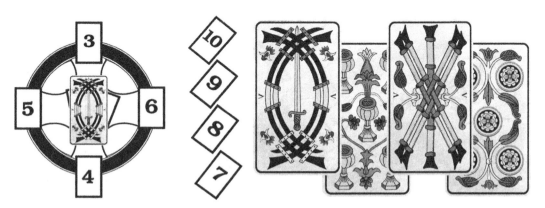

Blended with Position #1: *This position is meant to compliment position 1. Position 1 & 2 are read together to see the question more in depth. Therefore the meaning remains the same as above and is blended together with a second card for a combined interpretation. These two cards read together allow us to see new possible ways to see our question. Or at least to confirm that things are being seen clearly by the client.*

~ The Fives ~
• Change • Disruption • Adjustment •

Position #3 – Actions being taken

POSSIBLE INTERPRETATION: The seeker is attempting to alter the situation to their advantage. Stirring things up can be hectic but it can also be beneficial. Focus on the changes being positive ones. Calm and clear transition is key.

Position #4 – Immediate Objectives

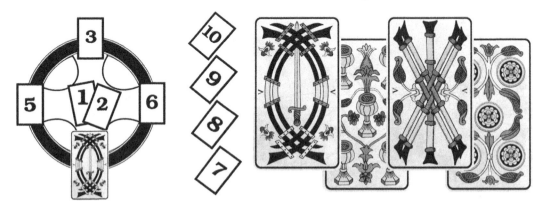

POSSIBLE INTERPRETATION: The immediate goal is to make a favorable change before proceeding further. Changes to set a good foundation to build upon. Changes take time and it is easy to become impatient. "In Time" is a good mantra for steady progress.

~ The Fives ~
• Change • Disruption • Adjustment •

Position #5 – An asset to the client

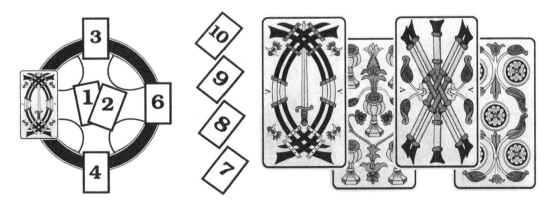

POSSIBLE INTERPRETATION: The seeker is in a good position to make changes. Stir things up. Rearrange the situation to one that is more favorable to your quest. Changing what is not working is key.

Position #6 – An opportunity still to come

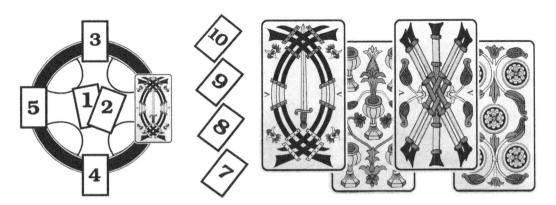

POSSIBLE INTERPRETATION: An opportunity for favorable change is coming. Opportunity knocks! Be ready to answer when it does. Taking action when opportunity knocks will be key.

~ The Fives ~
• Change • Disruption • Adjustment •

Position #7 – Client's viewpoint

POSSIBLE INTERPRETATION: The seeker sees this question as a change. Is it really? Or is it just the repetitive same ol – same ol? If the seeker is concerned about this change as being disruptive, look into how serious this change really is. It might not be as serious as the client perceives it to be.

Attempt to alter things in the seeker's favor. Measure the progress to decide how far to go with this change. Keep positive!

Position #8 – When to take action

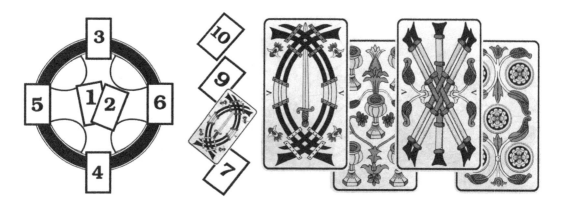

POSSIBLE INTERPRETATION: The time is now to act before opportunity is lost. Watch for changes to take place. Then act while things are shifting!

Things seem to be in constant motion at this time. Getting off or on this roller coaster might seem challenging.

~ The Fives ~
• Change • Disruption • Adjustment •

Position #9 – The real purpose of this quest

POSSIBLE INTERPRETATION: This shows a major shift in the seekers life. Important changes are sought by the seeker. Necessary shifts that need to be addressed. The quest is one that will bring about a significant transformation.

Position #10 – Closing remarks and finer details

POSSIBLE INTERPRETATION: Breakthroughs in remarkable ways will be available as you proceed on this path. This too shall pass. The cycle continues. This quest will bring about other changes not anticipated yet by the seeker.

~ Positional Influence ~

The Minor Arcana

The Sixes

INSIGHT: This is an important force that can break through challenges in front of your quest. Sixes are the energy of overcoming obstacles to our quest. Once these obstacles are taken on and eliminated the confidence of the Sevens is attained.

~ The Sixes ~
• Overcoming Obstacles • Challenging • Resolving •

Position #1 – The real question

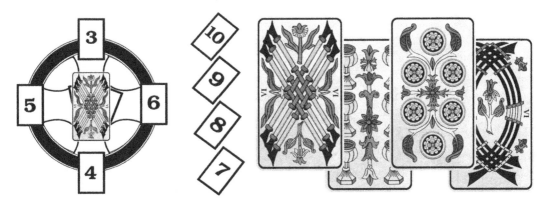

POSSIBLE INTERPRETATION: Overcoming an obstacle.
Dealing with a resistance to your goal. Know the resistance well and you can overcome it. A need to know exactly what it is you're dealing with. What challenges does the client face in this endeavor? The seeker is facing a challenge. Tough issues need to be addressed in order to proceed on this quest.

Position #2 – The real question cont'

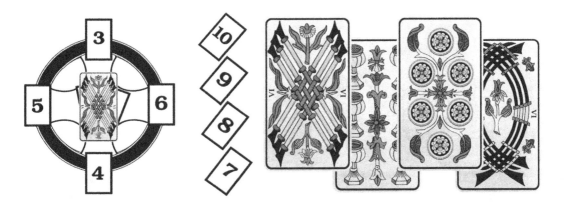

Blended with Position #1: *This position is meant to compliment position 1. Position 1 & 2 are read together to see the question more in depth. Therefore the meaning remains the same as above and is blended together with a second card for a combined interpretation. These two cards read together allow us to see new possible ways to see our question. Or at least to confirm that things are being seen clearly by the client.*

~ The Sixes ~
• Overcoming Obstacles • Challenging • Resolving •

Position #3 – Actions being taken

POSSIBLE INTERPRETATION: Planning how to take on the challenges ahead. Taking on the first challenges to move forward is key. The immediate goal is to smooth out any resistance the seeker feels is in the way. It is important to know what order to eliminate the blocks that are halting this quest. Setting priorities is key.

Position #4 – Immediate Objectives

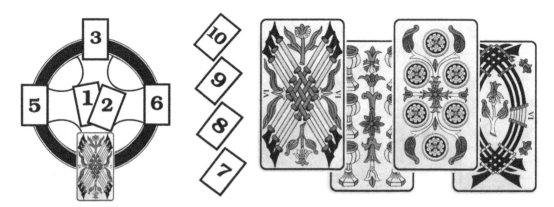

POSSIBLE INTERPRETATION: Persuading resisting parties to see things differently. Convincing others of your end result and ideas on this issue will be helpful to your quest. Eliminating resistance that is blocking your progress.

~ The Sixes ~
• Overcoming Obstacles • Challenging • Resolving •

Position #5 – An asset to the client

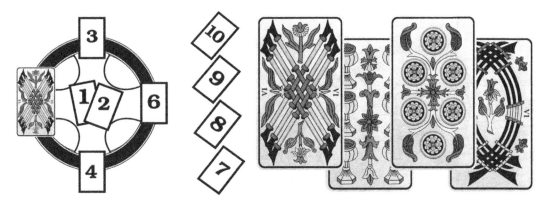

POSSIBLE INTERPRETATION: You have the ability to overcome the obstacles before you. The first step to overcome an obstacle is to accept it. Don't avoid this challenge. Embrace it. Your asset here is courage. Facing what you fear is key. Immediate failures can still be a path towards eventual success.

Position #6 – An opportunity still to come

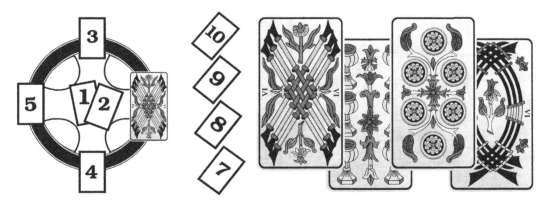

POSSIBLE INTERPRETATION: An opportunity to resolve differences is to come. Persistence is key. You will find opportunity to remove resistance putting things in your favor. Look for favorable opportunities to make themselves available as you proceed.

~ The Sixes ~
• Overcoming Obstacles • Challenging • Resolving •

Position #7 – Client's viewpoint

POSSIBLE INTERPRETATION: The seeker might be seeing this as a challenge to be addressed. Searching for solutions. Confidence might be challenged. A defeatist attitude will only bring about negative energy. Optimism is key. Stay positive and look for opportunities to sway this in your favor.

Position #8 – When to take action

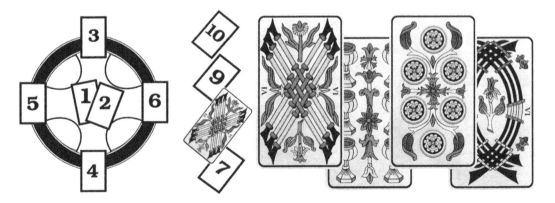

POSSIBLE INTERPRETATION: This is the time to face the challenges ahead of you. Addressing delays on your quest full force. Taking on any resistance to advance on this quest. Now is the time to act against opposition. Expressing your views on this quest is key at this time. But keep in mind that diplomacy and patience work best for success.

~ The Sixes ~
• Overcoming Obstacles • Challenging • Resolving •

Position #9 – The real purpose of this quest

POSSIBLE INTERPRETATION: A quest that involves freeing up restrictions on pursuits of happiness and fulfillment. Freedom to choose directions that have been restricted in the past. Free movement. Ideas, opinions and desires need to be recognized. Completing this quest resolves key issues of recognition and self worth for the seeker.

Position #10 – Closing remarks and finer details

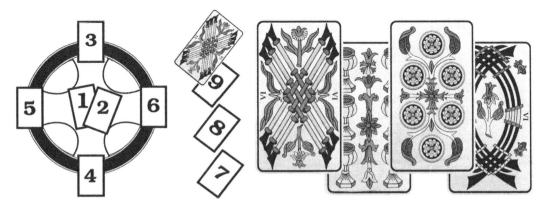

POSSIBLE INTERPRETATION: Obstacles not yet seen might still come your way. Be prepared for the unexpected. Be ready to take on unexpected resistance as you proceed. You may have to defend your ideas to others in the end. Be convincing. Know your quest well!

~ Positional Influence ~

The Minor Arcana

The Sevens

INSIGHT: The energy of the Sevens shows us believing in self is key for success. Not giving up is the path to accomplishment. The Sevens show an energy of confidence that allows the advancement of the eights.

~ The Sevens ~
• Confidence • Experience • Conviction •

Position #1 – The real question

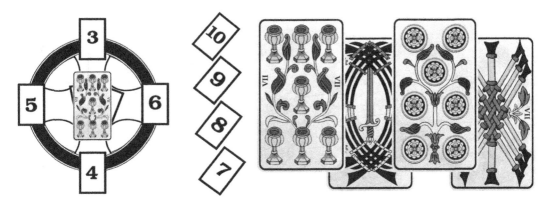

POSSIBLE INTERPRETATION: A promising endeavor. Fast progress.
A boost of energy. A strong energy of some type is seen with the Sevens. A confident situation is key. The seeker is in a strong position. Promising situation. An unstoppable energy with forward movement. Progress is seen quickly.

Position #2 – The real question cont'

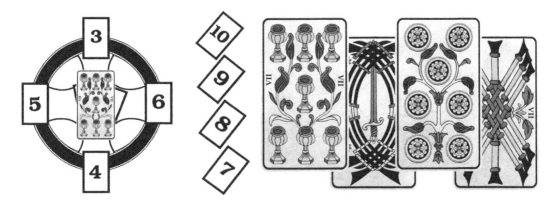

Blended with Position #1: *This position is meant to compliment position 1. Position 1 & 2 are read together to see the question more in depth. Therefore the meaning remains the same as above and is blended together with a second card for a combined interpretation. These two cards read together allow us to see new possible ways to see our question. Or at least to confirm that things are being seen clearly by the client.*

~ The Sevens ~
• Confidence • Experience • Conviction •

Position #3 – Actions being taken

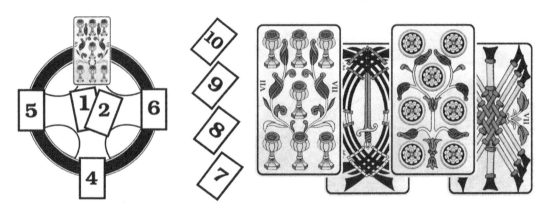

POSSIBLE INTERPRETATION: Striving forward in positive ways. Improvements are made from effective planning taken by the client. Fast progress because of wise decisions are possible. Sevens placed here show the client is in the process of positive achievements. A time of real confidence boosting on the quest. Actions that are taken show positive results.

Position #4 – Immediate Objectives

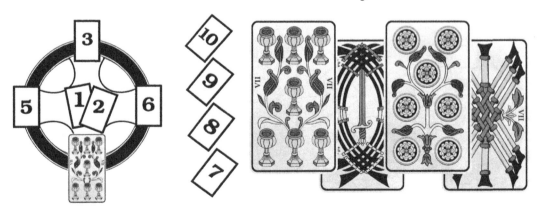

POSSIBLE INTERPRETATION: Your ability to succeed is key. Recognition by others will make the initial goals easier to attain. A time to demonstrate your capability with words and actions. A show of talent make things more convincing to others as a feasible objective.

~ The Sevens ~
• Confidence • Experience • Conviction •

Position #5 – An asset to the client

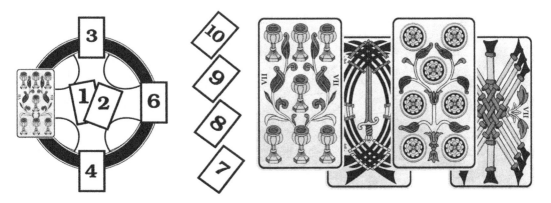

POSSIBLE INTERPRETATION: Focus on what you do best and enhance it to even higher levels. Focus should be made on your strong points not your weaknesses. Playing your game, not someone elses is key.

Position #6 – An opportunity still to come

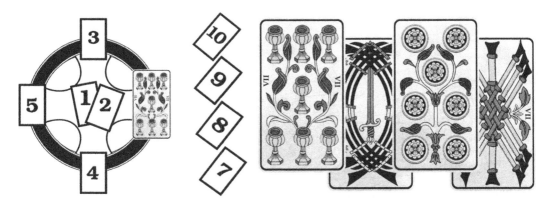

POSSIBLE INTERPRETATION: Watch for opportunities for progress to come soon. Your confidence will be a key factor. Improvements towards the goal! The client will see encouraging results coming on the efforts they are making. This will also continue to expand as time moves forward.

~ The Sevens ~
• Confidence • Experience • Conviction •

Position #7 – Client's viewpoint

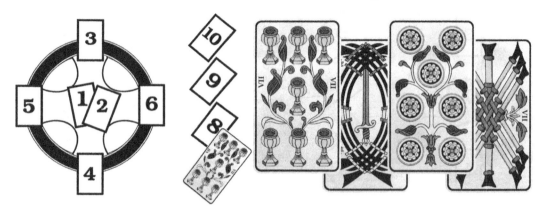

POSSIBLE INTERPRETATION: The seeker might be over confident on this issue. Or the seeker might need to have more confidence to proceed. Confidence is key on this quest. The client is seeing their own quest as very promising. Caution might be overlooked by the client at this time and should be warned of that weakness. Optimistic thinking is a strong asset but over confidence is easily acquired if not careful.

Position #8 – When to take action

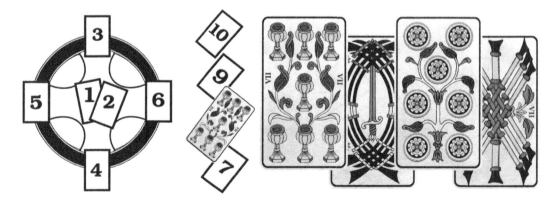

POSSIBLE INTERPRETATION: The time is now to show your ability to others. Things seem to be in place for a swift advance towards the quest. Don't lose the opportunity! A time for bold moves is now. Quick action brings quick results.

~ The Sevens ~
• Confidence • Experience • Conviction •

Position #9 – The real purpose of this quest

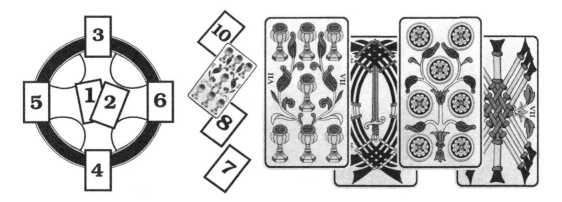

POSSIBLE INTERPRETATION: Advancing on a loved interest. Inspirational accomplishment is key to the seeker. Convincing others of your thinking on an important matter from the heart. Proficiency and confidence. Fulfilling a lifelong quest. Happiness and fulfillment of a goal. A working situation that is flawless can be accomplished through your confident action.

Position #10 – Closing remarks and finer details

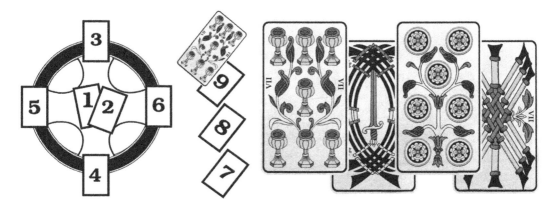

POSSIBLE INTERPRETATION: Confidence will be gained by moving forward on this goal. Whether the quest is completely accomplished or not, confidence will become stronger because of your efforts on this quest.

~ Positional Influence ~

The Minor Arcana

The Eights

INSIGHT: The Eights are seen as an energy of progress. Moving forward on some situation important to the seeker. Advancement is key with the Eights. The energy of the Eights shows us we can do anything we want if we choose to.

~ The Eights ~
• Advancement • Improvement • Elevation •

Position #1 – The real question

POSSIBLE INTERPRETATION: An advancement. Winds of change are an issue. Things are moving in another direction. The question involves an advancement of concern. Being for or against this advancement is key for finding answers.

Position #2 – The real question cont'

Blended with Position #1: *This position is meant to compliment position 1. Position 1 & 2 are read together to see the question more in depth. Therefore the meaning remains the same as above and is blended together with a second card for a combined interpretation. These two cards read together allow us to see new possible ways to see our question. Or at least to confirm that things are being seen clearly by the client.*

~ The Eights ~
• Advancement • Improvement • Elevation •

Position #3 – Actions being taken

POSSIBLE INTERPRETATION: Plans are needed to advance on this quest. The key is to stay focused on what is trying to be accomplished without distraction. Making sure the strategy in place will advance the issue in question.

Position #4 – Immediate Objectives

POSSIBLE INTERPRETATION: Key issues can be put into place by the seeker. Remember the path of least resistance to an end. Putting things in place for you advancing forward on this quest. Easy progress can be achieved if efforts are made. One step at a time is key.

~ The Eights ~
• Advancement • Improvement • Elevation •

Position #5 – An asset to the client

POSSIBLE INTERPRETATION: The seeker is in a good position to advance on this quest. Taking advantage of any steps that can me made to move forward is key.

Position #6 – An opportunity still to come

POSSIBLE INTERPRETATION: Watch for an opportunity to be clearly presented. Advancement will be offered. Be ready for it when it comes.

~ The Eights ~
• Advancement • Improvement • Elevation •

Position #7 – Client's viewpoint

POSSIBLE INTERPRETATION: Careful thought is wise before proceeding. The seeker may be seeing this issue as an easy quest to achieve. Remember that thinking that way could lead to surprise challenges. The seeker might be anxious to move on this issue. Move forward slow but steady. Building slowly helps build a strong lasting situation.

Position #8 – When to take action

POSSIBLE INTERPRETATION: Any moves that bring you closer to your quest should be done now. A time to make progress to bring you closer to the goal. Necessary steps to strengthen your position can be accomplished with swift progress at this time.

~ The Eights ~
• Advancement • Improvement • Elevation •

Position #9 – The real purpose of this quest

POSSIBLE INTERPRETATION: The seeker is trying to better themselves in a significant way. Something important based on sound judgement for a better quality of life. A major stepping stone is seen in the seeker's quest. A matter of significance to the client.

Position #10 – Closing remarks and finer details

POSSIBLE INTERPRETATION: This is a start to an important stage on the seeker's path. Just the beginning. The beginning of significant progress. Quick advances will be seen as you move forward from here.

~ Positional Influence ~

The Minor Arcana

The Nines

INSIGHT: The Nines can be seen as an energy of attainment. Acquiring something that will advance the seeker forward in a growing way. Although not all attainments are positive ones, Nines usually are seen as a pleasant gain for the seeker.

~ The Nines ~
• Attainment • Fulfilment • Ownership •

Position #1 – The real question

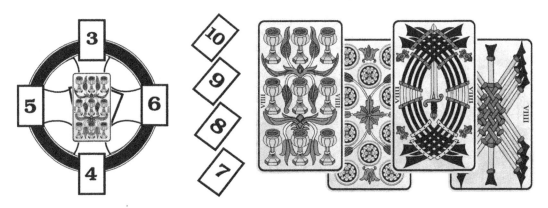

POSSIBLE INTERPRETATION: Acquiring an important objective. Significant opportunity to advance with a positive gain. Something that will change things is attained. New awareness is added to a situation. How can the question be seen as something being attained? What are these attainments?

Position #2 – The real question cont'

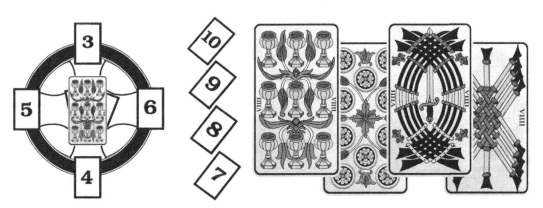

Blended with Position #1: *This position is meant to compliment position 1. Position 1 & 2 are read together to see the question more in depth. Therefore the meaning remains the same as above and is blended together with a second card for a combined interpretation. These two cards read together allow us to see new possible ways to see our question. Or at least to confirm that things are being seen clearly by the client.*

~ The Nines ~
• Attainment • Fulfilment • Ownership •

Position #3 – Actions being taken

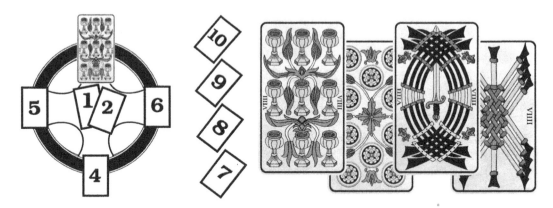

POSSIBLE INTERPRETATION: More is needed before proceeding. What needs to be attained before moving forward? Necessary elements need to be acquired and in place before action is taken.

Position #4 – Immediate Objectives

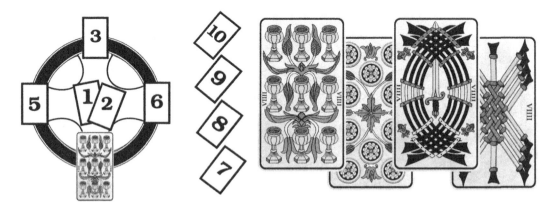

POSSIBLE INTERPRETATION: Taking inventory of what you have available at this time to work with is key. A clear focus on what needs to be gained for a successful outcome. What is needed to be attained to progress on this quest?
What still needs to be found?

~ The Nines ~
• Attainment • Fulfilment • Ownership •

Position #5 – An asset to the client

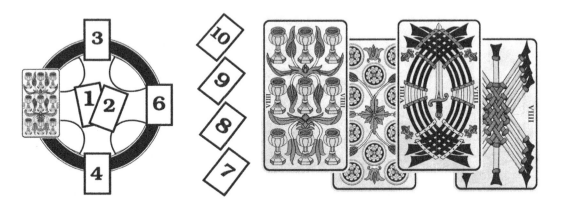

POSSIBLE INTERPRETATION: The seeker is in a good position to attain this quest. Remember that progress might not come all at once. But in steps. All changes work at different speeds.

Position #6 – An opportunity still to come

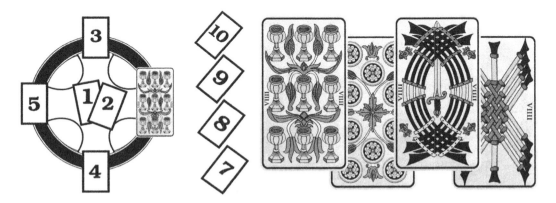

POSSIBLE INTERPRETATION: An opportunity to attain your quest will be coming to you. Attainment is yours in due time. Patience will be key.

~ The Nines ~
• Attainment • Fulfilment • Ownership •

Position #7 – Client's viewpoint

POSSIBLE INTERPRETATION: The seeker may be seeing this quest as a real attainment. A quest of real value is seen by the client. Take time to look deep before moving full force on this quest. A significant opportunity is seen by the client. This opportunity could be an important find for the seeker!

Position #8 – When to take action

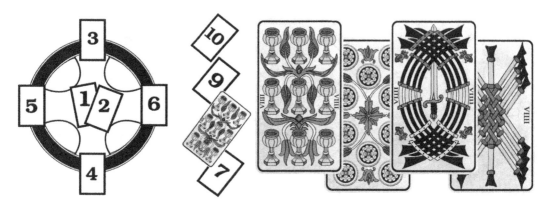

POSSIBLE INTERPRETATION: All is in place to move on this issue. The time seems right for progressive action. Attainment can be successful if action is taken at this time. Big gains are ready to be taken.

~ The Nines ~
• Attainment • Fulfilment • Ownership •

Position #9 – The real purpose of this quest

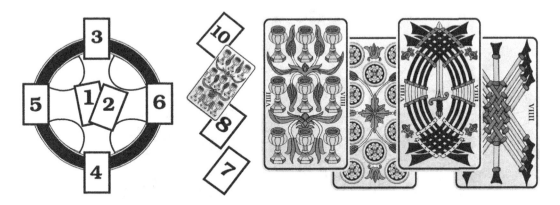

POSSIBLE INTERPRETATION: Great gifts are coming your way!
Efforts to what you truly desire will become reality because the quest is truly felt.

Position #10 – Closing remarks and finer details

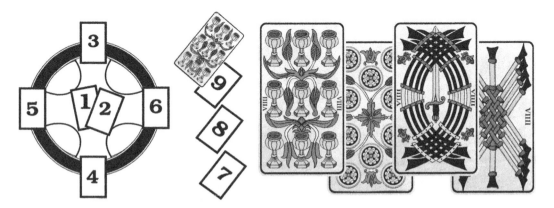

POSSIBLE INTERPRETATION: Attaining what is desired will bring the predicted happiness you anticipated. No surprises. A peaceful ending to a rewarding path taken by the seeker.

~ Positional Influence ~

The Minor Arcana

The Tens

INSIGHT: The Tens can be seen as things coming to a close. A completion. The end of the road to a goal or journey. A time to reflect on what has been accomplished. The Tens can be seen as an end to something significant.

~ The Tens ~
• Completion • Closure • Achievement •

Position #1 – The real question

POSSIBLE INTERPRETATION: How can we associate "Completion" to our quest? How do we complete a job well done. End of one cycle and the beginning of another. An opportunity to put things to rest that need to be closed. A peaceful outcome. Turning the page on an issue. Walking away.

Position #2 – The real question cont'

Blended with Position #1: *This position is meant to compliment position 1. Position 1 & 2 are read together to see the question more in depth. Therefore the meaning remains the same as above and is blended together with a second card for a combined interpretation. These two cards read together allow us to see new possible ways to see our question. Or at least to confirm that things are being seen clearly by the client.*

~ The Tens ~
• Completion • Closure • Achievement •

Position #3 – Actions being taken

POSSIBLE INTERPRETATION: Stages need to be complete before moving to the next step. Completion before moving forward is key. First things first. Don't get ahead of yourself in your planning.

Position #4 – Immediate Objectives

POSSIBLE INTERPRETATION: Key actions needs to be finished for further progress to take place. What action needs to be completed? Completely finishing initial goals before proceeding further is key.

~ The Tens ~
• Completion • Closure • Achievement •

Position #5 – An asset to the client

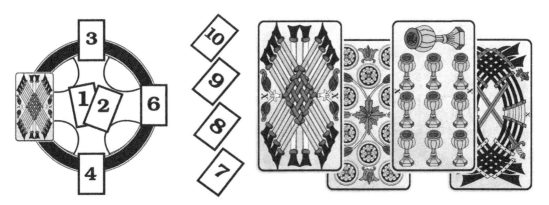

POSSIBLE INTERPRETATION: The seeker is in a good position to complete this quest. Ending one cycle means starting another. Success may bring on new challenges not yet seen. Remember that it will never be like it was. What was is past.

Position #6 – An opportunity still to come

POSSIBLE INTERPRETATION: An opportunity to complete the quest. Satisfying finish towards your quest.

~ The Tens ~
• Completion • Closure • Achievement •

Position #7 – Client's viewpoint

POSSIBLE INTERPRETATION: The client might be seeing this as a welcomed finish to something that needed to be completed for a long time now. Reward for efforts are accomplished. The seeker may be seeing this as all is lost! If so, look into ways to salvage what can be kept. How much damage has been done? What can be repaired on this issue?

Position #8 – When to take action

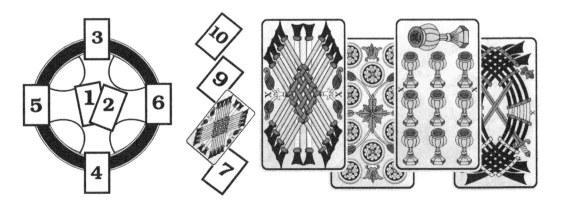

POSSIBLE INTERPRETATION: The time seems right to put things to rest. Finalizing issues. A time to complete issues of importance.
Wrapping up loose ends with others. Coming to agreements. Contracts are signed. A good time to make issues understood clearly.

~ The Tens ~
• Completion • Closure • Achievement •

Position #9 – The real purpose of this quest

POSSIBLE INTERPRETATION: A completion of a life long quest is key to the seeker. Attaining what you truly deserve. Keep a strong focus on the main purpose as you proceed.

Position #10 – Closing remarks and finer details

POSSIBLE INTERPRETATION: A gratifying experience should be expected because of all your efforts. The end of a wonderful chapter will be attained.
End of one cycle and the beginning of another.

~ Positional Influence ~

The Minor Arcana

The Pages

INSIGHT: The Pages can be seen as the essence of a new journey. Inexperience on a new and exciting quest. Much to learn but enthusiasm, makes the journey go easier.

~ The Pages ~
• New Path • Branching Out • Apprenticeship •

Position #1 – The real question

POSSIBLE INTERPRETATION: What value does a new path have to our question? An all new chosen environment for the seeker. A new experience for an old situation. A new direction on a chosen path. Inexperienced, but willing to move forward on this quest. Much to learn about a new interest.

Position #2 – The real question cont'

Blended with Position #1: *This position is meant to compliment position 1. Position 1 & 2 are read together to see the question more in depth. Therefore the meaning remains the same as above and is blended together with a second card for a combined interpretation. These two cards read together allow us to see new possible ways to see our question. Or at least to confirm that things are being seen clearly by the client.*

~ The Pages ~
• New Path • Branching Out • Apprenticeship •

Position #3 – Actions being taken

POSSIBLE INTERPRETATION: Searching for a new direction. Happiness is found with a new quest. A newly found quest is the focus of the seeker. Exciting situations are sought to fill a void.

Position #4 – Immediate Objectives

POSSIBLE INTERPRETATION: The first goal is to change direction. A new path is seen clearly as feasible. Approaches not yet used should be considered. A new direction could be helpful for initial goals.

~ The Pages ~
• New Path • Branching Out • Apprenticeship •

Position #5 – An asset to the client

POSSIBLE INTERPRETATION: The seeker is in a good position to take a new path into their quest. The seeker can let go of things holding them back. Releasing themselves of restrictive bonds that limit their pursuit. Weights are taken off your shoulders and replaced with a lighter more curious experience.

Position #6 – An opportunity still to come

POSSIBLE INTERPRETATION: An opportunity for a turn of events to prepare for. This change could be advantageous if acted on. New interest allows a change in plans for the better.

~ The Pages ~
• New Path • Branching Out • Apprenticeship •

Position #7 – Client's viewpoint

POSSIBLE INTERPRETATION: The client may be seeing their question as a whole new path. The issue is being seen as a new unexplored territory.
New situation. Exciting time ahead. A new learning experience for the seeker. Much will be learned in time if this path is traveled.

Position #8 – When to take action

POSSIBLE INTERPRETATION: A good time to start a new beginning. Timing looks good to move on this new quest. Timing looks good regardless of a lack of experience. Curiosity will spark success.

~ The Pages ~
• New Path • Branching Out • Apprenticeship •

Position #9 – The real purpose of this quest

POSSIBLE INTERPRETATION: Putting old issues to rest and moving on to better things. Reevaluating the situation brings new thinking into the scenario. An open mind is helpful for achieving this quest.

Position #10 – Closing remarks and finer details

POSSIBLE INTERPRETATION: A change of pace will be rewarding. New situations arise because of old thinking being let go. Doors open to a new lifestyle.

~ Positional Influence ~

The Minor Arcana

The Knights

INSIGHT: The Knights can be seen as an energy of action. Initiative without outside influences. Knights take on challenges that may seem too difficult to others. The Knights are dedicated to the quest no matter the odds.

~ The Knights ~
• Action • Initiative • Movement •

Position #1 – The real question

POSSIBLE INTERPRETATION: Decisions need to be made on actions to be taken. What are the options? Proceeding with a plan in place would be wise. Expect a challenge on this journey.

Position #2 – The real question cont'

Blended with Position #1: *This position is meant to compliment position 1. Position 1 & 2 are read together to see the question more in depth. Therefore the meaning remains the same as above and is blended together with a second card for a combined interpretation. These two cards read together allow us to see new possible ways to see our question. Or at least to confirm that things are being seen clearly by the client.*

~ The Knights ~
• Action • Initiative • Movement •

Position #3 – Actions being taken

POSSIBLE INTERPRETATION: Planning your actions carefully will bring about more clarity. A time to decide what initial actions need to be taken. Action needs to be taken for progress to follow. Delay is unwise.

Position #4 – Immediate Objectives

POSSIBLE INTERPRETATION: Action at this time brings promising results. Immediate goals can be accomplished if action is taken. Your deeds bring about new opportunity for success on this quest. Actions speak louder than words.

~ The Knights ~
• Action • Initiative • Movement •

Position #5 – An asset to the client

POSSIBLE INTERPRETATION: The seeker is in a good position to take action on the issue. Taking initiative is key. Following your heart will give you the strength to proceed. Your quest makes you who you are.

Position #6 – An opportunity still to come

POSSIBLE INTERPRETATION: An opportunity to take successful action on your goal. Positive results from initiative taken by the seeker will lead to progress towards the quest.

~ The Knights ~
• Action • Initiative • Movement •

Position #7 – Client's viewpoint

POSSIBLE INTERPRETATION: How to take action on this issue could be seen as the concern of the seeker? Should the client act on this issue? How? What actions should the seeker take pertaining to this issue? The seeker could be concerned about an action that has taken place? How should the client approach this issue?

Position #8 – When to take action

POSSIBLE INTERPRETATION: Taking action at this time is favorable. Believing in your quest will help your success. The heart of a knight is key as you move forward on this quest.

~ The Knights ~
• Action • Initiative • Movement •

Position #9 – The real purpose of this quest

POSSIBLE INTERPRETATION: The freedom to take action without resistance is key to the seeker. Freedom to share goals with others in a cooperative manner.

Position #10 – Closing remarks and finer details

POSSIBLE INTERPRETATION: This will open up the ability to move in ways not allowed before. A new freedom. A shift in responsibility is rewarded and recognized by others in your favor.

~ Positional Influence ~

The Minor Arcana

The Queens

INSIGHT: The Queens can be seen as an energy of exceptional patience and understanding. A persuasive but gentle approach to differences. A very wise and experienced energy can be seen in the Queens.

~ The Queens ~
• Patience • Diplomacy • Grace •

Position #1 – The real question

POSSIBLE INTERPRETATION: Patience and understanding is key.
The question needs to be subtly handled. Your feelings on this issue can become
catchy to others. Diplomacy and your insight will get you far.

Position #2 – The real question cont'

Blended with Position #1: *This position is meant to compliment position 1. Position 1 & 2 are read together to see the question more in depth. Therefore the meaning remains the same as above and is blended together with a second card for a combined interpretation. These two cards read together allow us to see new possible ways to see our question. Or at least to confirm that things are being seen clearly by the client.*

~ The Queens ~
• Patience • Diplomacy • Grace •

Position #3 – Actions being taken

POSSIBLE INTERPRETATION: Patience and understanding allows new ideas to come through with more clarity. Inaction is wise for now. Stop and think is best action at this time. Don't chase after answers. Allow the answers to come to you.

Position #4 – Immediate Objectives

POSSIBLE INTERPRETATION: Establishing a working relationship with outside influences would be an asset to the seeker. Clear communication and compromising attitude will get results. Understanding the total situation is key to building preliminary steps towards progress.

~ The Queens ~
• Patience • Diplomacy • Grace •

Position #5 – An asset to the client

POSSIBLE INTERPRETATION: Having patience and understanding is key for the seeker to focus on. Having patience and understanding of other's feelings will allow them to see your's as well. Eliminate your enemies by making them your friends. Grace is your key asset.

Position #6 – An opportunity still to come

POSSIBLE INTERPRETATION: Peace of mind with opportunity for calming results. Complete understanding opens up new doors of happiness.

~ The Queens ~
• Patience • Diplomacy • Grace •

Position #7 – Client's viewpoint

POSSIBLE INTERPRETATION: The client feels they see this issue very clearly. A caring concern about moving forward on the quest. A feeling of confidence about the endeavor in question. The seeker feels this issue can be completed successfully. A clear understanding of the causes and effects that have been put into place.

Position #8 – When to take action

POSSIBLE INTERPRETATION: A time of patience is key at this time. Biding your time will put things in your favor. Inaction at this time will be your best chance for success. Stay calm and wait for opportunity to come to you.

~ The Queens ~
• Patience • Diplomacy • Grace •

Position #9 – The real purpose of this quest

POSSIBLE INTERPRETATION: Truth and complete understanding of a situation is key for the seeker. Empathy for all that is involved. Forgiveness and compassion is a good path for success.

Position #10 – Closing remarks and finer details

POSSIBLE INTERPRETATION: You will be respected by others for the attitude you have on this issue in the end. A rewarding realization will be felt from this path you have taken.

~ Positional Influence ~

The Minor Arcana

The Kings

INSIGHT: The Kings can be seen as an energy of wisdom and knowledge being a key force. Experience and leadership is also present in the Kings. The Kings can also show vision that is difficult for most others to see. This is an influential force who sits in a good position to get things accomplished.

~ The Kings ~
• Knowledge • Leadership • Expertise •

Position #1 – The real question

POSSIBLE INTERPRETATION: Knowledge is key to the question.
A quest that seeks more information. Knowledge is power. The seeker has the knowledge to proceed on this quest. An issue of influence towards others. The seeker needs to attain more knowledge on this quest before proceeding further.

Position #2 – The real question cont'

Blended with Position #1: *This position is meant to compliment position 1. Position 1 & 2 are read together to see the question more in depth. Therefore the meaning remains the same as above and is blended together with a second card for a combined interpretation. These two cards read together allow us to see new possible ways to see our question. Or at least to confirm that things are being seen clearly by the client.*

~ The Kings ~
• Knowledge • Leadership • Expertise •

Position #3 – Actions being taken

POSSIBLE INTERPRETATION: A time to gain knowledge before proceeding. Information is key. Know what you're talking about before you speak. Your knowledge will generate influence upon others once you have it.

Position #4 – Immediate Objectives

POSSIBLE INTERPRETATION: Convincing others can be achieved if information is attained on the issue at hand. Leadership will be convincing if your knowledge of the issue is displayed to others involved.

~ The Kings ~
• Knowledge • Leadership • Expertise •

Position #5 – An asset to the client

POSSIBLE INTERPRETATION: Your knowledge and insight on the issue is key in influencing others to your side. Believe in the power you have. Leadership on the issue is yours for the taking. A clear successful strategy based on your vision is key.

Position #6 – An opportunity still to come

POSSIBLE INTERPRETATION: Valuable insight will be seen by you. Knowledge will be attained because of keen awareness. Look for an opportunity to impress others with your ideas on the issue at hand.

~ The Kings ~
• Knowledge • Leadership • Expertise •

Position #7 – Client's viewpoint

POSSIBLE INTERPRETATION: The client feels like they are capable of success on this endeavor. A feeling of being in a good position to move forward on this quest. Good information is key for a successful outcome. A knowledgeable person will make good progress on this quest.

Position #8 – When to take action

POSSIBLE INTERPRETATION: A time to acquire valuable information on the issue. Knowing this issue well before you act is key. Careful planning is best at this time.

~ The Kings ~
• Knowledge • Leadership • Expertise •

Position #9 – The real purpose of this quest

POSSIBLE INTERPRETATION: Having the opportunity to express your knowledge on this issue can bring success. Sharing your experience on this issue will benefit others involved and will be helpful for attaining what you seek.

Position #10 – Closing remarks and finer details

POSSIBLE INTERPRETATION: A feeling of a rewarding experience of accomplishment will be yours. This path can put you in a very strong position for the future.

The 22 Major Arcana

NOTE:

The Major Arcana may vary from one deck to another is slight ways. Here are some of the more common variances you may come across.

• The High Priestess II is titled The Popess or Lady Pope.
• The Hierophant V may be titled The Pope.
• The Magician I may be titled The Trickster
• The Lovers VI may be titled The Lover
• The Hermit VIIII can be titled Father Time
• Judgement is spelled using the old English version instead of Judgment

• You may also find the roman numeral ranks of the cards using the more modern method of numbering. Example would be the Hermit listed as IX instead of the old method of VIIII

• The numeric value of Strength and Justice may be transposed between 8 and 11

• I have also put The Fool first on the list here instead of listing it last as I did in Chapter 3 on card meanings. The Fool can be seen as number 0 or number 22.

These adjustments have no bearing on the cards meanings. Any deck you use and titles shown will work just fine. It would be up to your personal preference to how it is understood.

~ The Fool ~

The Fool 0

The Fool is a free spirit. A wanderer exploring new worlds with no knowledge of where they will lead. The Fool moves forward with no concerns about what may come to pass. He travels light with no obligations or responsibilities. The Fool is vulnerable to challenges that he did not prepare for. A carefree spirit that we all have admired to some degree in our lives. The Fool has no concerns of failure. He just moves on to the next path.

~ The Fool ~
• Carefree • Trusting • Inexperienced •

Position #1 – The real question

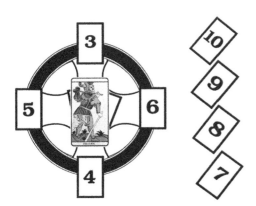

POSSIBLE INTERPRETATION:
A new venture. Inexperience. New ground. Carefree attitude on the issue at hand. Come-what-may attitude. A new approach to a quest without the experience needed to proceed. Exploring new possibilities.

Position #2 – The real question cont'

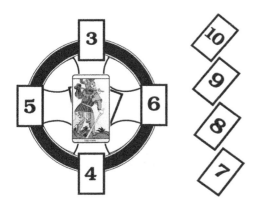

Blended with Position #1: *This position is meant to compliment position 1. Position 1 & 2 are read together to see the question more in depth. Therefore the meaning remains the same as above and is blended together with a second card for a combined interpretation. These two cards read together allow us to see new possible ways to see our question. Or at least to confirm that things are being seen clearly by the client.*

~ The Fool ~
• Carefree • Trusting • Inexperienced •

Position #3 – Actions being taken

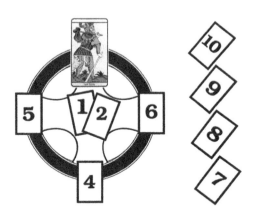

POSSIBLE INTERPRETATION: The seeker may be wanting to put themselves in a carefree stance on the issue. Seeking new answers or solutions. Looking for a new, trouble free solution. A need for less burden on the subject at hand. Let things flow naturally. Taking things at a more casual pace might help matters manifest.

Position #4 – Immediate Objectives

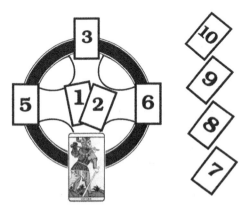

POSSIBLE INTERPRETATION: Attempting to create a new journey. A whole new scenario with no idea where it will lead. Taking the easiest path towards your goal seems to make sense to you. Striving to establishing a hunch with little to go on. "Something I feel I just want to do."

~ The Fool ~
• Carefree • Trusting • Inexperienced •

Position #5 – An asset to the client

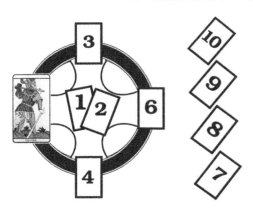

POSSIBLE INTERPRETATION: You are in a good position to remove obligations that stifle you from moving forward on this quest. Freedom to explore and speculate possibilities is easy at this time. Nothing substantial is holding you back. Having no fear of failure is key for your success. Not being afraid of looking foolish as you explore new ideas to things you have never done before.

Position #6 – An opportunity still to come

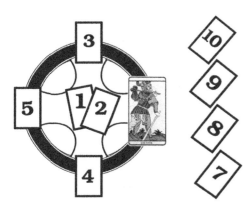

POSSIBLE INTERPRETATION: An opportunity to free up obligations that hinder your quest. More freedom of movement and less restrictions is near by. Look for things to start opening up in new ways favorable to your quest. Easy advancement into new realms of interest are close by.

~ The Fool ~
• Carefree • Trusting • Inexperienced •

Position #7 – Client's viewpoint

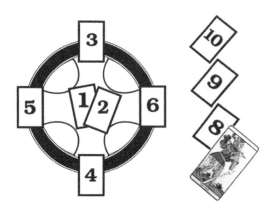

POSSIBLE INTERPRETATION: The seeker should check all aspects of this quest closely. Things might have been overlooked. If the quest seems like an easy task to the seeker it might be a red flag to double check the issue well. A quest where more information would be wise to get. Naive expectations should be looked at closely before moving forward on this journey.

Position #8 – When to take action

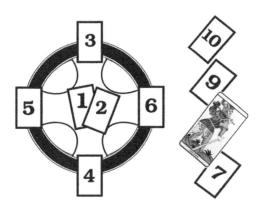

POSSIBLE INTERPRETATION: This is a good time to consider downsizing obligations and responsibilities. A carefree attitude is a good approach on this issue. Not a time to over think the issue. A time to free fall and let it all happen. Less is better at this time. A good time to explore ideas never tried before. A time to have fun and enjoy the ride.

~ The Fool ~
• Carefree • Trusting • Inexperienced •

Position #9 – The real purpose of this quest

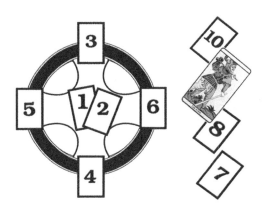 

POSSIBLE INTERPRETATION: I feel this quest will allow me to follow something close to my heart.'

Position #10 – Closing remarks and finer details

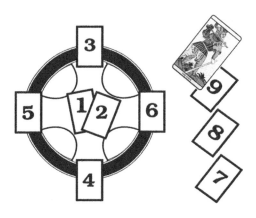 

POSSIBLE INTERPRETATION: This quest might go smoother than anticipated. Look for opportunities to lighten your load as you proceed. Keeping things simple might help.

~ The Magician ~

THE MAGICIAN

The Magician I

The Magician represents perfected action. The ability to perform with surprising results. Thought out plans that have been perfected in detail.

The ability to do what others thought was impossible is yours if carefully planned and mastered to an art. Observing what others overlook is key with this card.

~ Magician ~
• Mastership • Flawless Action • Illusion •

Position #1 – The real question

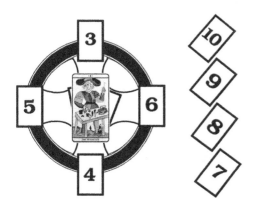 

POSSIBLE INTERPRETATION: An opportunity for a major accomplishment most have thought was not possible. Doing the impossible. A quest of influence. The ability to accomplish what others haven't. An opportunity of lasting impression.

Position #2 – The real question cont'

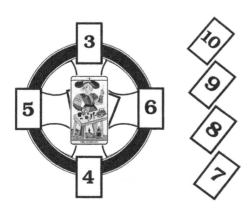 

Blended with Position #1: *This position is meant to compliment position 1. Position 1 & 2 are read together to see the question more in depth. Therefore the meaning remains the same as above and is blended together with a second card for a combined interpretation. These two cards read together allow us to see new possible ways to see our question. Or at least to confirm that things are being seen clearly by the client.*

~ The Magician ~
• Mastership • Flawless Action • Illusion •

Position #3 – Actions being taken

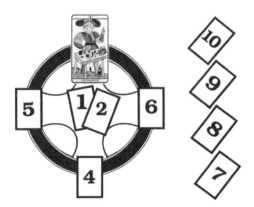 

POSSIBLE INTERPRETATION: A feeling that you have to pull a rabbit out of your hat! Expressing your ability will get you going in a good direction. Setting things up to perform the task at hand is key at this time. Meticulous preparation would be wise at this time. Know your subject well before you proceed.

Position #4 – Immediate Objectives

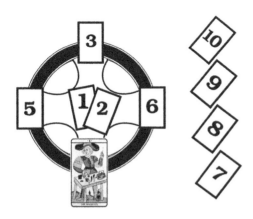 

POSSIBLE INTERPRETATION: Attempting to create a new quest that the seeker feels will impress others instantly once it is seen. A significant quest that is thought impossible to accomplish. Others feel this quest is an unlikely one. But you feel you can do it. Gratification in doing the impossible.

~ The Magician ~
• Mastership • Flawless Action • Illusion •

Position #5 – An asset to the client

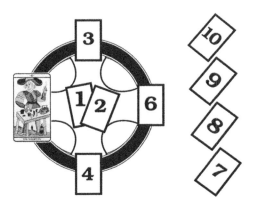 

POSSIBLE INTERPRETATION: Trust in your natural talent with this issue will get you far. You have the ability to manifest ideas into realities. Your position on this issue is powerful. Maybe more so than you realize. Surprising results are yours if you take action on this. Meticulous and well organized practice will be helpful as you proceed.

Position #6 – An opportunity still to come

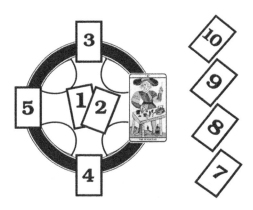 

POSSIBLE INTERPRETATION: Opportunity to perform your talents in impressive fashion. Materialization of new assets will be created by you as you proceed. Things will start to appear in your favor. You will find the ability to create what is needed. Look for hidden assets near by. They are there!

~ The Magician ~
• Mastership • Flawless Action • Illusion •

Position #7 – Client's viewpoint

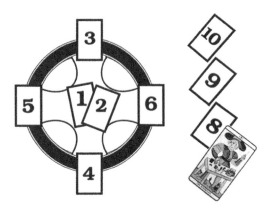

POSSIBLE INTERPRETATION: The client is seeing their own question with great confidence. The seekers talent in this issue seems strong. An ability to manipulate this issue to their advantage is key. The seeker is in a good position to perform the task at hand for success.

Position #8 – When to take action

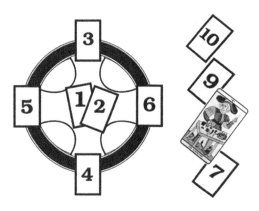

POSSIBLE INTERPRETATION: A time to make things happen. Expressing your expertise will be impressive to others. A time to start acquiring the things needed to perform effectively. A good time to create on this quest. Surprising results are within reach.

~ The Magician ~
• Mastership • Flawless Action • Illusion •

Position #9 – The real purpose of this quest

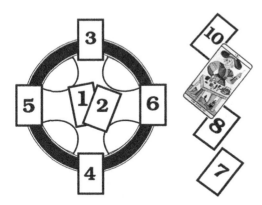 

POSSIBLE INTERPRETATION: I feel this quest will allow me to do what has been considered impossible. Major advances through your own sources. Perfection of the quest.

Position #10 – Closing remarks and finer details

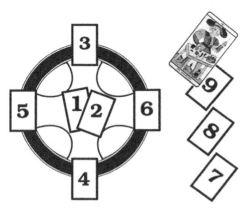 

POSSIBLE INTERPRETATION: Look for things to move in ways you never thought possible. Looks like you might pull a rabbit out of your hat and even surprise yourself! Things should fall into place nicely.

~ The High Priestess ~

The High Priestess II

The High Priestess is the card of hidden knowledge and wisdom. She is mysterious and unknown. Mystical energy is seen in this card exploring that which can't be seen. Deep wisdom that has great value is attained. Intuitive insight from the realm of dreams is key with this card.

~ The High Priestess ~
• Mystery • Hidden Knowledge • Secrecy •

Position #1 – The real question

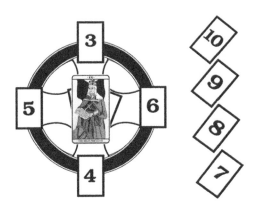 

POSSIBLE INTERPRETATION: Impressive stature. Hidden knowledge is yours. Tapping into knowledge from the subconscious. Power of the subconscious mind is key. A strong influence. Answers from dreams. Deep wisdom that is usually not exposed to others will be impressive to others when shared.

Position #2 – The real question cont'

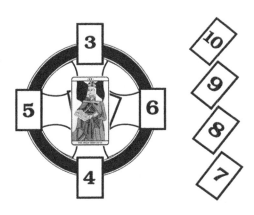 

Blended with Position #1: *This position is meant to compliment position 1. Position 1 & 2 are read together to see the question more in depth. Therefore the meaning remains the same as above and is blended together with a second card for a combined interpretation. These two cards read together allow us to see new possible ways to see our question. Or at least to confirm that things are being seen clearly by the client.*

~ The High Priestess ~
• Mystery • Hidden Knowledge • Secrecy •

Position #3 – Actions being taken

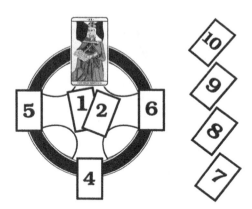 

POSSIBLE INTERPRETATION: Your knowledge and insight on this subject is best kept to yourself at this time. Secrecy is best until a later time. A time to keep plans protected and hidden. Don't let those challenging you know what you're up to yet.

Position #4 – Immediate Objectives

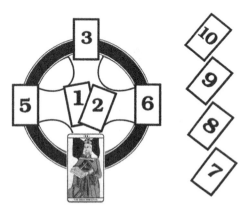 

POSSIBLE INTERPRETATION: You feel you can create a situation that others cannot see yet. Your quest has broad vision. Keep in mind that others cannot see your quest as well as you see it. Your insight alone is key.

~ The High Priestess ~
• Mystery • Hidden Knowledge • Secrecy •

Position #5 – An asset to the client

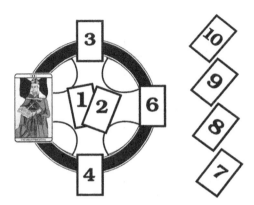 

POSSIBLE INTERPRETATION: Your hidden knowledge will be key as you proceed. Surprising others with your wisdom will encourage others to your side on this matter. Your wisdom is impressive once it is shown. Your very presence can influence things in your favor.

Position #6 – An opportunity still to come

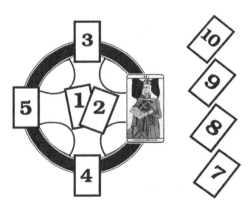 

POSSIBLE INTERPRETATION: Knowledge that has been hidden will be revealed that can be useful to your quest. Alliances in the background will come forward as you share your insight into your goal. Impressive progress based on new insight will be seen by others. Your deep understanding of the issue at hand can be expressed openly soon.

~ The High Priestess ~
• Mystery • Hidden Knowledge • Secrecy •

Position #7 – Client's viewpoint

POSSIBLE INTERPRETATION: The seeker has a dedication to this cause. The client is closely connected to this quest. A strong connection to the issue allows the seeker to shift details in key ways as they proceed. A flowing energy runs through the seeker on this quest making actions and intent very effective.

Position #8 – When to take action

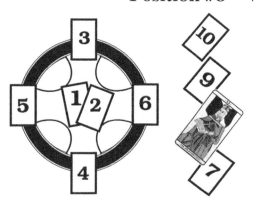

POSSIBLE INTERPRETATION: Your influence is magical at this time. Others will listen of you speak. Expressing your wisdom at this time will get favorable results. Things are in your reach if you choose to take them. Following your insight will bring positive results.

~ The High Priestess ~
• Mystery • Hidden Knowledge • Secrecy •

Position #9 – The real purpose of this quest

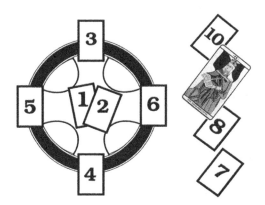 

POSSIBLE INTERPRETATION: I feel this quest will allow me to get in touch with my higher self. Fulfilling a quest that comes from the spirit within. Making your dream possible. Getting in touch with your spirituality.

Position #10 – Closing remarks and finer details

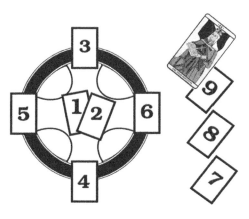 

POSSIBLE INTERPRETATION: Hidden factors may arise as you move on this. Welcome the good ones and prepare for the bad. You might have to explain any hidden intentions as you move forward.

~ The Empress ~

The Empress III

The Empress is the power of creativity. New ideas and exploring all possibilities. Flourishing life force that can create new situations from nothing but ideas. She is the power of motherhood and abundance.

~ The Empress ~
• Abundance • Innovation • Conception •

Position #1 – The real question

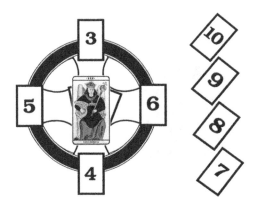

POSSIBLE INTERPRETATION: Creative energy is key. New ideas with real promise. A flourish of new thinking about your quest. A nurturing situation with much potential. Your seeds of ideas are planted well on this quest.

Position #2 – The real question cont'

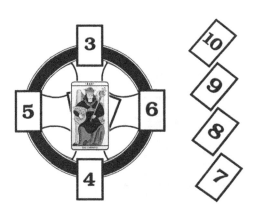

Blended with Position #1: *This position is meant to compliment position 1. Position 1 & 2 are read together to see the question more in depth. Therefore the meaning remains the same as above and is blended together with a second card for a combined interpretation. These two cards read together allow us to see new possible ways to see our question. Or at least to confirm that things are being seen clearly by the client.*

~ The Empress ~
• Abundance • Innovation • Conception •

Position #3 – Actions being taken

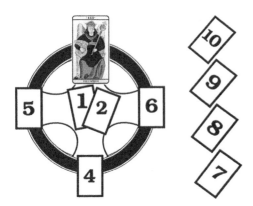 

POSSIBLE INTERPRETATION: A need to consider all aspects. Nothing is off the table at this time. Creating new options. Review new ideas to your final goal. Considering a new approach is key. Imagination can be beneficial on this issue.

Position #4 – Immediate Objectives

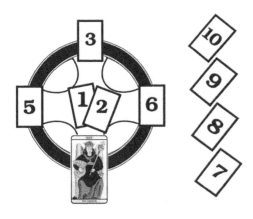 

POSSIBLE INTERPRETATION: The quest of the seeker is one that will flourish. Expanding on a already established situation will reap good rewards!
The seeker sees much potential in this endeavor. Innovative ideas will prove themselves bountiful if established.

~ The Empress ~
• Abundance • Innovation • Conception •

Position #5 – An asset to the client

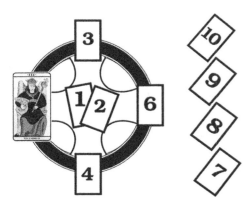

POSSIBLE INTERPRETATION: Your creative energy allows new opportunity to come to you naturally. If you move on this quest things will flourish automatically. Your original type thinking will bring about new concepts on this quest not seen before. New ideas will abound.

Position #6 – An opportunity still to come

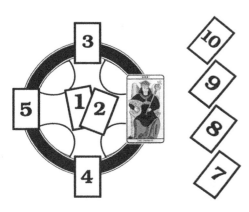

POSSIBLE INTERPRETATION: Things will start to take shape on this quest naturally. A growing interest on the issue will happen soon. An opportunity to nurture your quest with more care is near.

~ The Empress ~
• Abundance • Innovation • Conception •

Position #7 – Client's viewpoint

POSSIBLE INTERPRETATION: The seeker feels they can nurture this quest in important ways. The client truly cares about this issue and will care for it very well through any challenges that arise. A strong sense that this quest is unwavering and truly felt from the heart.

Position #8 – When to take action

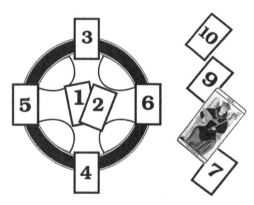

POSSIBLE INTERPRETATION: The time is now for the situation to be prepared. Growth is promising if things get put into place at this time. The seeker is in a good position to create things in their favor at this time. A time to plant ideas that have potential to grow.

~ The Empress ~
• Abundance • Innovation • Conception •

Position #9 – The real purpose of this quest

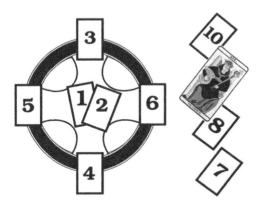 

POSSIBLE INTERPRETATION: I feel this quest will allow me to express my creative energy. Innovation of original concepts.

Position #10 – Closing remarks and finer details

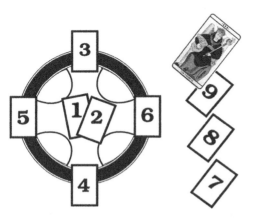 

POSSIBLE INTERPRETATION: New ideas will come as you proceed on this quest. The seeds you've planted will start to grow before this quest is completed.

~ The Emperor ~

The Emperor   IIII

The Emperor shows a power of building what has been planned. A force of leadership able to manifest ideas into realities. A energy able to move all that is needed in the direction of progress. This power has the force to create ideas into physical reality. Dreams turned into realizations are seen with this card.

~ The Emperor ~
• Leadership • Empowered • Influential •

Position #1 – The real question

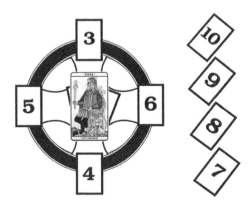

POSSIBLE INTERPRETATION: The power to turn ideas into realities is key. Leadership is strong. Taking the initiative will advance the quest. The ability to manifest this issue into a reality. Experience is strong. In a good position to succeed with cooperation from others. A position of leadership.

Position #2 – The real question cont'

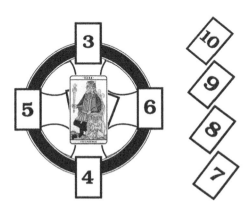

Blended with Position #1: *This position is meant to compliment position 1. Position 1 & 2 are read together to see the question more in depth. Therefore the meaning remains the same as above and is blended together with a second card for a combined interpretation. These two cards read together allow us to see new possible ways to see our question. Or at least to confirm that things are being seen clearly by the client.*

~ The Emperor ~
• Leadership • Empowered • Influential •

Position #3 – Actions being taken

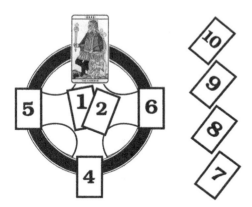 

POSSIBLE INTERPRETATION: A good time to set guidelines and understanding what needs to be accomplished and in what order. Persuading others to your side is in your power. Knowing what impressive actions will make the most impact. A sound strategy is key.

Position #4 – Immediate Objectives

POSSIBLE INTERPRETATION: An opportunity to manifest something worthwhile. Something the seeker can call their own. A significant building block to greater things. Something the seeker knows will be if accomplished. A sound and feasible plan with great potential is clear to the client.

~ The Emperor ~
• Leadership • Empowered • Influential •

Position #5 – An asset to the client

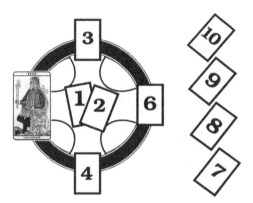 

POSSIBLE INTERPRETATION: In a good position to build what you desire. You have the resources available to manifest ideas into realities. You have the ability to do what you seek to accomplish. Leadership is your key asset on this quest. Exploring what can be done now will bring benefits to your cause. Results will be there for you if you act.

Position #6 – An opportunity still to come

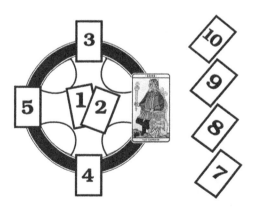 

POSSIBLE INTERPRETATION: Substantial development will start to take place soon. Well made plans start to pay off. The opportunity to manifest well made plans into realities. Leadership and pointing out sound ideas is necessary for things to move forward. Others start to listen to your ideas and see your progress is working.

~ The Emperor ~
• Leadership • Empowered • Influential •

Position #7 – Client's viewpoint

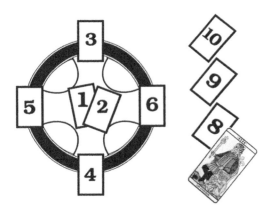 

POSSIBLE INTERPRETATION: The seeker is seeing this quest as a realistic goal. Things seem to be clearly feasible to the seeker. Confidence is expressed in wise ways on this endeavor. The seeker is ready to move forward in tangible ways on this objective.

Position #8 – When to take action

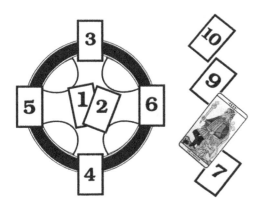 

POSSIBLE INTERPRETATION: This is a good time to build concepts into realities. The laying of a firm foundation to build on. Perfect time to lay the initial ground work for growth. Your influence is strong right now for successful leadership on the endeavor in question. Your plans are ready to be put into action.

~ The Emperor ~
• Leadership • Empowered • Influential •

Position #9 – The real purpose of this quest

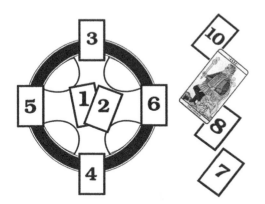

POSSIBLE INTERPRETATION: This quest will allow me to build and to lead others. Achieving a sense of honor and respect with self and others around me. Self gratification. A significant accomplishment is sought by the seeker.

Position #10 – Closing remarks and finer details

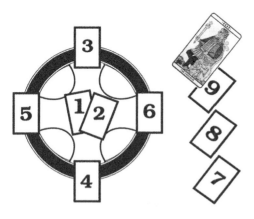

POSSIBLE INTERPRETATION: Your well planned ideas will attract cooperation from others to get things done. Your quest may attract others of influence to your cause as you proceed.

~ The Hierophant ~

The Hierophant V

The Hierophant shows influential guidance. Someone with authority would be beneficial to have in your corner who knows this quest well. A superior advisory is needed to move forward. This card can also show that you have the knowledge to make decisions on your quest with good accuracy and judgment. It can also mean a higher source of knowledge is near to help you if you seek it out.

~ The Hierophant ~
• Guidance • Established Authority • Conformity •

Position #1 – The real question

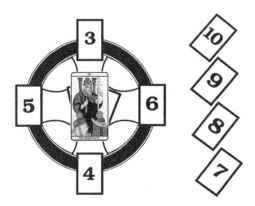 

POSSIBLE INTERPRETATION: Guidance will be key. Professional counsel on this issue will be an effective choice. A source of authority on a given subject. Traditional type strategy. Play it straight. Tried and true action is the best choice for success. Someone higher than you will help if you allow it.

Position #2 – The real question cont'

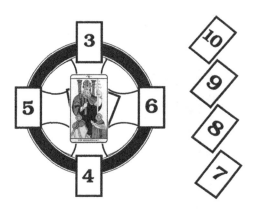 

Blended with Position #1: *This position is meant to compliment position 1. Position 1 & 2 are read together to see the question more in depth. Therefore the meaning remains the same as above and is blended together with a second card for a combined interpretation. These two cards read together allow us to see new possible ways to see our question. Or at least to confirm that things are being seen clearly by the client.*

~ The Hierophant ~
• Guidance • Established Authority • Conformity •

Position #3 – Actions being taken

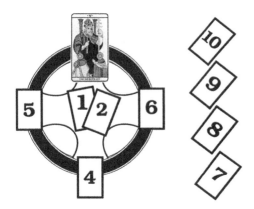

POSSIBLE INTERPRETATION: A time for sound guidance. Clear cut and well established authority will be helpful before proceeding. Affirming actions before they are done will be to your benefit. Planning things by the book is key at this time. Sound and time-tested procedures will lead to the best results.

Position #4 – Immediate Objectives

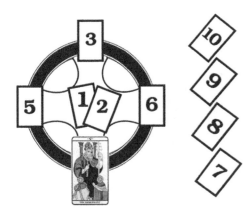

POSSIBLE INTERPRETATION: A well established task based on what has worked in the past. The seeker feels a promising situation can be achieved if the old ways are followed. The seeker feels this is a calling. The client feels guided by more than themselves.

~ The Hierophant ~
• Guidance • Established Authority • Conformity •

Position #5 – An asset to the client

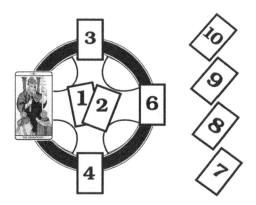 

POSSIBLE INTERPRETATION: You have good guidance on how to proceed. Capable support is in your realm. Effective direction from those around you will be helpful. Your reputation is strong on this quest. You have the insight to move efficiently. Others will respect your counsel on this issue.

Position #6 – An opportunity still to come

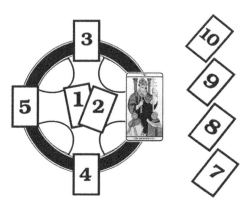 

POSSIBLE INTERPRETATION: An opportunity to lead others along your path. You will gain influence from others as you proceed. A force of authority prevails. Aligning yourself with this authority may be useful to your quest. Wise choices based on what was done in the past may influence this quest.

~ The Hierophant ~
• Guidance • Established Authority • Conformity •

Position #7 – Client's viewpoint

POSSIBLE INTERPRETATION: The seeker feels their quest is based on sound reason and truth. A feeling of being guided in secure ways for success.
A feeling of a journey based on real truths. Strong confidence of success based on truth. Seeking truth is wise as you proceed.

Position #8 – When to take action

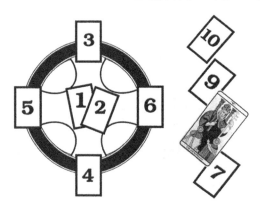 

POSSIBLE INTERPRETATION: This is a good time for the seeker to seek guidance on the issue. Advice from others who are familiar with the scenario is wise.
A time of qualified counsel from authorities on the subject.

~ The Hierophant ~
• Guidance • Established Authority • Conformity •

Position #9 – The real purpose of this quest

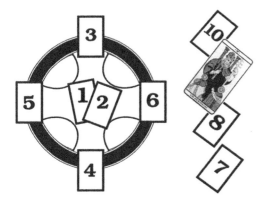 

POSSIBLE INTERPRETATION: The opportunity to guide others on something dear to you. To seek something you feel is bigger than yourself.

Position #10 – Closing remarks and finer details

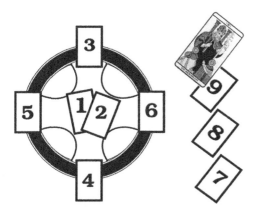 

POSSIBLE INTERPRETATION: Additional professional guidance could be available as you journey forward. This endeavor may attract others who follow your path. An opportunity of sound, established recognition could come your way.

~ The Lover ~

The Lover VI

Choices that needs to be made is seen with the Lover. In order for things to proceed decisions needs to be made. Sometimes these decisions can be difficult to make. Careful thought is wise when the Lover card appears in a reading. Following your heart can be seen as a true source to follow.

~ The Lover ~
• Commitment • Compromise • Selection •

Position #1 – The real question

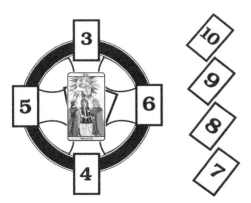 

POSSIBLE INTERPRETATION: Hard choices to be made. Good aspects to both sides of this coin. Careful thought takes time to see. Repercussions either way. Two distinct paths going in two distinct directions creates a need to make a crucial choice before proceeding.

Position #2 – The real question cont'

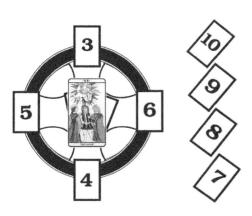 

Blended with Position #1: *This position is meant to compliment position 1. Position 1 & 2 are read together to see the question more in depth. Therefore the meaning remains the same as above and is blended together with a second card for a combined interpretation. These two cards read together allow us to see new possible ways to see our question. Or at least to confirm that things are being seen clearly by the client.*

~ The Lover ~
• Commitment • Compromise • Selection •

Position #3 – Actions being taken

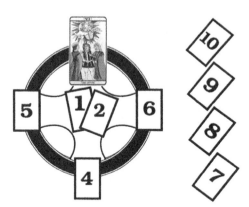

POSSIBLE INTERPRETATION: A time to make clear choices. Choices are critical for successful results. Seeking the correct path is key. Compromise is a good safety net before proceeding. See both sides clearly before choices are made.

Position #4 – Immediate Objectives

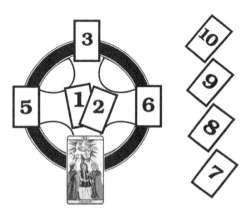

POSSIBLE INTERPRETATION: The seeker feels their counsel will help others make the right choice. Attempting to convince others of your way of thinking. Explaining your thinking to others can be convincing if shown clearly. Communicating with authority is key.

~ The Lover ~
• Commitment • Compromise • Selection •

Position #5 – An asset to the client

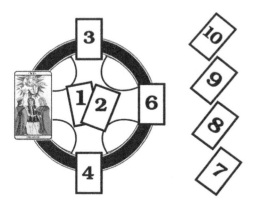

POSSIBLE INTERPRETATION: Seeing things clearly allows you to make sound choices on the quest. No confusion on direction once you think things over clearly. Wise decisions are made quickly by your insight in sync with the issue. No confusion on how to stand on this issue.

Position #6 – An opportunity still to come

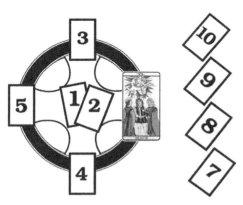

POSSIBLE INTERPRETATION: Look for opportunities to make clear choices that have been difficult to make in the past. Decisions are made soon on this issue. Clear direction based on wise choices will be there for you to make. Good choices will lead to progress.

~ The Lover ~
• Commitment • Compromise • Selection •

Position #7 – Client's viewpoint

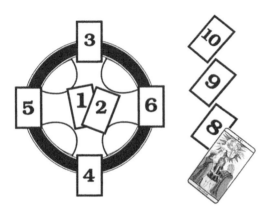

POSSIBLE INTERPRETATION: The seeker sees this quest depending on a choice being made by an outside source. How can the seeker influence that choice?
The seeker has a difficult choice to make before proceeding.

Position #8 – When to take action

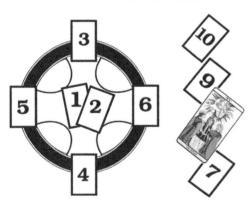

POSSIBLE INTERPRETATION: Sound choices can be made now with the information available to the seeker. Things can be seen clearly to make key decisions. Choices made will be accurate if they are followed through. A time to make decisions is key.

~ The Lover ~
• Commitment • Compromise • Selection •

Position #9 – The real purpose of this quest

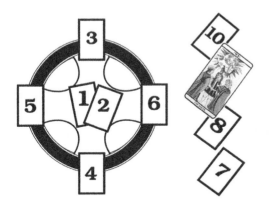

POSSIBLE INTERPRETATION: This quest will allow the seeker to make the right choices and to move in the best direction.

Position #10 – Closing remarks and finer details

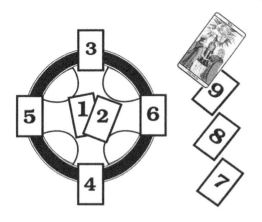

POSSIBLE INTERPRETATION: Better options and opportunity might come your way once things are in motion. Others like your direction. Opportunity for close relationships to come.

~ The Chariot ~

The Chariot VII

The Chariot is seen as a very powerful force that would be hard to stop once in motion. If you control the reins of this vehicle you better know what you're doing so not to lose control. This card holds a lot of influence on your quest. If handled well, you are in a good position to move forward on your quest. Quick progress from an unstoppable force is seen with this card.

~ The Chariot ~
• Forceful Position • Vigorous Action • Quick Progress •

Position #1 – The real question

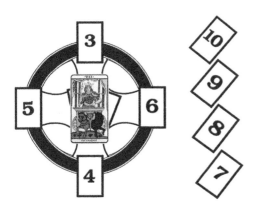 

POSSIBLE INTERPRETATION: In a strong position to advance without resistance. A show of strength would be wise. Easy progress if you advance on your quest with confidence. Swift action. In control of the situation. A time for covering much ground quickly.

Position #2 – The real question cont'

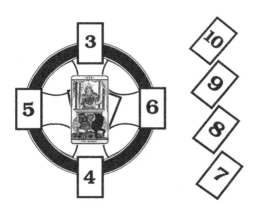 

Blended with Position #1: *This position is meant to compliment position 1. Position 1 & 2 are read together to see the question more in depth. Therefore the meaning remains the same as above and is blended together with a second card for a combined interpretation. These two cards read together allow us to see new possible ways to see our question. Or at least to confirm that things are being seen clearly by the client.*

~ The Chariot ~
• Forceful Position • Vigorous Action • Quick Progress •

Position #3 – Actions being taken

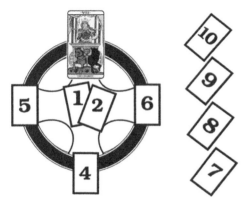 

POSSIBLE INTERPRETATION: Laying the groundwork for bold action. Your talent will be a strong point. Use it to it's fullest extent. It is very convincing once in motion. Gaining the confidence before proceeding is key to your success. Focus on your talents to attain that edge.

Position #4 – Immediate Objectives

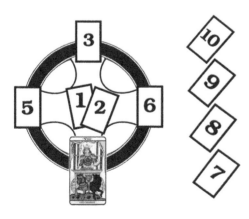 

POSSIBLE INTERPRETATION: Anxious to move forward on this quest. Things will fall into place once the ball starts rolling is the feeling of the seeker. Swift and effective initial progress should be taken soon. All is in place to proceed without delay.

~ The Chariot ~
• Forceful Position • Vigorous Action • Quick Progress •

Position #5 – An asset to the client

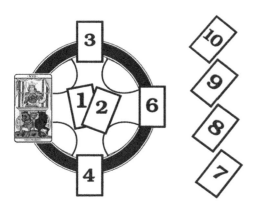 

POSSIBLE INTERPRETATION: Bold moves will work for you. Quick results are yours if you act with confidence. Your energy is unstoppable in your quest. Capabilities are strong and swift. Significant influence on those around you can be easily gained.

Position #6 – An opportunity still to come

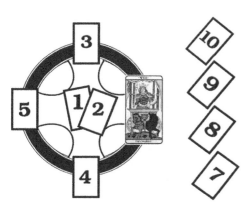 

POSSIBLE INTERPRETATION: Opportunities for quick progress develop fast. Your confidence in this quest will open doors to move forward.
A new unstoppable drive comes to your side. Look for alliances with strong influence to become available.

~ The Chariot ~
• Forceful Position • Vigorous Action • Quick Progress •

Position #7 – Client's viewpoint

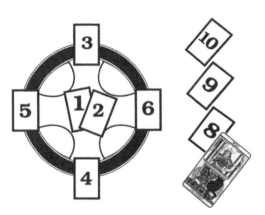 

POSSIBLE INTERPRETATION: The seeker feels strong on this issue. Expectation of quick progress and accomplishment. A chance for a strong victory.

An opportunity that would be foolish not to take is perceived by the seeker. Check all aspects before proceeding. Once it is started, it will be difficult to reverse actions in any way.

Position #8 – When to take action

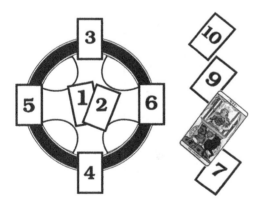 

POSSIBLE INTERPRETATION: Now is the time to take action. Effective progress can be made if action is taken now. A time to show your true strength.

A time for swift action towards the quest. The client is capable of swift progress on the issue.

~ The Chariot ~
• Forceful Position • Vigorous Action • Quick Progress •

Position #9 – The real purpose of this quest

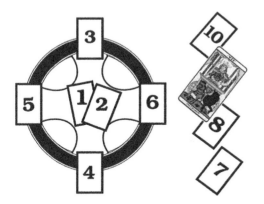 

POSSIBLE INTERPRETATION: I feel this quest will help to overcome things holding me back. To move forward in significant ways.

Position #10 – Closing remarks and finer details

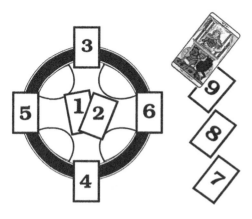 

POSSIBLE INTERPRETATION: Progress might happen quicker than expected. New ground might be broken unexpectedly.

~ Justice ~

Justice VIII

Justice represents universal truth. This energy can be seen as laws that cannot be ignored. Truth will come out in the end. This card can also be seen as legal situations being resolved. But those resolved issues happen because truth prevails in the end.

~ Justice ~
• Established Recognition • Fairness • Universal Truths •

Position #1 – The real question

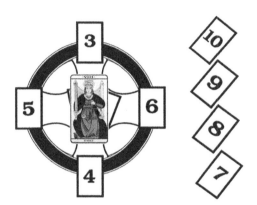

POSSIBLE INTERPRETATION: Truth of the matter is key. Understanding totally what you are dealing with before taking action. Knowing all the facts.
Looking into details is wise on your quest. Keeping no secrets on this issue helps things move correctly. Being open and honest is key.

Position #2 – The real question cont'

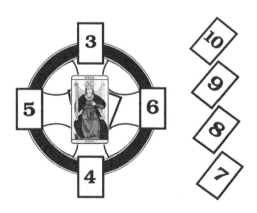

Blended with Position #1: *This position is meant to compliment position 1. Position 1 & 2 are read together to see the question more in depth. Therefore the meaning remains the same as above and is blended together with a second card for a combined interpretation. These two cards read together allow us to see new possible ways to see our question. Or at least to confirm that things are being seen clearly by the client.*

~ Justice ~
• Established Recognition • Fairness • Universal Truths •

Position #3 – Actions being taken

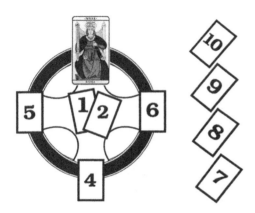 

POSSIBLE INTERPRETATION: Making sure you do not overstep bounds. Understanding your place in this quest at this time. Your responsibility will be acknowledged. Stay within your place of influence on this issue. Actions will be accounted for.

Position #4 – Immediate Objectives

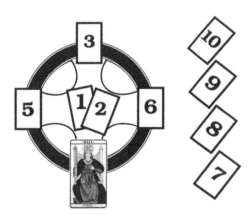 

POSSIBLE INTERPRETATION: A peaceful and harmonious situation that will always be in place allows a fulfilling quest to be followed. Establishing agreements that are fair to all. An open and true quest that more can be built on. Reliable and dedicated cooperation by all involved.

~ Justice ~
• Established Recognition • Fairness • Universal Truths •

Position #5 – An asset to the client

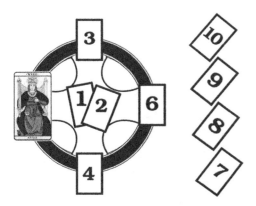 

POSSIBLE INTERPRETATION: The truth is on your side. Expressing your opinions to others will be hard to deny once they are seen. What is true will work successfully. Structured thinking is strong with you. Laying things out for all to see is to your benefit. Expressing your thoughts creates enthusiasm in your quest.

Position #6 – An opportunity still to come

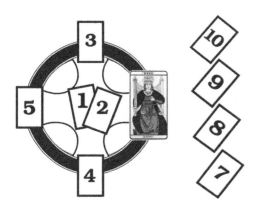 

POSSIBLE INTERPRETATION: Truth will prevail shortly. Strong support from established sources. Openness and expressing your views is key. Expressing the positive aspects of this quest to others creates a strong and influential ally.

~ Justice ~
• Established Recognition • Fairness • Universal Truths •

Position #7 – Client's viewpoint

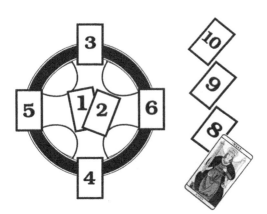 

POSSIBLE INTERPRETATION: The seeker truly believes in this quest. Make sure that all the facts are accurate. Taking the time to verify what is implied would be wise. What is thought to be true should be checked. More than a verbal agreement is key.

Position #8 – When to take action

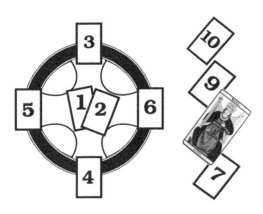 

POSSIBLE INTERPRETATION: A good time to examine all the factors of this quest carefully before taking action. Weighing out all aspects of the issue. Verifying what you feel you know about this issue would be wise. Truth is on your side on this quest.

~ Justice ~
• Established Recognition • Fairness • Universal Truths •

Position #9 – The real purpose of this quest

POSSIBLE INTERPRETATION: This quest will get you what you seek. A true meaning. Finding your truth. Having justice. To get what you deserve.

Position #10 – Closing remarks and finer details

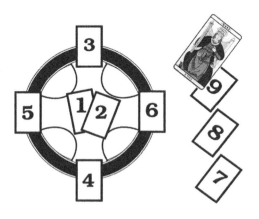

POSSIBLE INTERPRETATION: New information may come as you proceed. Established authority will side with your views. Legal agreements can be made.

~ Hermit ~

The Hermit VIIII

The Hermit represents a sense of inner searching. No one can walk with you on that soul searching quest. Isolation is needed to find direction in key situations. This solitude puts us on a higher position to see our path more clearly.

~ Hermit ~
• Isolation • Solitude • Separation •

Position #1 – The real question

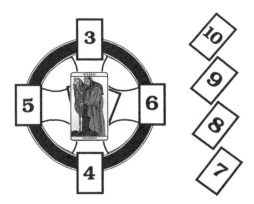 

POSSIBLE INTERPRETATION: A time of solitude. Looking within for answers is key. A journey taken alone is to your advantage. Answers are found by isolation from others. Putting yourself in a position to think clearly without disruption is key.

Position #2 – The real question cont'

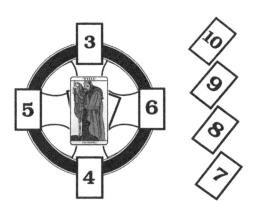 

Blended with Position #1: *This position is meant to compliment position 1. Position 1 & 2 are read together to see the question more in depth. Therefore the meaning remains the same as above and is blended together with a second card for a combined interpretation. These two cards read together allow us to see new possible ways to see our question. Or at least to confirm that things are being seen clearly by the client.*

~ Hermit ~
• Isolation • Solitude • Separation •

Position #3 – Actions being taken

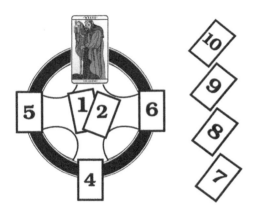

POSSIBLE INTERPRETATION: Other's influences may be a distraction at this time. Looking within self for planning future action is best. Isolation can be a calming space for you now. Clearing away disruption and delays.

Position #4 – Immediate Objectives

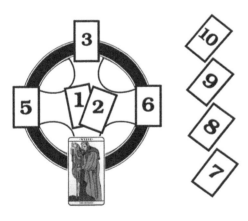

POSSIBLE INTERPRETATION: An environment of peace allows more to be done. Creating a peaceful environment. Clear and focused thinking is key for things to move forward. The seeker may feel surrounded by disruption at this time.

~ Hermit ~
• Isolation • Solitude • Separation •

Position #5 – An asset to the client

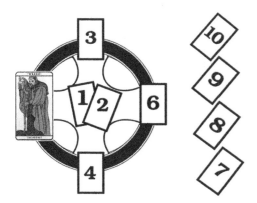 

POSSIBLE INTERPRETATION: Your knowledge on this idea sets you apart from others around you. Vision is your key. You are in a good position to see more than others around you. Share your knowledge selectively. Many others may not be ready to see your deep vision of this quest like you do.

Position #6 – An opportunity still to come

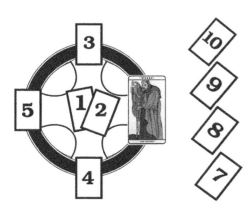 

POSSIBLE INTERPRETATION: Progress without assistance from others is possible. Opportunity for isolation can create a positive advance. Insight from a new source will come into play. Assets that were hidden now become available. Signs from a different source bring new direction not previously seen.

~ Hermit ~
• Isolation • Solitude • Separation •

Position #7 – Client's viewpoint

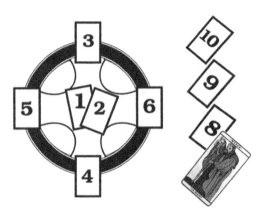 

POSSIBLE INTERPRETATION: The seeker feels they have inside information on this issue. Keeping things to themselves for now is wise. Your unique position on this issue is key. The seeker is on a higher plane than those around them. Not a time to share ideas with others. Seeing something others don't see.

Position #8 – When to take action

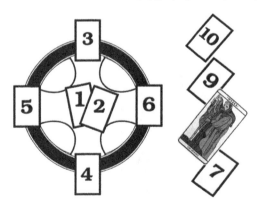 

POSSIBLE INTERPRETATION: A time to close out outside influences and look within for what is right for you. A look at your interest on this issue is what is key. Not the concerns of others involved. A need to follow your own feelings and not those of others. Your personal feelings on this quest are sharp at this time.

~ Hermit ~
• Isolation • Solitude • Separation •

Position #9 – The real purpose of this quest

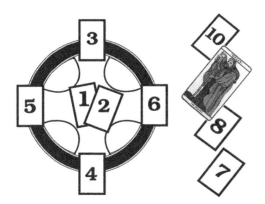 

POSSIBLE INTERPRETATION: I feel this quest will allow me to find peace and solitude. A place to think. Peaceful environment.

Position #10 – Closing remarks and finer details

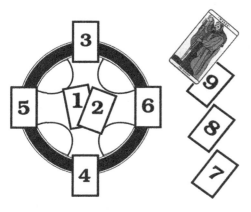 

POSSIBLE INTERPRETATION: This quest may leave you standing alone for awhile before success is final. Feedback from others might be scarce until substantial progress is made.

~ The Wheel of Fortune ~

The Wheel of Fortune X

Evolution is key to our progress. All things evolve as time goes on. The wheel keeps spinning. But it only spins in a forward direction. Not backwards. Things move forward in positive ways. The Wheel only turns forward.

~ The Wheel of Fortune ~
• Progress • Turning Point • In Motion •

Position #1 – The real question

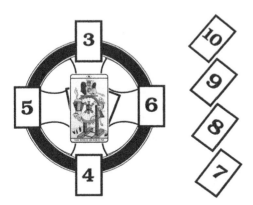 

POSSIBLE INTERPRETATION: Putting things in motion. Evolving situations could create promising situations for your quest. Necessary advancement is in motion. Luck is in your corner at this time. An evolving situation can stimulate a rearrangement of things. Stirring things up.

Position #2 – The real question cont'

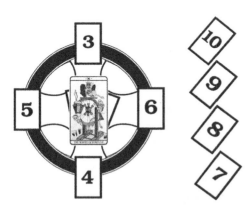 

Blended with Position #1: *This position is meant to compliment position 1. Position 1 & 2 are read together to see the question more in depth. Therefore the meaning remains the same as above and is blended together with a second card for a combined interpretation. These two cards read together allow us to see new possible ways to see our question. Or at least to confirm that things are being seen clearly by the client.*

~ The Wheel of Fortune ~
• Progress • Turning Point • In Motion •

Position #3 – Actions being taken

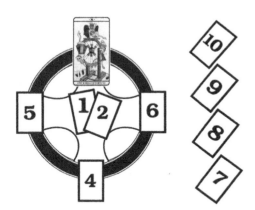 

POSSIBLE INTERPRETATION: Watching for what is in place to improve the issue. Opportunity will shift quickly. Watching when to grab it when it is right. Waiting for your luck to change is wise before moving on your quest. Waiting for shifts in the situation to your favor before proceeding.

Position #4 – Immediate Objectives

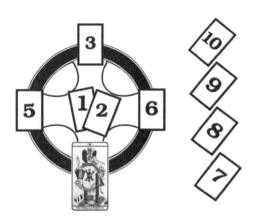 

POSSIBLE INTERPRETATION: Accepting the changes before us is key. Adjustments can be made for further progress on this endeavor. Making things compatible to the situation. Recognizing things will change in time. Dealing with the ever changing environment will be helpful to the cause.

~ The Wheel of Fortune ~
• Progress • Turning Point • In Motion •

Position #5 – An asset to the client

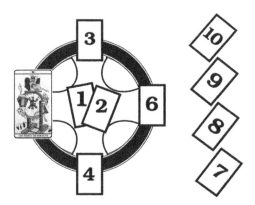 

POSSIBLE INTERPRETATION: You're in a good position to rearrange things in your favor. The ball will start rolling easily if you take the initiative. Rearranging priorities may be helpful at this time. You can turn things around in your favor. Cracking open new opportunities can be done at key times. A watchful eye is key at this time,

Position #6 – An opportunity still to come

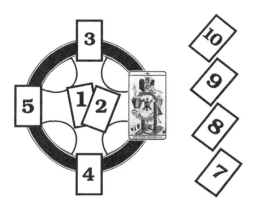 

POSSIBLE INTERPRETATION: An opportunity to shift things in your favor on this quest is coming. The wheels will soon be in motion towards progress. Luck comes your way if you keep moving on this quest. The ability to get things moving will come to pass. Keep it going once it starts showing itself.

~ The Wheel of Fortune ~
• Progress • Turning Point • In Motion •

Position #7 – Client's viewpoint

POSSIBLE INTERPRETATION: The seeker is seeing this quest as a goal that is ever changing. A time of significant improvement is seen by the client. A time to move things along is key. Success comes from adjusting a move to another position.

Position #8 – When to take action

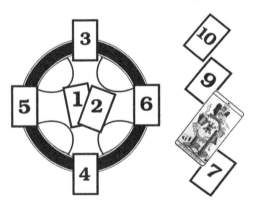 

POSSIBLE INTERPRETATION: This is a good time to put things in motion. Timing is key. A time to synchronize effort for all who are involved. Dates and schedules should be planned now. The time is now to act before situations change. Time slots are seen clearly if looked at.

~ The Wheel of Fortune ~
• Progress • Turning Point • In Motion •

Position #9 – The real purpose of this quest

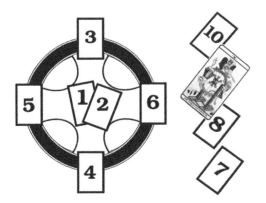 

POSSIBLE INTERPRETATION: This quest will allow the seeker to put themselves in a positive position. Advancement.

Position #10 – Closing remarks and finer details

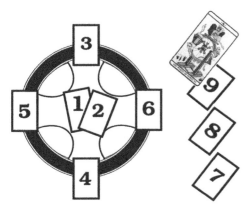 

POSSIBLE INTERPRETATION: Being in the right place at the right time seems likely on key issues in this quest. Lady Luck is on your side!

~ Strength ~

Strength XI

The Strength card shows the power of free-will. Reaching deep to grasp temptation and put it on hold can be done once we recognise the power we all have within us. This card represents an inner strength of will. Coming to grips with ourselves is seen in this card.

~ Strength ~
• A Good Position • Taking Hold • Strong-Willed •

Position #1 – The real question

POSSIBLE INTERPRETATION: Putting your self in a strong position will create a promising outcome. Self discipline is key and will influence others to follow. Focus and hone your strengths before you proceed. Preparation is key. Making ready would be wise.

Position #2 – The real question cont'

Blended with Position #1: *This position is meant to compliment position 1. Position 1 & 2 are read together to see the question more in depth. Therefore the meaning remains the same as above and is blended together with a second card for a combined interpretation. These two cards read together allow us to see new possible ways to see our question. Or at least to confirm that things are being seen clearly by the client.*

~ Strength ~
• A Good Position • Taking Hold • Strong-Willed •

Position #3 – Actions being taken

POSSIBLE INTERPRETATION: Strengthening your position for the challenges still to come is key. Putting yourself in a stronger position before acting on your quest. Understanding your challenge well will give you the strength needed to succeed.

Position #4 – Immediate Objectives

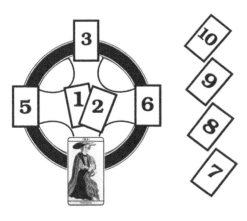 

POSSIBLE INTERPRETATION: A need to be in a stronger position on the issue at hand. Getting a better grip on the direction of this quest. A more influential stand needs to be established. A firm foothold is key before more can be done.

~ Strength ~
• A Good Position • Taking Hold • Strong-Willed •

Position #5 – An asset to the client

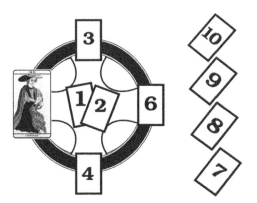 

POSSIBLE INTERPRETATION: Your position is strong. Use this strength to advance on things moving in your favor. Assert your influence when given the chance. Your strength is recognized by others and cooperation will come in time if you stay strong.

Position #6 – An opportunity still to come

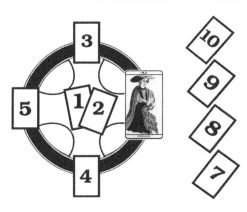 

POSSIBLE INTERPRETATION: You will be in a stronger position as you proceed. Compassionate but assertive actions help shape things in your favor,
An opportunity to use your means in an effective way will come. Your strength on this quest improves giving you motivation to advance.

~ Strength ~
• A Good Position • Taking Hold • Strong-Willed •

Position #7 – Client's viewpoint

POSSIBLE INTERPRETATION: The seeker sees themselves in a strong position on this quest. A feeling of control allows the seeker to make key changes in their life. In a good position to influence others. The seeker feels they are in a good position to succeed.

Position #8 – When to take action

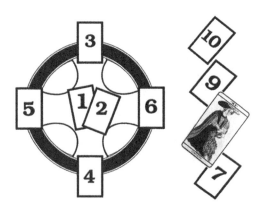 

POSSIBLE INTERPRETATION: You are in a strong position to act now. Move slow and steady and things will progress nicely. Gentle assertion will get you cooperation. Your hold on the issue is good for moving forward at this time.

~ Strength ~
• A Good Position • Taking Hold • Strong-Willed •

Position #9 – The real purpose of this quest

POSSIBLE INTERPRETATION: This quest will put the seeker in a stronger position than before. Efforts will pay off.

Position #10 – Closing remarks and finer details

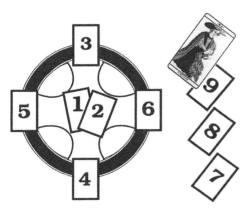 

POSSIBLE INTERPRETATION: Look for opportunities to strengthen your position as you move forward.

~ The Hanged Man ~

The Hanged Man XII

The Hanged Man shows how seeing things differently from others can put you in a difficult position. Keeping your focus during these challenging times can eventually allow others to see things the same as you. Standing up for a principle means facing the consequences. Standing firm on this issue can create consequences. In a state of limbo until things loosen up.

~ The Hanged Man ~
• Standing Alone • Reversal • Consequences •

Position #1 – The real question

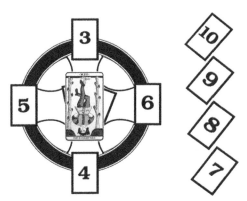

POSSIBLE INTERPRETATION: Putting yourself in a good position to see both sides of the question. A tilted perception of the issue will bring new light. Seeing other angles is key. A time of inaction. Observation is your best choice at this time. Wait for an opportunity to arise. Accepting what needs to be addressed.

Position #2 – The real question cont'

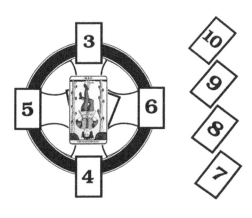

Blended with Position #1: *This position is meant to compliment position 1. Position 1 & 2 are read together to see the question more in depth. Therefore the meaning remains the same as above and is blended together with a second card for a combined interpretation. These two cards read together allow us to see new possible ways to see our question. Or at least to confirm that things are being seen clearly by the client.*

~ The Hanged Man ~
• Standing Alone • Reversal • Consequences •

Position #3 – Actions being taken

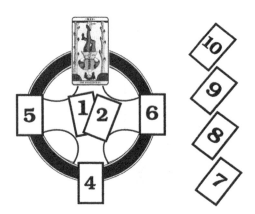 

POSSIBLE INTERPRETATION: Seeing all aspects before proceeding. Searching for what may be hidden before action is taken. Making a switch in your position before moving forward. Recently seeing things differently than before brings new insight.

Position #4 – Immediate Objectives

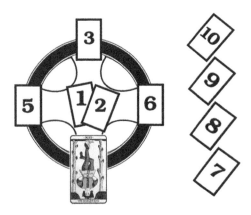 

POSSIBLE INTERPRETATION: Changing opinions on the current situation brings new light into the quest. Trying to see a new look at an old way of thinking. Shifting old actions into a different direction. A change of thinking creates a time of inaction until things become clearer. Inaction and biding your time.

~ The Hanged Man ~
• Standing Alone • Reversal • Consequences •

Position #5 – An asset to the client

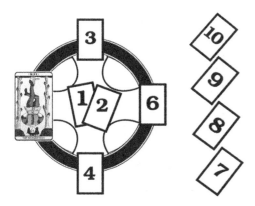 

POSSIBLE INTERPRETATION: You have time to think of how to shift things to be more in your favor. Take time to use what you know to figure new strategies. In a good place to see things differently than others do. View points not seen by others are seen by you clearly.

Position #6 – An opportunity still to come

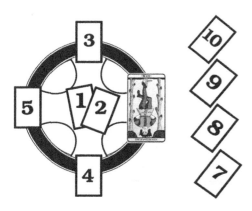 

POSSIBLE INTERPRETATION: A reversal in your environment will give you a glimpse of new insight to take advantage of. A time of standing alone on this issue will bring you the opportunity to lead others in time. Seeing things from a different angle shows new awareness on your quest. Sacrifices and perseverance start to pay off.

~ The Hanged Man ~
• Standing Alone • Reversal • Consequences •

Position #7 – Client's viewpoint

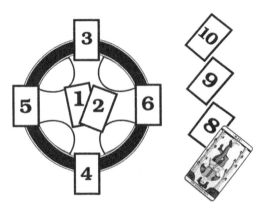 

POSSIBLE INTERPRETATION: The seeker is seeing things in limbo. Not moving because of blocks in the way. Action is limited. Hoping for things to change. Restrictions hold you back. Eventually things will loosen up and movement on this quest will be accomplished easier than the present time allows.

Position #8 – When to take action

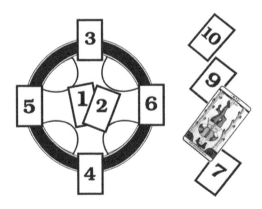 

POSSIBLE INTERPRETATION: Moving at this time may be difficult. Things are restricted making it hard to change in your favor. A good time to observe and not make big moves for now. Seeing other options could be beneficial to you.

~ The Hanged Man ~
• Standing Alone • Reversal • Consequences •

Position #9 – The real purpose of this quest

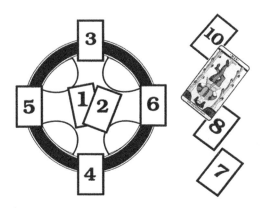 

POSSIBLE INTERPRETATION: This quest will allow the seeker to prove a point of importance.

Position #10 – Closing remarks and finer details

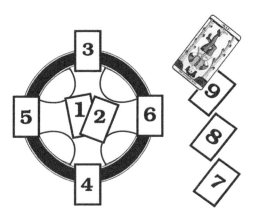 

POSSIBLE INTERPRETATION: Be prepared to be put into uncomfortable positions as you move forward on this quest.

~ Death ~

Death XIII

Death is seen today as things changing. Sweeping away what is seen as clutter around your quest is wise. Some things must pass to bring in a better situation. Nothing remains the same forever. A cleansing of the old to bring in the new is key. Sometimes this is seen as a radical change that needs to be made in order to succeed.

~ Death ~
• Major Shift • Cleansing • Elimination •

Position #1 – The real question

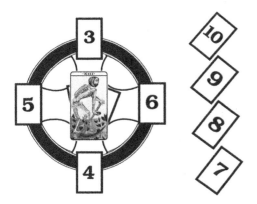

POSSIBLE INTERPRETATION: A time of major transformation. Harvesting away old energy to bring in the new. Big changes will be to your advantage in time. Sweeping changes are necessary for a better position to take hold.

Position #2 – The real question cont'

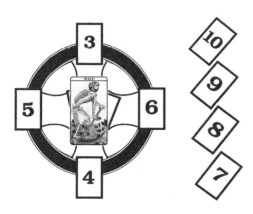

Blended with Position #1: *This position is meant to compliment position 1. Position 1 & 2 are read together to see the question more in depth. Therefore the meaning remains the same as above and is blended together with a second card for a combined interpretation. These two cards read together allow us to see new possible ways to see our question. Or at least to confirm that things are being seen clearly by the client.*

~ Death ~
• Major Shift • Cleansing • Elimination •

Position #3 – Actions being taken

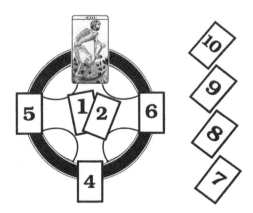

POSSIBLE INTERPRETATION: Wanting to make major changes before moving forward. Sweeping away unnecessary baggage before proceeding further.
Efforts being made for a fresh start. Cleaning the slate for a better position on your quest.

Position #4 – Immediate Objectives

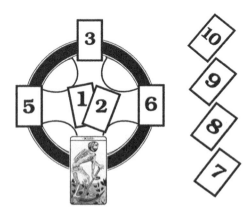

POSSIBLE INTERPRETATION: Cleaning house. Old energy becomes baggage that can slow your progress down. Clearing out confusing energy.
Less is better at this time. Simplifying the quest's initial objectives will be beneficial. Focus on first-things-first goals.

~ Death ~
• Major Shift • Cleansing • Elimination •

Position #5 – An asset to the client

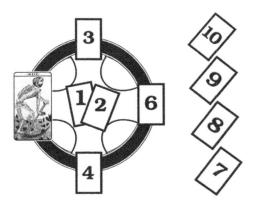 

POSSIBLE INTERPRETATION: You are in a good place to make major shifts in your environment. Nothing is stopping you from making big changes toward this issue. Your influence is undeniable. Inevitable conclusions will be accepted in your favor if you act.

Position #6 – An opportunity still to come

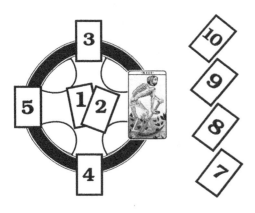 

POSSIBLE INTERPRETATION: Opportunity for major changes are near! Reaping what you've sown is coming. Your influence on others is inevitable.
Things will change without your influence. The shift is the end of a major cycle. You will have the opportunity to eliminate what is not needed.

~ Death ~
• Major Shift • Cleansing • Elimination •

Position #7 – Client's viewpoint

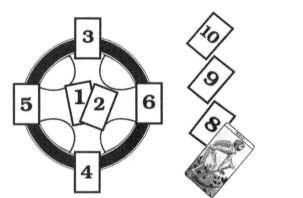 

POSSIBLE INTERPRETATION: The seeker is seeing this issue as a major change. Take advantage of transformations at this time and shift them to your advantage. Concern about what will be is key. A time of transition. A whole new world awaits the client. Go with the flow and enjoy the ride!

Position #8 – When to take action

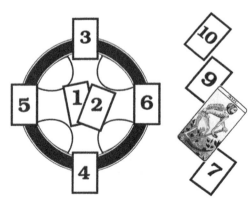 

POSSIBLE INTERPRETATION: A time of sweeping changes that are easy to get caught up in may rush you along. Stay up with the changes at present but move at your own pace. Many changes in many different directions may cause confusion. Not a good time for making guesses on actions to take. Slow movement is best for now. A time of big changes allows you to act on your quest unnoticed.

~ Death ~
• Major Shift • Cleansing • Elimination •

Position #9 – The real purpose of this quest

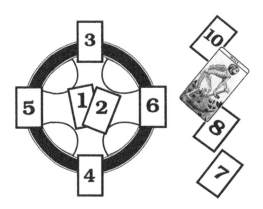 

POSSIBLE INTERPRETATION: This quest will allow the seeker to change their life in significant ways. Look for opportunities to make sweeping transitions and eliminating old baggage.

Position #10 – Closing remarks and finer details

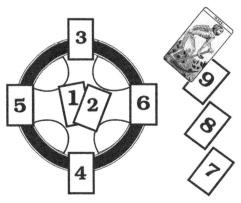 

POSSIBLE INTERPRETATION: More changes than you anticipated can result from this endeavor.

~ Temperance ~

Temperance XIIII

Temperance is a major force of inspiration on your quest. The feeling that nothing will get in the way that can't be rectified. The unquenchable thirst driving you forward is seen in this powerful card. Trying to keep things balanced as you pursue your quest without ignoring other responsibilities can be challenging but is seen as a key factor in Temperance.

~ Temperance ~
• Vibrant Energy • Guiding Force • Higher Sources •

Position #1 – The real question

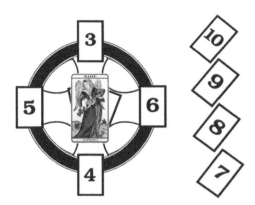 

POSSIBLE INTERPRETATION: The seeker is inspired by the quest. A quest from the heart is a key strength. Inspiration can be contagious and the seeker can be influential to support from others. A energy that is catchy!

A shift of balance. Influential to others involved. A cause that benefits others as well as the client. Peaceful transactions with good harmony.

Position #2 – The real question cont'

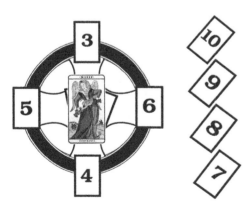 

Blended with Position #1: *This position is meant to compliment position 1. Position 1 & 2 are read together to see the question more in depth. Therefore the meaning remains the same as above and is blended together with a second card for a combined interpretation. These two cards read together allow us to see new possible ways to see our question. Or at least to confirm that things are being seen clearly by the client.*

~ Temperance ~
• Vibrant Energy • Guiding Force • Higher Sources •

Position #3 – Actions being taken

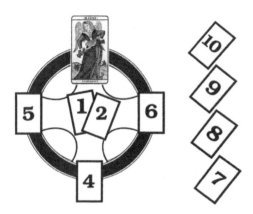

POSSIBLE INTERPRETATION: Perfect balance of energy will bring positive results. Good focus for better movement. Seek a strong foothold on what needs to be accomplished before taking the first step.

Position #4 – Immediate Objectives

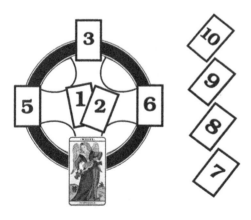

POSSIBLE INTERPRETATION: Trying to get others inspired about your quest. Attempting to get motivated on resolving the challenge at hand. Moving on this quest creates excitement in others involved. Create motivation by showing a balanced path to this journey.

~ Temperance ~
• Vibrant Energy • Guiding Force • Higher Sources •

Position #5 – An asset to the client

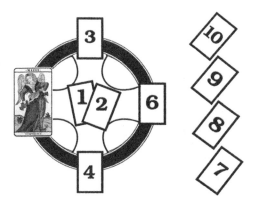 

POSSIBLE INTERPRETATION: You have the ability to inspire others about your quest. Share your ideas and enthusiasm. Your inspiration is insatiable once things start moving on this quest. Your quest is well grounded with dream like possibilities.

Position #6 – An opportunity still to come

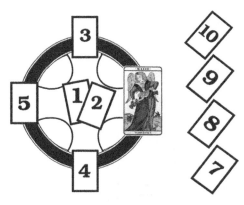 

POSSIBLE INTERPRETATION: Sharing your quest with others will be accepted well, Your ideas will be viewed as special if you share them soon. Exchange of ideas brings good results. Time to hone and balance your priorities. Opportunities will become available to you soon that allow you to heighten expectations quickly.

~ Temperance ~
• Vibrant Energy • Guiding Force • Higher Sources •

Position #7 – Client's viewpoint

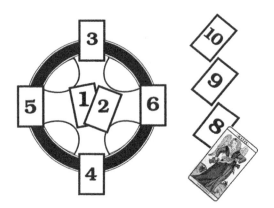 

POSSIBLE INTERPRETATION: The client is inspired by this quest. Looking at this issue clearly and with scepticism is wise before proceeding. The client's desires may be clouding what is real. Staying true to the quest is an unwavering strength of the seeker. Seeing this issue from a higher level may bring new insight into the quest.

Position #8 – When to take action

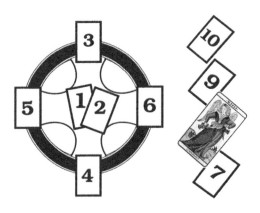 

POSSIBLE INTERPRETATION: Things move freely now. Take advantage of all things fitting into place nicely. Smooth transactions are possible at this time.
Take advantage of the positive energy that is in place on this issue to make big changes in your favor.

~ Temperance ~
• Vibrant Energy • Guiding Force • Higher Sources •

Position #9 – The real purpose of this quest

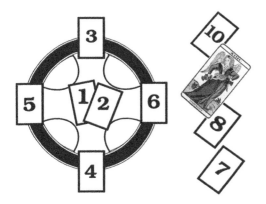 

POSSIBLE INTERPRETATION: I feel this quest will give me inspiration. To be inspired in something I truly believe in.

Position #10 – Closing remarks and finer details

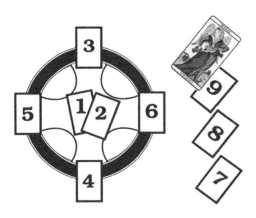 

POSSIBLE INTERPRETATION: Good balance on the issue is key as you proceed. Opportunities to make the peace will develop as you move forward.

~ The Devil ~

The Devil XV

The Devil is in all of us to some extent. Self doubt. Denial. Low self esteem. Clinging to superficial values can delay your progress. Not facing truths can become harmful. These things can all be eliminated if we choose to let them go.

~ The Devil ~
• Denial • Negative Influences • Obsessions •

Position #1 – The real question

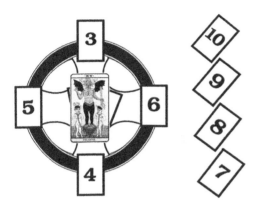 

POSSIBLE INTERPRETATION: Self doubt causes inability to act. Procrastination and excuses can become setbacks. A time to address delays in moving forward. False fears, denial. Self limitations can be limiting yourself from your quest. Dark thinking can cause despair. Surrounding yourself in negative energy can be harmful to your pursuits of real happiness.

Position #2 – The real question cont'

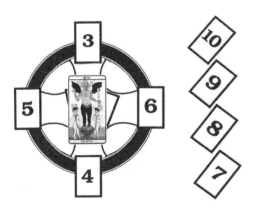 

Blended with Position #1: *This position is meant to compliment position 1. Position 1 & 2 are read together to see the question more in depth. Therefore the meaning remains the same as above and is blended together with a second card for a combined interpretation. These two cards read together allow us to see new possible ways to see our question. Or at least to confirm that things are being seen clearly by the client.*

~ The Devil ~
• Denial • Negative Influences • Obsessions •

Position #3 – Actions being taken

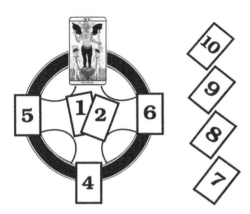

POSSIBLE INTERPRETATION: Clearing up any negativity before moving forward allows for less confusion down the road. Dealing with things that are being avoided is wise at this time. Self defeating issues are understood. Striving to be an example of clear vision on your quest. No hidden agendas.

Position #4 – Immediate Objectives

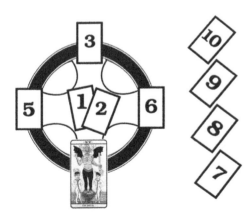

POSSIBLE INTERPRETATION: Recognizing the down side of this quest and measuring the consequences. Getting rid of false dependencies is key.
Dealing with negative limitations. Freeing up bondage and unnecessary restrictions.

~ The Devil ~
• Denial • Negative Influences • Obsessions •

Position #5 – An asset to the client

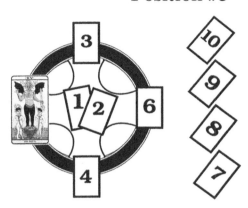

POSSIBLE INTERPRETATION: Outside negative influences have no effect on you. You are not in self denial on this issue. You detect insincerity immediately on this issue. You have the ability to overcome any negative influences on this issue. Be wary of procrastination. You may feel dependant on others to succeed on this quest. Having no fcar is key.

Position #6 – An opportunity still to come

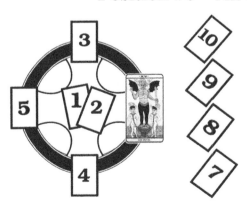

POSSIBLE INTERPRETATION: This particular time may bring thoughts of self doubt. Earlier set backs may haunt you. This is a great time to test your own resolve and strengthen your position. Pass these tests and nothing will stop your success. Facing a challenging time. False fears can set you back. Opportunity will come to shed light on lingering weaknesses.

~ The Devil ~
• Denial • Negative Influences • Obsessions •

Position #7 – Client's viewpoint

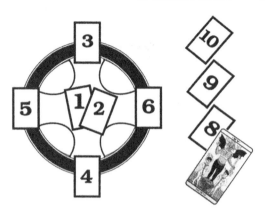

POSSIBLE INTERPRETATION: A release of bondage is key. The client may be seeing this issue as a dark influence on them. This influence is only there by their choice and can be released. A fear of moving forward. Fear of failure can hinder wonderful accomplishments. Self esteem on this issue may be low.

Position #8 – When to take action

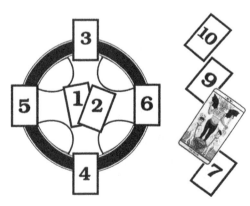

POSSIBLE INTERPRETATION: Much still needs to be understood. Limits are not allowing all to be seen at this time. Points of view need to be explained more clearly. Many good possibilities but more needs to be seen before commitments are made. A time to release self inflicted limitations and improve confidence. Wait for a more strategic time to act.

~ The Devil ~
• Denial • Negative Influences • Obsessions •

Position #9 – The real purpose of this quest

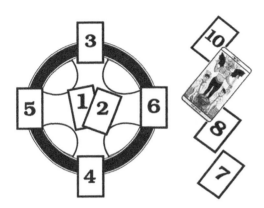 

POSSIBLE INTERPRETATION: I feel this quest will allow me to better myself. Gained willpower to challenge inner conflicts.

Position #10 – Closing remarks and finer details

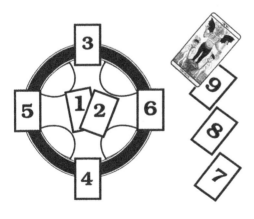 

POSSIBLE INTERPRETATION: Challenges not known to you yet may arise as you move forward.

~ The Tower ~

The Tower XVI

The Tower card shows us disruption. Delays happen and making ready for them is wise. Preparation will pay off before things happen. Unexpected challenges can be met head on if you watch for them. Waiting out the storm is wise.

~ The Tower ~
• Rude Awakenings • Abrupt Changes • Disruption •

Position #1 – The real question

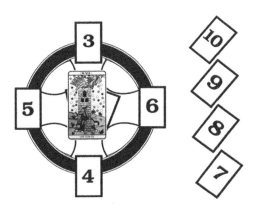

POSSIBLE INTERPRETATION: Disruption can cause delays and confusion.
Be prepared to ride out the storm. Don't be discouraged by setbacks.
A major bump in the road. This too shall pass. Not a good time to make big moves.
Dealing with challenging times.

Position #2 – The real question cont'

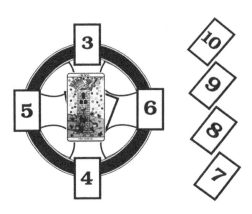

Blended with Position #1: *This position is meant to compliment position 1. Position 1 & 2 are read together to see the question more in depth. Therefore the meaning remains the same as above and is blended together with a second card for a combined interpretation. These two cards read together allow us to see new possible ways to see our question. Or at least to confirm that things are being seen clearly by the client.*

~ The Tower ~
• Rude Awakenings • Abrupt Changes • Disruption •

Position #3 – Actions being taken

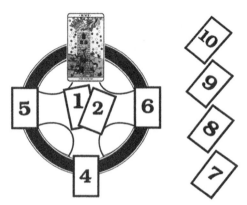 

POSSIBLE INTERPRETATION: Preparing for any worst case scenarios that may occur. Safe guarding against any disruptions still to come is wise. Being prepared for the worst but expecting the best. Considering all the consequences before moving forward on this quest.

Position #4 – Immediate Objectives

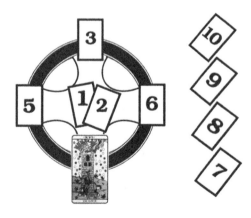 

POSSIBLE INTERPRETATION: Meeting disruptions head on. Ironing out the delays and setbacks. Resolving threatening issues that can diminish the success of this quest is key. Quick action is key before things become out of hand. Take care of problems before they start.

~ The Tower ~
• Rude Awakenings • Abrupt Changes • Disruption •

Position #5 – An asset to the client

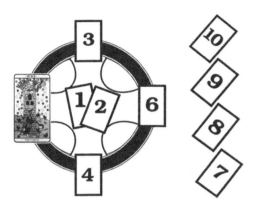 

POSSIBLE INTERPRETATION: Being well prepared to take on challenges would be wise. Your ability to make snap judgment calls is sharp.
Be prepared to ride out the storm. Don't be discouraged by setbacks. Your confidence will keep you on track. Staying focused is key.

Position #6 – An opportunity still to come

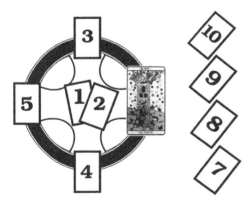 

POSSIBLE INTERPRETATION: A time to test what you're up against can bring great advancement onto your quest. Riding out the storm might be in the near future. Being prepared to take on new and surprising challenges that may occur would be wise.

~ The Tower ~
• Rude Awakenings • Abrupt Changes • Disruption •

Position #7 – Client's viewpoint

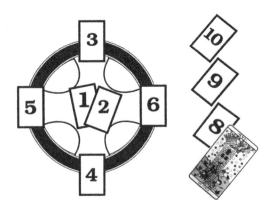 

POSSIBLE INTERPRETATION: Disruption is key. The seeker may be seeing this issue as being vulnerable. Repercussions are feared.
Fear creates inaction. Concerns that the consequences will be high if this path is taken. Clear thinking will bring solutions to this challenge.

Position #8 – When to take action

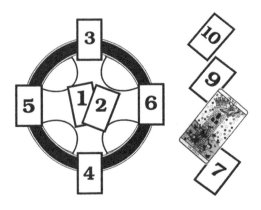 

POSSIBLE INTERPRETATION: A time to lay low and wait for the dust to settle. Let things settle down before you make moves. A time to wait for better days to come. A time to correct wrong directions into more accurate routes.
Improvement need to be made before action is taken. A time to try to keep things stable and calm.

~ The Tower ~
• Rude Awakenings • Abrupt Changes • Disruption •

Position #9 – The real purpose of this quest

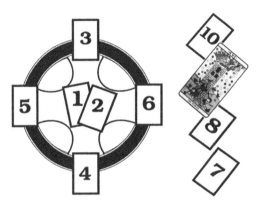 

POSSIBLE INTERPRETATION: This quest will allow the seeker to take on challenges that have disrupted their life. Be prepared for unexpected challenges as you proceed.

Position #10 – Closing remarks and finer details

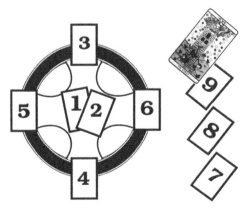 

POSSIBLE INTERPRETATION: Tearing down old ways too quickly can result in more than you anticipated.

~ The Star ~

The Star XVII

The Star card shows us a sense of direction. Our path becomes clear. Following our own shining star is now in sight. Look and you will see your path clearly. Then it's just a matter of taking the steps forward to follow your quest. Aimless direction is now eliminated.

~ The Star ~
• Guiding Light • New Hope • On Course •

Position #1 – The real question

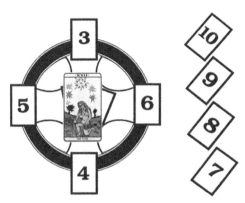 

POSSIBLE INTERPRETATION: A clear direction is seen on your quest. Clear itinerary of steps that need to be taken for success. A path is near if you seek it out. Keep your focus on the real purpose of your quest and follow it well.

Position #2 – The real question cont'

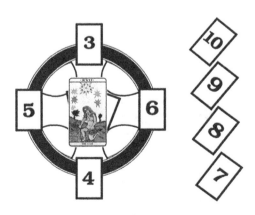 

Blended with Position #1: *This position is meant to compliment position 1. Position 1 & 2 are read together to see the question more in depth. Therefore the meaning remains the same as above and is blended together with a second card for a combined interpretation. These two cards read together allow us to see new possible ways to see our question. Or at least to confirm that things are being seen clearly by the client.*

~ The Star ~
• Guiding Light • New Hope • On Course •

Position #3 – Actions being taken

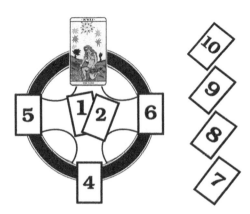 

POSSIBLE INTERPRETATION: Seeking clear direction before proceeding.
Knowing exactly where you are going before starting your journey is key.
Keeping an eye out for your guiding star. Looking for direction on your quest.

Position #4 – Immediate Objectives

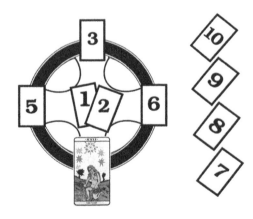 

POSSIBLE INTERPRETATION: Establishing a focused set of goals.
Clear and efficient set of plans need to be put in place before proceeding.
Staying focused on the finished objective. Not getting distracted with other issues.
Creating a well planned itinerary.

~ The Star ~
• Guiding Light • New Hope • On Course •

Position #5 – An asset to the client

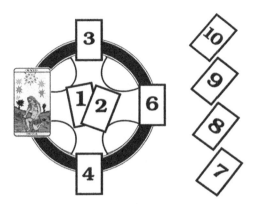 

POSSIBLE INTERPRETATION: You have clear insight on the goals you want to accomplish. You see clearly what you want to attain. Clear paths are seen by you easily on this quest. Keep your vision alive. It is a worthwhile quest.

Position #6 – An opportunity still to come

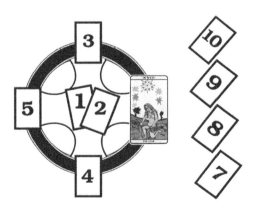 

POSSIBLE INTERPRETATION: Answers are found! New direction with clear insight is seen. The end is in sight. New hope comes into the picture for those who can see it. Keep your eyes open for good news to come your way. A shining star is coming!

~ The Star ~
• Guiding Light • New Hope • On Course •

Position #7 – Client's viewpoint

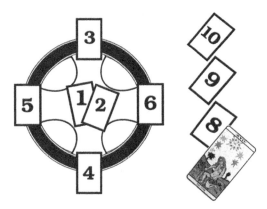 

POSSIBLE INTERPRETATION: The seeker is seeing the quest is in sight.
The client likes the direction this endeavor is going. Vision is strong.
Staying focused and on track is key. Enthusiasm is strong and distraction can be a weakness at this time. Staying on course is wise.

Position #8 – When to take action

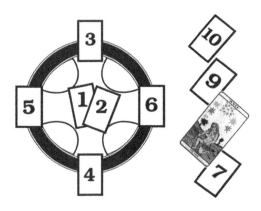 

POSSIBLE INTERPRETATION: A good time to take the path seen most clearly.
Good progress can be made on the path that makes itself the clearest.
A time of new hope is close. Watch for turns in your favor to come.

~ The Star ~
• Guiding Light • New Hope • On Course •

Position #9 – The real purpose of this quest

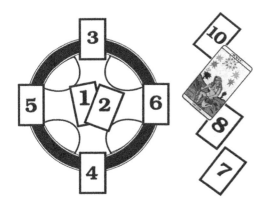 

POSSIBLE INTERPRETATION: This quest will allow the seeker to find a sense of hope and direction.

Position #10 – Closing remarks and finer details

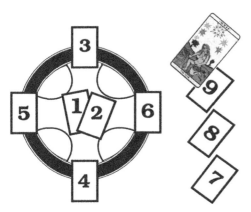 

POSSIBLE INTERPRETATION: Your plans seem to stay on course throughout until completion. More details will appear as you get closer to your quest.

~ The Moon ~

The Moon XVIII

The Moon card is seen in many different ways from good to bad. The moon cast an illusion of light but the light is only a reflection from the sun. The Moon card can represent mystery on your quest. Sure footed steps are wise. Things not seen clearly. Illusion shifts our perception of what is seen before our eyes. Intriguing mystery is always a curiosity.

~ The Moon ~
• Vague Strategy • Unknown Direction • Intrique •

Position #1 – The real question

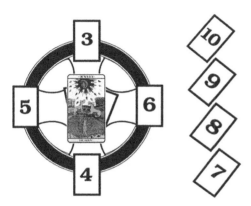 

POSSIBLE INTERPRETATION: Mysterious territory. Not all answers are seen clearly at this time. Move forward with caution. New opportunity is still to be found once more light is with you. Enjoy the not knowing and the mystery of this experience. The path will be clear in time.

Position #2 – The real question cont'

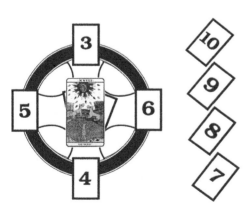 

Blended with Position #1: *This position is meant to compliment position 1. Position 1 & 2 are read together to see the question more in depth. Therefore the meaning remains the same as above and is blended together with a second card for a combined interpretation. These two cards read together allow us to see new possible ways to see our question. Or at least to confirm that things are being seen clearly by the client.*

~ The Moon ~
• Vague Strategy • Unknown Direction • Intrique •

Position #3 – Actions being taken

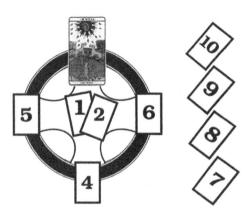

POSSIBLE INTERPRETATION: Exploring the possibilities! Many things still to be known before advancing on this exciting quest. Mystery still prevails.
The path is not well lit and progress moves slowly at this time. A promising quest still has much to be known.

Position #4 – Immediate Objectives

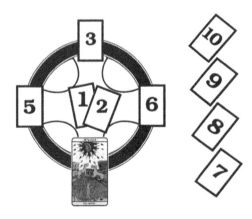

POSSIBLE INTERPRETATION: Putting more light into the direction this quest is going. Finding answers not yet seen is key. Feeling your way through for better direction and planning. Much is still not known. Putting key factors in place that are still not available.

~ The Moon ~
• Vague Strategy • Unknown Direction • Intrigue •

Position #5 – An asset to the client

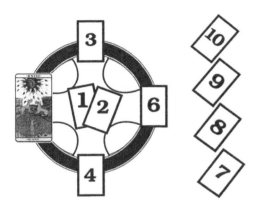 

POSSIBLE INTERPRETATION: Sure footed steps are taken carefully by you. Caution is key as you proceed. Mystery awaits your curiosity. No fear as you move into uncharted territory. Your intrigue allows you to discover new insight on your quest.

Position #6 – An opportunity still to come

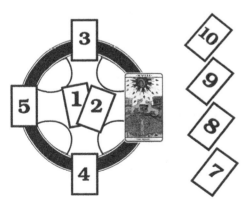 

POSSIBLE INTERPRETATION: Uncovering unanswered questions about your quest. Slow but steady progress is possible if done carefully. An opportunity to uncover new treasures not seen before. Move slowly and keep your eyes open for hidden jewels of opportunity.

~ The Moon ~
• Vague Strategy • Unknown Direction • Intrique •

Position #7 – Client's viewpoint

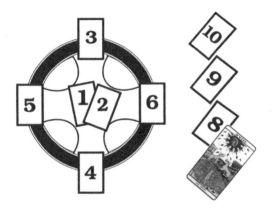 

POSSIBLE INTERPRETATION: The client may not be seeing everything involved at this time. Curiosity is strong. Caution is key. Mystery of the situation may be intriguing. The devil is in the details. Looking closely before proceeding might be a wise choice.

Position #8 – When to take action

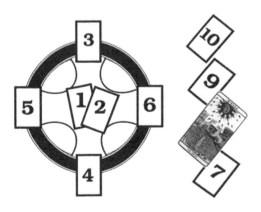 

POSSIBLE INTERPRETATION: A time to look at where you are exactly on your quest. A time to set an itinerary in place. A good time to observe what is around you and where you stand right now before moving in any direction.

~ The Moon ~
• Vague Strategy • Unknown Direction • Intrique •

Position #9 – The real purpose of this quest

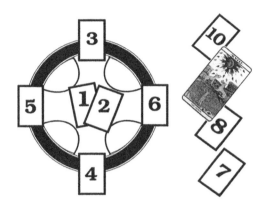 

POSSIBLE INTERPRETATION: This quest will allow the seeker to fully explore a mystery of interest that has been close to their heart for a long time.

Position #10 – Closing remarks and finer details

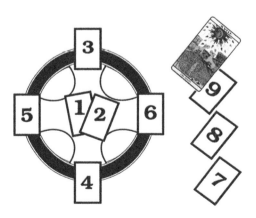 

POSSIBLE INTERPRETATION: Be prepared for progress to move slowly. Direction might become vague at times on your quest. Don't change course when feelings become unsure.

~ The Sun ~

The Sun XVIIII

The Sun cards show us in a nurturing position. Growth, warmth and solace are forces seen in this card. The life giving light of the sun can be measured in many ways. This card puts us in a good space.

~ The Sun ~
• Nurturing Environment • Comfort • Growing •

Position #1 – The real question

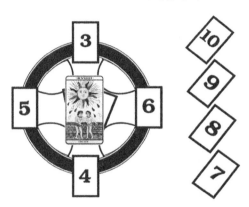 

POSSIBLE INTERPRETATION: You are in a good position with your quest. Nurturing situation with others can be accomplished. Growth and abundance. Comfort and solace. This journey is clearly seen. An important step is in play for growth at this time.

Position #2 – The real question cont'

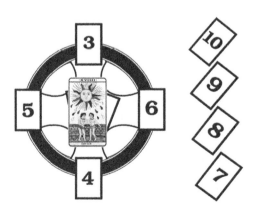 

Blended with Position #1: *This position is meant to compliment position 1. Position 1 & 2 are read together to see the question more in depth. Therefore the meaning remains the same as above and is blended together with a second card for a combined interpretation. These two cards read together allow us to see new possible ways to see our question. Or at least to confirm that things are being seen clearly by the client.*

~ The Sun ~
• Nurturing Environment • Comfort • Growing •

Position #3 – Actions being taken

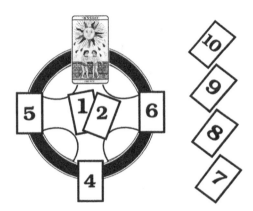

POSSIBLE INTERPRETATION: Putting yourself in a good position before action is taken. Attempting to shed more light on this subject before decisions are made. A nurturing space for expanding the horizons is wise before proceeding further. Growth will happen quickly once you proceed if all is in order.

Position #4 – Immediate Objectives

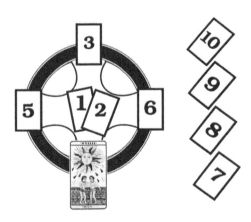

POSSIBLE INTERPRETATION: A need to put more light on the subject. Being in a well exposed position when things are in motion will allow others to see more. More direct exposure to the situation needs to be established. Being in the right places at the right time is key.

~ The Sun ~
• Nurturing Environment • Comfort • Growing •

Position #5 – An asset to the client

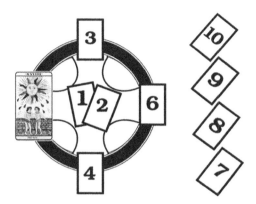

POSSIBLE INTERPRETATION: You generate positive light around this issue that is catchy to others. The position you are in allows growth on the issue,
Things will eventually grow in time if you keep on track and don't give up. The situation is good for growth.

Position #6 – An opportunity still to come

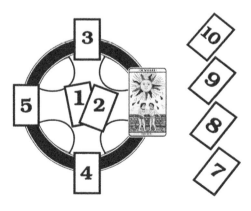

POSSIBLE INTERPRETATION: New light will be shed on your quest. Things fall into place. Stay exposed on your quest to others around you. Being in the open and "out there" will bring new life to your endeavor. Warm response from others will be found.

~ The Sun ~
• Nurturing Environment • Comfort • Growing •

Position #7 – Client's viewpoint

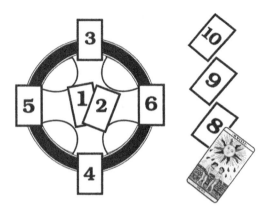 

POSSIBLE INTERPRETATION: The client may feel optimistic about the situation. Positive thinking has advantages on this quest. The seeker may feel they are on a wonderful journey. The clear and well lit direction shows this quest looks promising.

Position #8 – When to take action

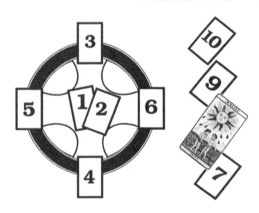 

POSSIBLE INTERPRETATION: Easy movement at this time. A good time to take advantage of the light shining on you. Good progress can be seen at this time if you act. A warm and safe energy surrounds you allowing easy progress at this time.

~ The Sun ~
• Nurturing Environment • Comfort • Growing •

Position #9 – The real purpose of this quest

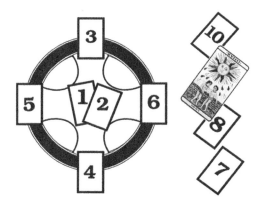 

POSSIBLE INTERPRETATION: This quest will allow the seeker to create a more nurturing lifestyle. Doing what truly makes the seeker happy.

Position #10 – Closing remarks and finer details

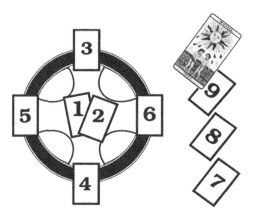 

POSSIBLE INTERPRETATION: Your quest looks promising as the days go by. Good progress by the summer.

~ Judgement ~

Judgement XX

The Judgement card shows a new level of understanding. Judgment from a higher source. All things will be seen clearly in the end. Nothing is overseen. Authority of the highest level will oversee what is relevant with the energy of Judgment XX.

~ Judgement ~
• Resurrection • New Understanding • Evaluation •

Position #1 – The real question

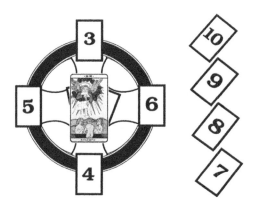 

POSSIBLE INTERPRETATION: Close evaluation of the situation is key. Weighing out all options is wise. Judging what is real and what isn't. Others will judge you on this quest. Be true to self and others will be true to you as well. Good judgment and support from others is feasible on this issue.

Position #2 – The real question cont'

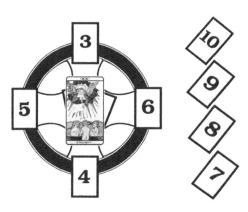 

Blended with Position #1: *This position is meant to compliment position 1. Position 1 & 2 are read together to see the question more in depth. Therefore the meaning remains the same as above and is blended together with a second card for a combined interpretation. These two cards read together allow us to see new possible ways to see our question. Or at least to confirm that things are being seen clearly by the client.*

~ Judgement ~
• Resurrection • New Understanding • Evaluation •

Position #3 – Actions being taken

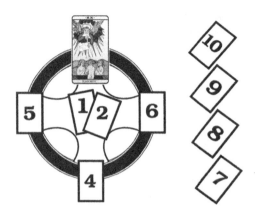 

POSSIBLE INTERPRETATION: Weighing out all the facts before proceeding. Sound judgment is key on this issue. Concern how others will judge the seeker could be an unnecessary concern. Don't judge yourself too harshly on your ability for this quest.

Position #4 – Immediate Objectives

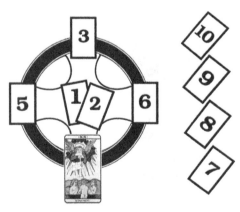 

POSSIBLE INTERPRETATION: Calling attention from others to consider this promising quest. Encourage others to judge this quest and share opinions.
A time for all to look at the feasibility of this matter. Measuring out both sides of the matter is advised before going further.

~ Judgement ~
• Resurrection • New Understanding • Evaluation •

Position #5 – An asset to the client

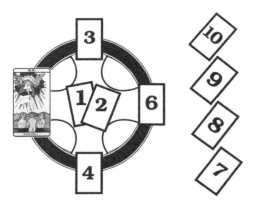 

POSSIBLE INTERPRETATION: Your judgment on this quest is sound. Good insight into what you are attempting to accomplish. Being open to reevaluating small details can refine the quest into a better situation. Judging what others cannot see yet can be a key asset.

Position #6 – An opportunity still to come

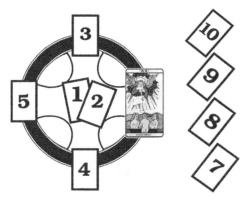 

POSSIBLE INTERPRETATION: Positive recognition is in your favor as you move forward. A sound judgment on your quest makes things move smoothly.
Sharing your progress and ideas will bring good results in the future. Keeping things open for judgment of others is key.

~ Judgement ~
• Resurrection • New Understanding • Evaluation •

Position #7 – Client's viewpoint

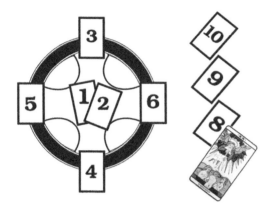 

POSSIBLE INTERPRETATION: A time to make sound judgment is key. Careful evaluation is wise. Seeing all aspects on this journey will take away any surprises. Unbiased opinions from others might be wise. A clear vision of the end result will be beneficial.

Position #8 – When to take action

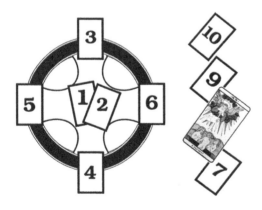 

POSSIBLE INTERPRETATION: Things fall your way for action to begin. Your quest is seen favorably by others who give good support. A time to judge actions carefully before moving forward. Actions taken with sound judgment will pay off.

~ Judgement ~
• Resurrection • New Understanding • Evaluation •

Position #9 – The real purpose of this quest

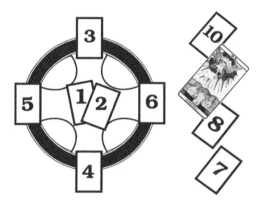

POSSIBLE INTERPRETATION: This quest will allow the seeker to be recognized. A rewarding accomplishment that is praised by others.

Position #10 – Closing remarks and finer details

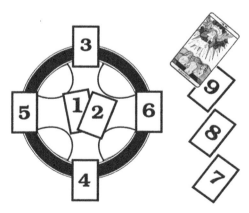

POSSIBLE INTERPRETATION: Judgment will be in your favor in the end. Be prepared to explain your actions to others of importance on this quest.

~ The World ~

The World XXI

The World card shows things come together in perfect harmony. A very positive conclusion to life's journey. This card can signify a completion. In the end all things seem to come together nicely. Perfect balance in all aspects of a quest is seen in The World card. The dance of life is done well.

~ The World ~
• Accomplished • Celebration • Happiness •

Position #1 – The real question

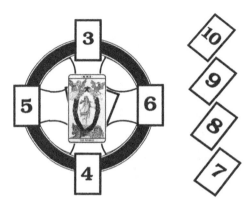 

POSSIBLE INTERPRETATION: Reaping the rewards of a job well done. Happiness at the end of this journey. No regrets. A happy ending from your efforts will be celebrated by others. Positive recognition from others if this quest is pursued.

Position #2 – The real question cont'

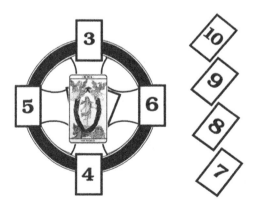 

Blended with Position #1: *This position is meant to compliment position 1. Position 1 & 2 are read together to see the question more in depth. Therefore the meaning remains the same as above and is blended together with a second card for a combined interpretation. These two cards read together allow us to see new possible ways to see our question. Or at least to confirm that things are being seen clearly by the client.*

~ The World ~
• Accomplished • Celebration • Happiness •

Position #3 – Actions being taken

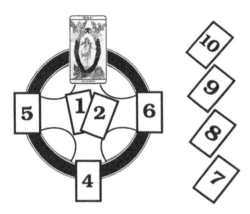

POSSIBLE INTERPRETATION: Putting yourself in the perfect scenario before moving on this quest. Patience is key to a perfect situation. Good ideas take time to manifest into realities. Finding the perfect time to finish this endeavor could be your challenge once all is in motion.

Position #4 – Immediate Objectives

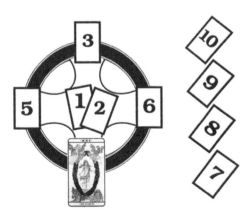

POSSIBLE INTERPRETATION: The seeker truly feels this quest is a perfect scenario. Confirm this thinking by sharing your ideas with others involved.
A time of celebration. Traveling through this journey can be shared by all involved in positive ways if done correctly. The right team for success is key.

~ The World ~
• Accomplished • Celebration • Happiness •

Position #5 – An asset to the client

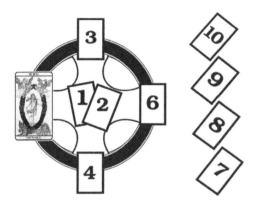

POSSIBLE INTERPRETATION: Optimism creates excitement from others around you. Completion is something others want as well as you. Shared interest will create a happy environment making it a joyous journey for all. Express your talents. Others will share in your energy making the quest more powerful.

Position #6 – An opportunity still to come

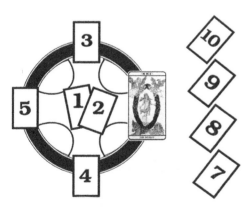

POSSIBLE INTERPRETATION: An opportunity to look back at positive progress made for all involved on this quest. Optimism will be seen soon.
Taking hold of the positive aspects and celebrating how far you have come to this point helps your chances of future success,

~ The World ~
• Accomplished • Celebration • Happiness •

Position #7 – Client's viewpoint

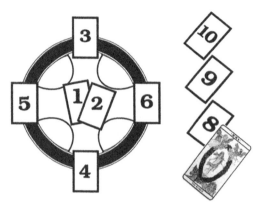 

POSSIBLE INTERPRETATION: The client is seeing every thing coming together nicely. Celebration to a positive direction on the quest at hand. The seeker is in a happy space when looking at the possibilities. This attitude is a strength that will go far!

Position #8 – When to take action

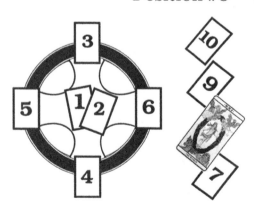 

POSSIBLE INTERPRETATION: Actions taken will bring positive results at this time. A time to dance to your quest. Happy advancement with no resistance.
A vision of your quest allows you to see the end result as positive. A time to follow your dreams. You deserve it!

~ The World ~
• Accomplished • Celebration • Happiness •

Position #9 – The real purpose of this quest

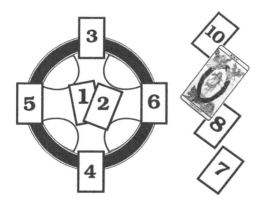 

POSSIBLE INTERPRETATION: This quest will allow the seeker to have all that they strive for. To put themselves at the center of what they love.

Position #10 – Closing remarks and finer details

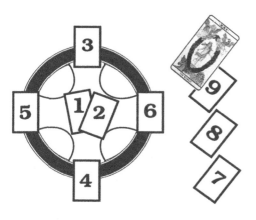 

POSSIBLE INTERPRETATION: You will not be celebrating this quest alone. Good company shares in your success,

In Closing

In the chapter on card meanings I took the time to list what the cards meanings were in the 1960's and 1980's. I felt it was interesting to show how much things have changed in such a short period of time. Short in relation to the time Tarot has been around anyway. I wanted to do that to show the perception of these cards and what they mean is not etched in stone.

I have seen these changes come about first hand.
I've seen the shifts and how they just smoothly adjust without so much as a whisper. Like styles in clothing, things just gradually change. No one really gives it too much attention but it does happen. I've been reading these cards long enough to see it over time.

So with the knowledge that these cards have gone through changes we can assume that they will continue to keep changing. Change also means progress. In 1969 there was hardly any clearly written information on these cards. Now look at what we have today! Information on the Tarot right at your finger tips. Now the challenge has become what information is to follow. There are many wonderful authors out there today.

My main goal in writing my books is to explain why this system works. I feel today we can explain that mystery and I hope I have shown you that in these pages.

The most important thing I have to share with you is my experience. I can truly say it has been a wonderful ride! I hope that shows in these pages.

It is my hope that my work will inspire others to look even deeper into understanding these fascinating cards.

ABOUT THE AUTHOR

Vincent Pitisci and his wife Lynda Spino have been reading professionally in the Chicago area since 1993. Vincent also teaches the subject both in class rooms settings and in private sessions.

Other works by the author available on Amazon:
• Genuis of the Tarot – A Guide to Divination with the Tarot
• The Essential Tarot – Unlocking the Mystery
• Stray Tarot – How to Survive as a Tarot Reader
• Radical Tarot – Breaking all the Rules

• Tarot Reader's Log – A diagrammatic journal of your Tarot readings and predictions
• Tarot Maps – Chartered Predictions with the Celtic Cross

The Tarot deck used in this book is the authors own creation.
"The Tarot of Marseilles by Pitisci" is available from his website TAROTMAPS.com

The deck is registered as a Creative Commons work and is available commercially royalty free for all starving Tarot authors. It is his gift to the Tarot community for others wishing to write on the Tarot. A free, print ready high resolution file of the complete deck is available for download at TarotMaps.com as well.

Quick Reference Tarot Card Meanings

Major Arcana

Card	Meaning
0 The Fool	Carefree
1 The Magician	Awareness
2 The High Priestess	Mystery
3 Empress	Creativity
4 Emperor	The Builder
5 Hierophant	Guidance
6 The Lover	Duality
7 The Chariot	Progression
8 Justice	Truth
9 The Hermit	Soul Searching
10 The Wheel	Evolvement
11 Strength	Strength of Will
12 The Hanged Man	Sacrifice
13 Death	Transition
14 Temperance	Inspiration
15 The Devil	Temptation
16 The Tower	Disruption
17 The Star	Direction
18 The Moon	Mysterious Paths
19 The Sun	Nurturing
20 Judgement	New Awareness
21 The World	Peace & Harmony

Quick Reference Tarot Card Meanings

Minor Arcana

Card	Meaning
Aces	New Concept
Twos	Choice
Threes	Creativity
Fours	Stability
Fives	Change
Sixes	Overcoming Obstacles
Sevens	Achievement
Eights	Advancement
Nines	Attainment
Tens	Completion
Pages	New Path
Knights	Action
Queens	Patience & Understanding
Kings	Knowledge

The Four Suits

Suit	Definition
Swords/Spades	Thought
Pentacles/Diamonds	Physical/Material
Wands/Clubs	The Spirit
Cups/Hearts	Emotion

Made in the USA
Las Vegas, NV
27 April 2024

89215547R00260